Computer Forensics
JumpStart

Second Edition

Computer Forensics JumpStart

Second Edition

Michael G. Solomon

K Rudolph

Ed Tittel

Neil Broom

Diane Barrett

WILEY

Wiley Publishing, Inc.

Acquisitions Editor: Agatha Kim
Development Editor: Stef Jones
Technical Editor: Neil Broom
Production Editor: Dassi Zeidel
Copy Editor: Sara E. Wilson
Editorial Manager: Pete Gaughan
Production Manager: Tim Tate
Vice President and Executive Group Publisher: Richard Swadley
Vice President and Publisher: Neil Edde
Book Designer: Judy Fung
Compositor: James D. Kramer, Happenstance Type-O-Rama
Proofreader: Publication Services, Inc.
Indexer: Nancy Guenther
Project Coordinator, Cover: Katherine Crocker
Cover Designer: Ryan Sneed
Cover Image: © Tetra Images / Getty Images

Copyright © 2011 by Wiley Publishing, Inc., Indianapolis, Indiana

Published simultaneously in Canada

ISBN: 978-0-470-93166-0
ISBN: 978-1-118-06757-4 (ebk.)
ISBN: 978-1-118-06765-9 (ebk.)
ISBN: 978-1-118-06764-2 (ebk.)

10 9 8 7 6 5 4 3 2 1

Dear Reader,

Thank you for choosing *Computer Forensics JumpStart, Second Edition*. This book is part of a family of premium-quality Sybex books, all of which are written by outstanding authors who combine practical experience with a gift for teaching.

Sybex was founded in 1976. More than 30 years later, we're still committed to producing consistently exceptional books. With each of our titles, we're working hard to set a new standard for the industry. From the paper we print on, to the authors we work with, our goal is to bring you the best books available.

I hope you see all that reflected in these pages. I'd be very interested to hear your comments and get your feedback on how we're doing. Feel free to let me know what you think about this or any other Sybex book by sending me an email at nedde@wiley.com. If you think you've found a technical error in this book, please visit http://sybex.custhelp.com. Customer feedback is critical to our efforts at Sybex.

Best regards,

Neil Edde
Vice President and Publisher
Sybex, an Imprint of Wiley

To begin with, I'd like to welcome Mary Kyle to our merry band, and to thank her for bull-dogging this project in fine fashion. Thanks also to Kim Lindros, Agatha Kim, Jeff Kellum, and the rest of the Sybex/Wiley gang. Dearer to my heart, I'd like to thank my lovely wife, Dina, and my son, Gregory, for once again putting up with the old man when he's in the throes of creating and finishing another book. You two make everything else worthwhile, and I'm really looking forward to a fun, frenetic, and distraction-free holiday season. Best to one and all, and thanks to our readers who provide the justification for all this learning and hard work. May it do much good, and very little harm!

—Ed Tittel

To God, who has richly blessed me in so many ways, and to my wife and best friend, Stacey.

—Michael G. Solomon

To Richard Kane

—K Rudolph

To my mother, you gave me everything. I love you.

—Neil Broom

Acknowledgments

The authors of this book are a sizable and rowdy crowd, including Michael G. Solomon, Diane Barrett, K Rudolph, Neil Broom, and Ed Tittel. We'll start off by thanking each other for hanging together, rather than separately, in compiling this second edition. Next, we'd like to thank our able and capable project managers, Mary Kyle Inks and Kim Lindros, both of whom help herd the rest of us cats across the finish line. To our Waterside agent, Carole Jelen, who help put the deal together and shot trouble whenever and wherever she saw it: Thanks, and keep up the good work! After that, it's time for the folks at Sybex/Wiley to take a bow and accept our thanks, too: Agatha Kim, our intrepid acquisitions editor; Stef Jones, our masterful development editor; Jenni Housh, our editorial assistant and Jill of all processes and procedures; Dassi Zeidel, our amazing production editor; as well as Pete Gaughan, our dazzling editorial manager. We're sure there are plenty of others we would be thanking, if only we knew their names and roles. Please accept this shout out, in lieu of something more personal and informed. Believe it or not, we are quite grateful! And finally, to all the vendors who contributed software, hardware, and even the rights to reproduce screenshots or photographs: Thanks for creating the technologies that helped to make this book possible, and we hope also, its contents useful. We literally could not have done it without you.

—*Ed Tittel*

Thanks to the wonderful team that made this a fun and productive project. Mary did an outstanding job of managing the flow of tons of content and materials, as well as managing the authors and editors. Our technical editor, Neil, made all of our work better through his insightful comments and suggestions. And finally, Ed and K are both outstanding authors who make it all look easy. I'd love to work with this team again.

—*Michael G. Solomon*

This book would not have been possible without the support of Mary Kyle, Michael G. Solomon, Ed Tittel, Neil Broom, John B. Ippolito, Sam Carter, and Richard Kane. I am deeply grateful for their fantastic suggestions and unbelievable patience. I am fortunate and happy to be surrounded by such great people.

—*K Rudolph*

Thank you to my aunt, Jeanne Starnes, for your great advice, help, and love throughout the years. Special thanks to Gary Harbin for showing me how to build my first computer—look what you started. Bryan Bain, Lee Ann Bain, David Klukowski, Kenny Wilkins, and Doug Moore, you all made my first IT job great. Thank you for helping me get started in the field. Thanks to Brad Reninger and Will Dean for working so hard every day to make TRC successful. Your professionalism, dedication, and friendship are what make the company great. It is always a pleasure to work with legal professionals as dedicated as Jennifer Georges, Brian Saulnier, Hank Fellows, and Christine Tenley. Shauna Waters, thank you for always being upbeat and for teaching me how to sell. Thanks to the wonderful people at Intelligent Computer Solutions, especially Ezra Kohavi, Gonen Ravid, San Casas, Karen Benzakein, and Viviana Meneses, who help me stay on the cutting edge of new technology in this ever-changing field. Thank you, Amber Schroader and Shannon Honea at Paraben, for all the support. And finally, thank you to Ted Augustine and Chris Brown at Technology Pathways. Chris, you have been a great friend and a wonderful mentor.

—*Neil Broom*

About the Authors

Ed Tittel is a 28-year veteran of the IT industry. After spending his first seven years writing code (mostly for database engines and applications), he switched to a networking focus. After working for Excelan/Novell from 1987 to 1994, he became a full-time freelance writer, consultant, and trainer. He has contributed to more than 100 books on a variety of subjects, including the Sybex *CISSP Study Guide, Fifth Edition*, and many *For Dummies* titles. He also blogs regularly for TechTarget.com, and writes for a variety of IT certification-oriented Web sites.

Michael G. Solomon, CISSP, PMP, CISM, GSEC, is a full-time security speaker, consultant, and author specializing in achieving and maintaining secure IT environments. An IT professional and consultant since 1987, he has worked on projects for more than 100 major organizations and authored and contributed to numerous books and training courses. From 1998 to 2001, he was an instructor in the Kennesaw State University's Computer Science and Information Sciences (CSIS) department, where he taught courses on software project management, C++ programming, computer organization and architecture, and data communications. Michael holds an M.S. in Mathematics and Computer Science from Emory University (1998), a B.S. in Computer Science from Kennesaw State University (1987), and is currently pursuing a Ph.D. in Computer Science and Informatics at Emory University. He has also contributed to various security certification books for LANWrights, including *TICSA Training Guide* (Que, 2002) and an accompanying Instructor Resource Kit (Que, 2002), *CISSP Study Guide* (Sybex, 2003), as well as *Security+ Training Guide* (Que, 2003). Michael coauthored *Information Security Illuminated* (Jones & Bartlett, 2005), *Security+ Lab Guide* (Sybex, 2005), *Computer Forensics JumpStart* (Sybex, 2005), *PMP ExamCram2* (Que, 2005) and authored and provided the on-camera delivery of LearnKey's CISSP Prep and PMP Prep e-Learning course.

K Rudolph is the founder and CIO (Chief Inspiration Officer) of Native Intelligence, Inc. She is a Certified Information Systems Security Professional (CISSP) with a degree from Johns Hopkins University. K creates entertaining educational materials that have been presented to more than 400,000 learners and translated into five languages. She has contributed to eight books on security topics including the *Handbook of Information Security*, *Computer Security Handbook*, *System Forensics, Investigation, and Response*, and NIST Special Publication 800–16, *Information Technology Security Training Requirements: A Role- and Performance-Based Model*. K has presented at numerous conferences, including the Computer Security Institute Security Exchange (CSI SX) Conference, CSI Annual Security Conferences, New York Cyber Security Conferences, and Information Assurance and Security Conferences held by the FISSEA, FIAC, and eGOV. She has been a speaker for Security Awareness Day events held by the Army, Census Bureau, DLA, IHS, IRS, NOAA, NRC, and the government of Johnson County, Kansas. K volunteers with (ISC)²'s Safe and Secure Online program, which brings awareness presentations for 11- to 14-year-olds to local schools. In March 2006, the Federal Information Systems Security Educators' Association (FISSEA) honored K as the Security Educator of the Year. K is interested in just about everything, including contact juggling, mind mapping, storytelling, core work, aviation, teaching analogies, and photography.

Neil Broom is the President and Laboratory Director of Technical Resource Center, Inc. (www.trcglobal.com) in Atlanta, Georgia. TRC is the only private lab east of the Mississippi that earned the prestigious ASCLD/LAB accreditation in the field of Digital Evidence (Computer Forensics) from the American Society of Crime Laboratory Directors/Laboratory Accreditation Board as an expert witness, investigator, speaker, trainer, course director, and consultant in the fields of computer forensics, network and computer security, information assurance, and professional security testing. Neil has more than 15 years of experience providing investigative, technical, educational, and security services to the military, attorneys, law enforcement, the health care industry, financial institutions, and government agencies. Neil is a Certified Computer Examiner (CCE), Certified Information Systems Security Professional (CISSP), and Certified Fraud Examiner (CFE). He is a licensed Georgia private detective and private detective instructor. TRC is a licensed Georgia private detective agency. Neil has presented testimony as an expert witness many times. He has also provided training in the fields of computer forensics and information security to more than 3,000 students in the U.S. government, U.S. military, U.S. intelligence agencies, and Fortune 500 companies in the United States and abroad. Neil was the Chairman of the Digital Evidence Subcommittee for the International Association for Identification (IAI) and is a current member of the ASCLD/LAB Delegate Assembly. His past employment includes the U.S. Navy as a submariner, a law enforcement officer for the Gainesville Police Department, system administrator for the S1 Corporation, and a security trainer for Internet Security Systems (now a division of IBM).

Diane Barrett has been involved in the IT industry for about 20 years and has been active in education, security, and forensics for the past 10 years. She holds an M.S. degree in Technology with a specialization in Information Security and will be starting Ph.D. dissertation work shortly. Diane is currently a forensic trainer for Paraben and has been doing contract forensic work for the past several years in the Phoenix area. In addition to developing forensic curriculum for American Military University, she was the program champion for the Technology Forensics program at the University of Advancing Technology. She holds many industry certifications including CISSP, ISSMP, and DCFP. Diane has either coauthored or been the lead author on several computer forensics and security books. She is also a regular committee member for the Conference on Digital Forensics, Security and Law and presenter at Paraben's Forensic Innovations Conference.

Contents

Introduction

Want to know what computer forensic examiners really do? This book covers the essentials of computer forensics, and it's especially designed for those new to the field or who simply wish to learn more about undertaking this type of work. Many news stories and television shows highlight the role of forensic investigators in solving cases. It all seems so exciting, doesn't it? Computer forensics is really not that different from what you see on TV. Although it's quite a bit less glamorous, you'll find similarities in the real world.

After a crime or incident that involves a computer occurs, a specialist trained in computer forensics examines the computer to find clues about what happened. That is the role of the computer forensic examiner. This specialist may work with law enforcement or with a corporate incident response team. Although the rules governing each activity can be dramatically different depending on who your client is, the approach to the investigation remains roughly the same.

This book covers the basic elements, concepts, tools, and common activities to equip you with a solid understanding of the field of computer forensics. Although this book is not a definitive training guide for specific forensic tools, you will learn about the most common tasks that you'll encounter during any investigation. After reading this book, you will be able to participate in investigations and understand the process of finding, collecting, and analyzing the evidence gathered.

A heightened awareness of security in the wake of the attacks on September 11, 2001, has also provided many nontechnical people with an awareness of security issues previously known only in security specialist circles. Computers play a central role in all activities, both legal and illegal. The material in this book can be applied to both criminal investigations and corporate incident response. You don't have to be a member of law enforcement to benefit from the material presented here. Nontechnical people can also benefit from this book because it covers the basic approach computer examiners take in an investigation.

If you like the introduction to computer forensics we present in this book, you can pursue the topic further in several ways. Most major forensic tools vendors offer training on their own products and teach how to use them in investigations. See Chapter 8, "Common Forensic Tools," and Appendix D, "Forensic Tools," for more information. Appendix B, "Forensic Resources," contains many references to resources where you can obtain more information. If you decide to pursue computer forensic certification, Appendix C, "Forensic Certifications and More," provides a list of common certifications and contact information for each. If your job involves computer investigations, this book can help you expand your knowledge and abilities. Keep it handy as a resource as you acquire more experience and knowledge. And good luck with your pursuit!

Who Should Read This Book

Anyone fulfilling, or aspiring to fulfill, the responsibilities of a computer forensic examiner can benefit from this book. Also, if you just want to know more about what computer forensic examiners do, this book will fill you in on the details. The material is organized to provide a high-level view of the process and methods used in an investigation. Both law enforcement personnel and non-law enforcement can benefit from the topics presented here.

Because you are reading this introduction, you must have some interest in computer forensics. Why are you interested? Are you just curious, do you want to start working in computer forensics, or have you just been given the responsibility of conducting or managing an investigation? This book addresses readers in all of these categories.

Although we recommend that you read the book from start to finish for a complete overview of the topics, you can jump right to an area of interest. If you bought this book for a concise list of forensic tools, go right to Chapter 8. But don't forget the other chapters! You'll find a wealth of information in all chapters that will expand your understanding of computer forensics.

What This Book Covers

Chapter 1: "The Need for Computer Forensics"   This chapter lays the foundation for the rest of the book. It discusses the need for computer forensics and how the examiners' activities meet the need.

Chapter 2: "Preparation—What to Do Before You Start"   This chapter addresses the necessary knowledge you must have before you start. When you finish this chapter, you will know how to prepare for an investigation.

Chapter 3: "Computer Evidence"   This chapter discusses computer evidence and focuses on identifying, collecting, preserving, and analyzing evidence.

Chapter 4: "Common Tasks"   Most investigations include similar common tasks. This chapter outlines those tasks you are likely to see again and again. It sets the stage for the action items you will use in your activities.

Chapter 5: "Capturing the Data Image"   This chapter covers the first functional step in many investigations. You will learn the reason for and the process of creating media images for analysis.

Chapter 6: "Extracting Information from Data"   After you have an exact media image, you can start analyzing it for evidence. This chapter covers the basics of data analysis. You will learn what to look for and how to find it.

Chapter 7: "Passwords and Encryption"   Sooner or later, you will run into password-protected resources and encrypted files. This chapter covers basic encryption and password issues and discusses how to deal with them.

Chapter 8: "Common Forensic Tools"   Every computer forensic examiner needs a toolbox. This chapter covers many popular hardware and software forensic tools.

Chapter 9: "Pulling It All Together"   When the analysis is done, you need to present the results. This chapter covers the elements and flow of an investigation report.

Chapter 10: "How to Testify in Court"   If your evidence ends up in court, you need to know how to effectively present it. This chapter covers many ins and outs of being an expert witness and presenting evidence in court.

Appendix A: "Answers to Review Questions"   Answers to the Review Questions

Appendix B: "Forensic Resources"   A list of forensic resources you can use for further research

Appendix C: "Forensic Certifications and More"   A list of computer forensic certifications and contact information

Appendix D: "Forensic Tools"   A summary list of forensic tools, several of which are discussed in the text, with contact information

Glossary   A list of terms used throughout the book

Making the Most of This Book

At the beginning of each chapter you'll find a list of topics that the chapter covers. You'll find new terms (specific terminology) defined in the margins of the pages to help you quickly get up to speed on computer forensics. In addition, several special elements highlight important information:

Notes provide extra information and references to related information.

NOTE

Tips are insights to help you perform tasks more easily and effectively.

TIP

Warnings let you know about things you should—or shouldn't—do as you perform computer investigations.

WARNING

You'll find Review Questions at the end of each chapter to test your knowledge of the material covered. The answers to the Review Questions may be found in

Appendix A. You'll also find a list of Terms to Know at the end of each chapter to help you review key terms introduced in that chapter. These terms are also included in the Glossary at the end of this book.

You'll also find special sidebars in each chapter titled "Tales from the Trenches," written by Neil Broom. These are war stories Neil has acquired throughout his career as a computer forensic examiner. They are written in first person, so you'll really get a sense of what it's like to go "on scene" and get your hands dirty. Enjoy!

How to Contact the Authors

The authors welcome feedback from you about this book or about books you'd like to see in the future. You can reach the authors by writing to them at the addresses below. For more information about their work, please visit their respective Web sites.

Ed Tittel: ed@edtittel.com; learn more about Ed at http://www.edtittel.com.

Michael G. Solomon: michael@solomonconsulting.com; learn more about Michael at http://www.solomonconsulting.com/.

K Rudolph: Kaie@NativeIntelligence.com; learn more about K at www.NativeIntelligence.com.

Neil Broom: nbroom@trcglobal.com; learn more about Neil at www.trcglobal.com.

Sybex strives to keep you supplied with the latest tools and information you need for your work. Please check their Web site at www.sybex.com, where we'll post additional content and updates that supplement this book if the need arises. Enter Computer Forensics in the Search box (or type the book's ISBN—**9780470931660**), and click Go to get to the book's update page.

Chapter 1

The Need for Computer Forensics

Computer forensics is a fascinating field. As enterprises become more complex and exchange more information online, high-tech crimes are increasing at a rapid rate. The computer forensic industry has taken off in recent years, and it's no surprise that a profession once regarded as a vague counterpart of network security has grown into a science all its own. In addition, numerous companies and professionals now offer computer forensic services as a main line of business.

A computer forensic technician is a combination of a private eye and a computer scientist. Although the ideal background for this field includes legal, technical, and law enforcement experience, many industries as well as government and military organizations use professionals with investigative intelligence and technology proficiency. A computer forensic professional can fill a variety of roles such as private investigator, corporate compliance professional, or law enforcement official.

This chapter introduces you to the concept of computer forensics, while addressing computer forensic needs from two views—corporate policy and law enforcement. It will present some real-life examples of computer crime. It will help you assess your organization's needs and discuss various training methods used for practitioners and end users.

Defining Computer Forensics

computer forensics
Computer investigation and analysis techniques that involve the identi-fication, preservation, extraction, documentation, and interpretation of computer data to determine potential legal evidence.

The digital age has produced many new professions, but one of the most unusual is computer forensics. Computer forensics deals with the application of law to a science. The New Shorter Oxford English Dictionary defines *computer forensics* as "the application of forensic science techniques to computer-based material." In other words, forensic computing is the process of identifying, preserving, analyzing, and presenting digital evidence in a manner that is acceptable in a legal proceeding. At times, it is more science than art; other times, it is more art than science.

Although it is similar to other forms of legal forensics, the computer forensics process requires a vast knowledge of computer hardware, software, and proper techniques to avoid compromising or destroying evidence. Computer forensic review involves the application of investigative and analytical techniques to acquire and protect potential legal evidence; therefore, a professional within this field needs to have a detailed understanding of the local, regional, national, and sometimes even international laws affecting the process of evidence collection and retention. This is especially true in cases involving attacks that may be waged from widely distributed systems located in many separate regions.

intrusion
Any unauthorized access to a com-puter, including the use, alteration, or disclosure of programs or data residing on the computer.

Computer forensics can also be described as the critical analysis of a computer hard disk drive after an *intrusion* or crime. This is mainly because specialized software tools and procedures are required to analyze, after the fact, the various areas where computer data is stored. Often this involves retrieving deleted data from hard drives and servers that have been subpoenaed to appear in court or seized by law enforcement.

electronic discovery or e-discovery
The process whereby electronic documents are collected, prepared, reviewed, and distributed in asso-ciation with legal and government proceedings.

During the course of forensic work, you will run into a practice that is called *electronic discovery*, or *e-discovery*. Electronic discovery produces electronic documents for litigation. Data that is created or stored on a computer, computer network, or other storage media are included in e-discovery. Examples of such are e-mail, word-processing documents, plaintext files, database files, spreadsheets, digital art, photos, and presentations. Electronic discovery using computer foren-sic techniques requires in-depth computer knowledge and the ability to logically dissect a computer system or network to locate the desired evidence. It may also require expert witness testimony to explain to the court the exact method or methods by which the evidence was obtained.

Computer forensics has become a hot topic in computer security circles and in the legal community. It's a fascinating field with far more information available than can be analyzed in a single book, although this book will provide you with an understanding of the basic skills you'll need as a forensic investigator. Key skills in computer forensics are knowing the best places to look for evidence, and knowing when to stop looking. These skills come with time and experience.

In looking at the major concepts behind computer forensics, the main emphasis is on data recovery. To do that you must:

◆ Identify meaningful evidence

◆ Determine how to preserve the evidence

◆ Extract, process, and interpret the evidence

◆ Ensure that the evidence is acceptable in a court of law

All of these concepts are discussed in great detail throughout this book. Because computer-based information is fragile and can be easily fabricated, the simple presence of incriminating material is not always evidence of guilt. Electronic information is easy to create and store, yet computer forensics is a science that requires specialized training, experience, and equipment.

 Real World Scenario

Tales from the Trenches: Why Computer Forensics Matters

A computer forensic examiner might be called upon to perform any of a number of different types of computer forensic investigations.

We have all heard of or read about the use of computer forensics by law enforcement agencies to help catch criminals. The criminal might be a thief who was found with evidence of his crime when his home or office computer was searched, or a state employee who was found to have stolen funds from public accounts by manipulating accounting software to hide funds transfers.

Most of us know that computer forensics is used every day in the corporate business world to help protect the assets and reputation of large companies. Forensic examiners are called upon to monitor the activities of employees, assist in locating evidence of industrial espionage, and provide support in defending allegations of misconduct by senior management.

Government agencies hire computer forensic specialists to help protect the data the agencies maintain. Sometimes, it's as simple as making sure IRS employees don't misuse the access they have been granted to view your tax information by periodically reviewing their activities. Many times, it's as serious as helping to defend the United States to protect the most vital top secret information by working within a counterintelligence group.

Every day, divorce attorneys ask examiners to assist in the review of personal computers belonging to spouses involved in divorce proceedings. The focus of such investigations usually is to find information about assets that the spouse may be hiding and to which the other spouse is entitled.

Continues

More recently, defense attorneys have asked forensic examiners to reexamine computers belonging to criminal defendants. Computer forensic experts have even been asked to reexamine evidence used in a capital murder case that resulted in the defendant's receiving a death sentence. Such reexaminations are conducted to refute the findings of the law enforcement investigations.

Although each of these areas seems entirely unique, the computer forensic examiner who learns the basics, obtains appropriate equipment, follows proper procedures, and continues to educate himself or herself will be able to handle each of these investigations and many other types not yet discussed. The need for proper computer forensic investigations is growing every day as new methods, technologies, and reasons for investigations are discovered.

Computer Crime in Real Life

An endless number of computer crime cases is available for you to read. Most of the crimes presented in the following sections come from the Department of Justice Web site, online at www.cybercrime.gov. In these cases, we'll look at several types of computer crime and how computer forensic techniques were used to capture criminals. The cases presented here illustrate some of the techniques that you will learn as you advance through this book. As a forensic investigator, you never know what you may come across when you begin an investigation. As the cases in this section show, sometimes you find more than you could have ever imagined.

Hacker Sentenced for Identity Thefts from Payment Processor and Retail Networks

Alberto Gonzalez, 28, led a hacking and identity theft ring that compromised record-breaking numbers of credit cards. For his part in the crimes, Gonzalez received the longest sentence imposed for criminal hacking to date. In March 2010, in separate cases, U.S. District Court judges sentenced Gonzalez to two 20-year prison terms for hacking into several retail networks and a major payment processor.

Gonzalez committed access device fraud, aggravated identity theft, computer fraud, conspiracy, and wire fraud. He and his associates hacked into major U.S. retailers, including the TJX Companies, BJ's Wholesale Club, OfficeMax, Boston Market, Barnes & Noble, and Sports Authority. He also led the group that breached the Dave and Buster's restaurant chain electronic payment systems. The second prison sentence, 20 years and one day, was for two counts of conspiracy for assisting others in breaching the networks of card processor Heartland Payment Systems, supermarket chain, Hannaford Brothers Co. Inc., and nationwide convenience store chain, 7-Eleven.

Between July 2005 and his arrest in May 2008, Gonzalez and his group hacked into retail credit card payment systems by installing sniffer programs that captured payment card numbers used at the stores and by wardriving. Wardriving involves driving around in a car with a laptop computer looking for unsecured wireless computer networks. Gonzalez and his co-defendants stole more than 40 million credit and debit card numbers from major retailers. They sold the numbers and also committed ATM fraud by encoding the stolen data onto blank cards and then withdrawing cash from ATMs.

Gonzalez's ring hid and laundered their fraudulent gains by moving the money through bank accounts in Eastern Europe and using anonymous Internet-based currencies in the United States and abroad.

Gonzalez gave malware to other hackers that enabled them to bypass firewalls and anti-virus programs to break into companies' networks. (Malware is discussed in the Security Awareness section below.) Gonzalez admitted that his assistance allowed his co-conspirators to steal tens of millions of card numbers, adversely impacting hundreds of financial institutions.

In the largest investigation to date of its kind, the U.S. Secret Service worked abroad and in the United States using computer forensics to solve these cases. In July 2007, Secret Service in Turkey worked with Turkish agents to obtain Ukrainian suspect Maksym Yastremskiy's laptop while he danced at a nearby nightclub. After downloading data, U.S. agents returned the computer to Yastremskiy's hotel room. Instead of user names, Yastremskiy's accomplices used secure communication networks with numerical IDs.

Detectives noted Yastremskiy's chats with an American who sold millions of stolen credit card numbers to Yastremskiy. The American used the identity "201679996." The detectives worked with Carnegie Mellon University experts to link the numbers to a Russian e-mail address that belonged to Gonzalez. Ironically, Gonzalez had been working with the Secret Service as a consultant since 2003.

Shortly thereafter, the Secret Service arrested an Estonian hacker and found more than 40 million unsold credit card numbers linked to the break-ins at U.S. companies on two Latvian servers.

For months, Gonzalez hid in the National Hotel where he was living off more than $400,000 cash. He had buried another $1.1 million in the back yard of his parents' house. On May 7, 2008, agents raided Gonzalez's hotel room, condo, and parents' home. Gonzalez was then arrested.

Source: Wired.com, August 17, 2009, http://www.wired.com/threatlevel/2009/08/tjx-hacker-charged-with-heartland; U.S. Department of Justice, Office of Public Affairs, http://www.justice.gov/opa/pr/2010/March/10-crm-329.html.

NOTE

Man Charged with Operating Online Scheme to Steal Income Tax Refunds

In June 2010, Mikalai Mardakhayeu was arrested and charged for his alleged role in an online phishing scam. The international scam was designed to steal U.S. taxpayer income tax refunds. Mardakhayeu is a Belarusian national living in Massachusetts. He was charged with conspiracy and wire fraud.

As alleged in the indictment, in 2006 and 2007, Mardakhayeu and his co-conspirators operated Web sites that offered lower-income taxpayers online tax return preparation and electronic tax return filing services at no cost. The fraudulent Web sites claimed to be authorized by the Internal Revenue Service (IRS). Co-conspirators in Belarus allegedly collected the data entered by taxpayers and then changed the returns so that the legitimate tax refund payments would be redirected to U.S. bank accounts that Mardakhayeu controlled. In some cases, his co-conspirators increased the amount of the claimed refund.

Allegedly, his co-conspirators electronically filed the modified returns with the IRS and various state treasury departments. As a result, the U.S. Treasury and state treasury departments deposited stolen refunds of approximately $200,000 into bank accounts that Mardakhayeu controlled. If convicted, he could be sentenced to 20 years in prison.

NOTE Source: U.S. Department of Justice, Computer Crime and Intellectual Property Section (CCIPS), http://www.justice.gov/criminal/cybercrime/mardakhay euIndict.htm.

In this case, the forensic examiner might have found the files used to create the fraudulent Web sites. If the files were deleted, parts or all of them could have been recovered. Other evidence might include the actual data entered by the victims. The server logs and bank deposit records might have recorded who accessed the accounts. The forensic examiner has a wide variety of tools available to extract data and deleted information.

Newell Rubbermaid Network Hacked for Botnet and Adware Scams

In June 2008, a federal judge sentenced 21-year-old Robert Matthew Bentley to 41 months in prison and payment of $65,000 in restitution for conspiracy and computer fraud. Bentley and others (who are still being investigated) infected hundreds of computers in Europe with adware. The cost to detect and neutralize the adware was tens of thousands of dollars. Bentley and his co-conspirators were paid for installing the adware through a Western European-based operation called "Dollar Revenue."

The investigation began when the U.S.-based Newell Rubbermaid Corporation and at least one other European-based company reported a computer intrusion against the companies' European networks to the London Metropolitan Police.

This complex, multiyear, international criminal investigation also involved the U.S. Secret Service, the Finland National Bureau of Investigation, London's Metropolitan Police Computer Crime Unit, and the Federal Bureau of Investigation (FBI). Each of these law enforcement organizations detected and responded to botnets of computers secretly controlled by Bentley and his co-conspirators. Evidence was found on computers in Florida that were used in the actual intrusions and to receive payment for placing the adware.

NOTE

See U.S. Department of Justice, Computer Crime and Intellectual Property Section (CCIPS), http://www.justice.gov/criminal/cybercrime/bentleySent.pdf. **See also "Hacker Pleads Guilty to Computer Fraud" at** http://pcworld.about.com/od/adware/Hacker-Pleads-Guilty-to-Comput.htm.

This case spanned several countries. National and international law enforcement agencies had to work together to track the illicit computer accesses. By installing the adware and accepting payments, the suspect unwittingly left a trail of forensic evidence. The evidence may have included items such as the parts of the program used to control the botnets.

Former Intel Employee Indicted for Alleged Heist of $1B in Trade Secrets

This case involves employee theft of valuable intellectual property. Stealing and selling proprietary information has become big business. When proprietary information is stolen, a computer forensic investigator may work in tandem with corporate human resources and compliance professionals to help examine not only how the theft occurred, but also provide evidence for prosecution. This case shows that the FBI takes a tough line against stealing data from former employers.

In 2008, Biswamohan Pani, 33, a former Intel employee, was indicted for wire fraud and the theft of more than $1 billion worth of trade secrets from Intel. The stolen information was valued in research and development costs and included mission-critical details about Intel's processes for designing its newest microprocessors. According to the affidavit, Pani told Intel management that he was resigning to work for a hedge fund and that he would use his accrued vacation until his termination date on June 11, 2008.

Pani remained on Intel's payroll through June 11, 2008, but he started work at Intel rival Advanced Micro Devices, Inc. (AMD) on June 2, 2008. From June 8 until June 11, 2008, Pani used his Intel laptop to access Intel's servers and download commercially sensitive data, including more than 100 sensitive documents, 13 of which were classified by Intel as "Top Secret." He also downloaded a document explaining how the encrypted Intel documents could be reviewed from an external hard drive after he left Intel. The indictment also alleged that Pani attempted to access Intel's computer network again two days after his last day at Intel. On July 1, 2008, proprietary Intel documents were located at Pani's home.

During his June 11 exit interview, Pani acknowledged his confidentiality obligations and falsely told Intel that he had returned all of Intel's property, including any documents or computer data.

Per the indictment, AMD personnel neither requested the stolen information nor knew that Pani had taken or would take it. Pani may have planned to use the information to further his career, with or without his employer's knowledge. Both Intel and AMD have assisted the FBI investigation.

If convicted, Pani faces up to 10 years on the trade secret charge, and an additional 20 years on each of the wire fraud counts.

NOTE

See U.S. Department of Justice, Computer Crime and Intellectual Property Section (CCIPS), http://www.justice.gov/usao/ma/Press%200f"ce%20-%20Press %20Release%20Files/Nov2008/PaniBiswamohanIndictmentPR.html. **See also** *Secure Computing Magazine*, **September 18, 2008,** http://www.securecomputing.net.au/ News/123155,amd-worker-charged-with-intel-theft.aspx.

In this case, computer forensic evidence may include the date and time the files were downloaded as well as access information showing that Pani logged into the Intel servers. Time and date stamps are an important part of the computer forensic process. You will learn about these and other forensic techniques later in the book.

Figure 1.1 is from the Web site of the Computer Crime and Intellectual Property Section of the Criminal Division of the U.S. Department of Justice (http://cybercrime.gov). Here you can find a lot of useful information and additional cases.

The following examples illustrate that computer forensic investigators have no idea where their cases will end up. As a computer sleuth, you may be required to work across state lines and with various agencies. You may end up working with several companies in various countries. You may wind up at a dead end because it takes too long to get the information you need or the employer decides not to prosecute. The computer forensic world is full of surprises.

disaster recovery
The ability of an organization to recover from an occurrence inflicting widespread destruction and distress.

best practices
A set of recommended guidelines that outline a set of controls to improve internal and business processes, performance, quality and efficiency.

Figure 1.1   cybercrime.gov Web site *(U.S. Department of Justice)*

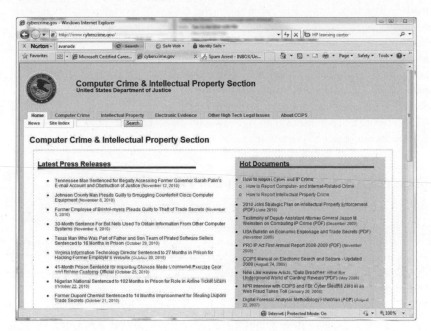

Corporate versus Law Enforcement Concerns

The needs of the corporate world and those of law enforcement differ on several levels. Law enforcement officials work under more restrictive rules than corporate agents or employees. If you assist law enforcement in an investigation, you may be considered "an agent of law enforcement" and you may be bound by the same restrictions that they encounter. When working with law enforcement, it's important to be aware of these ramifications, especially if you're working without a court order. This scenario could also open you up to civil litigation when complying with such requests, so it's always advisable to seek legal counsel. In the corporate world, all that is generally required to begin an investigation—to access servers, network systems, routers, and so forth—is the written approval of the corporate agent with the appropriate level of authority for such activities. On the other hand, law enforcement is subject to multiple laws regarding not only how but under what circumstances evidence can be seized. Often, forensic investigators working in law enforcement need a court order before they may examine computer systems, networks, routers, and so on. Face it: There is a big difference between a company deciding to log router traffic and a local or federal law enforcement officer asking the company to log the traffic.

incident
A threatening computer security breach that can be recovered from in a relatively short period of time.

incident response
The action taken to respond to a situation that can be recovered from relatively quickly.

Both law enforcement and corporate practitioners follow a set of *best practices* set forth by various agencies. For law enforcement, a set of best practices exists for electronic discovery and proper retrieval of data. The corporate world also established best practices for security and best practices for determining what comprises an *incident*. These best practices inform *incident response* procedures, which describe how to react to an incident. Because disasters are usually of a larger magnitude, best practices for disaster recovery may affect both electronic discovery and retrieval of data. The focus of this book is to provide information that can be used in either discipline—corporate computer forensics or law enforcement computer forensics—and is not specifically aimed at law enforcement.

Corporate Concerns: Detection and Prevention

intrusion detection
Using software and hardware agents to monitor network traffic for patterns that may indicate an attempt at intrusion.

Every day new articles are written about network security and vulnerabilities in software and hardware. This visibility has caused security to become a priority in most companies. Corporate efforts to make sure a network is secure generally are focused on how to implement hardware and software solutions, such as *intrusion detection*, web filtering, spam elimination, and patch installation. The SQL Slammer *worm* infected 200,000 computers running Microsoft's SQL Server. Ninety percent of all vulnerable servers were infected in the first 10 minutes after the worm was released on the Internet. Dealing with the threat of network damage through an intrusion or *virus* is a part of everyday life for corporate IT professionals, whereas forensic experts focus on the examination, analysis, and evaluation of computer data to provide relevant and valid information to the courts.

security policies
Specifications for a secure environment, including such items as physical security requirements, network security planning details, a detailed list of approved software, and human resources policies on employee hiring and dismissal.

Corporate focus is on minimizing the potential damage that may result from unauthorized access attempts through the prevention, detection, and identification of an unauthorized intrusion. This is done mainly by putting *security policies* in place that dictate the level of security for various areas and computers. Along with these policies, incident response and disaster recovery plans set forth procedures for investigations, including when, who, and how to contact law enforcement.

Companies can access Web sites to find out about new vulnerabilities or security best practices. It is in the best interest of any company to assign someone to check this information on a regular basis to ensure that the network is protected.

virus
A program or piece of code that is loaded onto a computer without the user's knowledge and is designed to attach itself to other code and replicate. The virus replicates when an infected file is executed or launched.

You'll find in many corporate environments that incidents are not reported, often due to the issue of legal liability. The "Let's just quietly fix it" approach to security incidents is common in the corporate world. Some laws now hold senior management responsible for data breaches. A company is potentially liable for damages caused by a hacker's using one of its computers, and a company might have to prove to a court that it took reasonable measures to defend itself from hackers.

The following federal laws address security and privacy and affect nearly every organization in the United States.

> The Health Insurance Portability and Accountability Act (HIPAA) of 1996 was enacted on August 21, 1996, to ensure the portability, privacy, and security of medical information. HIPAA dictates that only patients, agents they designate, and their health-care providers have access to the patients' medical information. HIPAA requires that Patient Health Information (PHI) be kept private and secure. It imposes stiff fines and jail time both for health-care institutions and individuals who disclose confidential health information to unauthorized parties.

> The Gramm-Leach-Bliley (GLB) Act requires financial institutions to ensure the security and confidentiality of the personal information that they collect. This includes information such as names, addresses, phone numbers, income, and Social Security numbers. Basically, financial institutions are required to secure customer records and information regardless of size of the information files. Among other institutions, GLB covers check-cashing businesses, mortgage brokers, real estate appraisers, professional tax preparers, courier services, and retailers that issue credit cards to consumers.

> The Sarbanes-Oxley Act, named for the two Congressmen who sponsored it, was passed to restore the public's confidence in corporate governance by requiring chief executives of publicly traded companies to personally validate financial statements and other information. Congress passed the law to prevent future accounting scandals such as those committed by Enron and WorldCom. Under the law, executives who sign off on internal controls can face criminal penalties if a breach is detected. In other words, if someone can easily get into a secure or private part of your system because you use a three-character password such as "dog," you will be noncompliant with Sarbanes-Oxley.

Compliance is becoming more important to businesses, which face an increasing number of laws and regulations that involve e-discovery obligations and data breach notification laws. For example, a new Massachusetts law protects residents' personal data from breaches and sets a fine of $5,000 for each record lost. This means a company could be fined $1 million for losing a laptop computer containing personal data on 200 Massachusetts residents.

The new law applies to businesses in Massachusetts and to any company that keeps personal data on the state's residents. The law requires companies to act to prevent breaches, not just to notify victims after a breach has occurred. Businesses must encrypt data in motion and at rest, including information on portable devices such as USB drives, laptop computers, and smartphones.

worm
Similar in function and behavior to a virus, except that worms do not need user intervention. A worm takes advantage of a security hole in an existing application or operating system and then finds other systems running the same software and automatically replicates itself to the new hosts.

Often, a company that is the victim of a security breach does not know which law enforcement entity to call. Company management might feel that the local or state police will not be able to understand the crime and that the FBI and Secret Service are not needed. In addition, management might be afraid that the intrusion will become public knowledge, harming investor confidence and chasing away current and potential customers. They might also fear the effect of having critical data and computers seized by law enforcement.

An investigation can seriously jeopardize the normal operations of a company, not only for the customers but for employees as well. A disruption in the workplace causes confusion and upsets employee schedules. Furthermore, cases are often hard to pursue if a suspect is a juvenile or an intruder is from another country. In many states, the damages inflicted by an intruder are too small to justify prosecution. Last, pursuing such matters takes a long time and can be costly.

NOTE   **Many businesses perceive that there is little benefit to reporting network intrusions.**

Law Enforcement Concerns: Prosecution

Whereas the corporate world focuses on prevention and detection, the law enforcement realm focuses on investigation and prosecution. Each state has its own set of laws that govern how cases should be prosecuted. For cases to be prosecuted, evidence must be properly collected, processed, and preserved. In later chapters, we'll go through these procedures. Technology has dramatically increased the universe of discoverable electronic material, thereby making the job of law enforcement much more complex. Electronic evidence can include any and all electronically stored information that is in digital, optical, or analog form. Not only does evidence include electronic data, it also includes electronic devices such as computers, CD-ROMs, floppy disks, cellular telephones, pagers, and digital cameras.

 Real World Scenario

22-Year Old Tennessee Man Convicted for Hacking into Sarah Palin's E-mail Account

On April 30, 2010, a federal jury in Tennessee convicted David C. Kernell, now 22, of intentionally obtaining unauthorized access to Sarah Palin's e-mail account. Kernell, the son of a Tennessee state Representative, was also convicted of obstruction of justice. Kernell was found not guilty of wire fraud. The judge declared a mistrial on the identity theft charge because the jury was unable to reach a verdict on that charge. Kernell turned himself into federal authorities.

Continues

> Evidence presented at trial showed that on Sept. 16, 2008, Kernell accessed Palin's personal e-mail account. He reset her account password by providing Palin's birth date and zip code to Yahoo's password retrieval system. According to the evidence, Kernell read the contents and captured screenshots of the e-mail directory, e-mail content, and other personal information. Kernell posted screenshots of Palin's personal information and e-mail messages to a public Web site. Kernell also changed her password to a new one and posted the new password, allowing the account to be accessed by others.
>
> Evidence also showed that after he became aware of a possible investigation by the FBI, Kernell deleted electronic evidence to obstruct the imminent FBI investigation. As of the writing of this book, Kernell's sentencing is scheduled for late October 2010. Kernell faces a maximum of one year in prison and a $100,000 fine for unauthorized access as well as 20 years in prison and a $250,000 fine for obstruction of justice.
>
> Source: U.S. Department of Justice, Federal Bureau of Investigation, Knoxville, http://knoxville.fbi.gov/dojpressrel/pressrel10/kx043010.htm

For a case to stand up in court, most evidence must be attested to by a witness. In the case of electronic evidence, who is the witness of a computer making a log entry? How can a law enforcement officer show that the other 15 accounts logged in at the time didn't commit the deed? Despite the relative infancy of the law, electronic data is finding its way into the courtroom and is profoundly impacting many cases.

Courts are generally not persuaded by challenges to the authenticity, best evidence rule, chain of custody, and so on of electronic data introduced at trial. This type of issue has been brought up in court several times. A good example is *United States v. Tank*. The court addressed the question of the authentication of Internet chat room logs that were maintained by one of the co-defendants. The defendant claimed that the government did not have a sufficient foundation for the admission of the logs. The government provided evidence linking the screen name used by the defendant to the defendant. The government evidence also included testimony from one of the co-defendants about the method he used to create the logs and his recollection that the logs appeared to be an accurate representation of the conversations among the members. The court ruled in favor of the government, declaring that the government made a satisfactory showing of the relevance and authenticity of chat room log printouts.

With the increase of cybercrime, keeping up with caseloads has become nearly impossible. Department of Public Safety (DPS) crime lab personnel barely have time to answer the phone. How does law enforcement determine the priority of the complaints that they investigate and prosecute? Generally speaking, the following factors help determine which cases get priority:

The Amount of Harm Inflicted   Crimes against children or violent crimes usually get high priority, along with crimes that result in large monetary loss.

Crime Jurisdiction   Crimes that affect the local populace are usually chosen, especially when resources are taken into consideration.

Success of Investigation   The difficulty of investigation and success of the outcome weigh heavily in determining which cases are investigated.

Availability and Training of Personnel   Often crime investigations that don't require a large amount of manpower or very specific training take precedence.

Frequency   Isolated instances take a lower priority than those that occur with regular frequency.

In addition, some associations offer help and guidance not only to law enforcement but the corporate world as well. The High Technology Crime Investigation Association (HTCIA) is one such organization. The national Web site, `http://htcia.org`, links to chapters throughout the world, which include information on local laws associated with computer crimes.

Training

To fight cybercrime effectively, everyone who deals with it must be educated. This includes the criminal justice and the IT communities, as well as everyday users. Imagine what would happen to evidence if a law enforcement officer wasn't properly trained and, as a result of his or her actions, a good portion of evidence was destroyed. Many times, the judge or jury does not understand the topics discussed or lacks the technical expertise to interpret the law. What would happen in a complex case if the jury, prosecutor, and judge did not understand computer-related evidence? More likely than not, the defendant would end up getting away with the crime.

We are faced with many scenarios where this is true, but probably none more vexing than cases involving child pornography. Child pornography issues present circumstances in which the prosecution might have to prove that a photograph is one of a real child owing to rulings on virtual pornography. Pornographic pictures and videos with images that look like children need to be evaluated to determine if the subject is a minor and whether or not the subject is real or virtual. A defendant may claim that the images are of adults or virtual children. Experts may render opinions based on experience and training. Forensic investigators may use techniques such as skin tone analysis or verification against a database of items already recognized as real. The National Center for Missing and Exploited Children (NCMEC) (`http://www.missingkids.com/missingkids/servlet/Public HomeServlet?LanguageCountry=en_US`) maintains a database of real images against which law enforcement personnel can compare alleged child pornographic images for verification. A complete analysis may also include more standard forensic tasks, such as generating file listings, extracting web browser histories, processing email and text messages, manually reviewing pictures and videos, and extracting metadata. However, not all cases go to court, and the role of a forensic investigator can vary.

Before deciding what type of specific training you need, evaluate the role you want to fill so you get the most benefit. Here are common roles that can involve computer forensics:

◆ Law enforcement officials

◆ Legal professionals

◆ Corporate human resources professionals

◆ Compliance professionals

◆ Security consultants providing incident response services

◆ System administrators performing incident response

◆ Private investigators

The next sections discuss the types of computer forensic employees in both the corporate and law enforcement worlds and the types of training available for them.

Forensic Practitioners

The following types of people and organizations sometimes hire computer forensic specialists:

◆ Civil litigators can utilize personal and business computer records in cases involving fraud, divorce, and harassment.

◆ Insurance companies can sometimes reduce costs by using computer evidence of possible fraud in accident, arson, and workman's compensation cases.

◆ Corporations hire computer forensic specialists to obtain evidence of embezzlement, theft, and misappropriation of trade secrets.

◆ Individuals sometimes hire computer forensic specialists to support claims of wrongful termination, sexual harassment, and age discrimination.

◆ Law enforcement officials sometimes require assistance in pre-search warrant preparation and post-seizure handling of computer equipment.

◆ Prosecutors and defense attorneys in criminal and civil proceedings often use evidence uncovered by computer forensic specialists.

◆ Criminal prosecutors use computer evidence in cases such as financial fraud, drug and embezzlement record-keeping, and child pornography.

All of these industries rely on properly trained computer forensic investigators. The following sections describe some of the training available to both corporate and law enforcement worlds. The role that you play as a computer forensic investigator will ultimately decide which type of training is right for you.

Law Enforcement

The position an individual holds in the criminal justice community dictates the type of training required. Here are some examples of the types of training needed in several professions:

- ◆ Legislators need to understand the laws that are proposed and that they are passing.
- ◆ Prosecuting attorneys should have training on electronic discovery and digital data, and how to properly present computer evidence in a court of law.
- ◆ Detectives should have hands-on training in working with data discovery of all types and on various operating systems.

When law enforcement professionals are originally trained at the academy, they should receive some type of basic training on computer crime and how to investigate such crimes. Ideally, all criminal justice professionals would receive training in computer crimes, investigations, computer network technologies, and forensic investigations. Here are some ways to get the training needed to pursue a career in computer forensics:

- ◆ Key Computer Service Certified Computer Examiner (CCE) BootCamp: http://www.cce-bootcamp.com/
- ◆ The SANS Institute's computer security training courses: www.sans.org
- ◆ The International Association of Computer Investigative Specialists (IACIS) forensic examiner courses: http://www.iacis.com

Many local community colleges and universities offer classes in computer forensics. Law enforcement professionals can take advantage of them without having to pay the high cost of classes offered by private firms. An excellent resource for law enforcement is the International Association for Computer Investigative Specialists (IACIS), online at http://www.iacis.com/.

Corporate

Frequently, security and disaster recovery projects aren't funded because they don't produce revenue. An Ernst & Young annual security survey of 1,400 organizations states that only 13 percent think that spending money on IT training is a priority. This shows that training is needed not only for IT professionals but for management as well.

In the corporate world, just as in the criminal justice world, the position an individual holds in an organization dictates the type of training they need. For end users to buy into security, management must buy in first. Managers have a legal responsibility to police what is happening within their own computer systems, as demonstrated by the Sarbanes-Oxley Act. Management training is usually geared more toward compliance issues and the cost of putting preventative measures in place. IT professionals, on the other hand, need training geared more toward return on investment (ROI) in order to obtain funding for security projects and computer crime awareness, which includes new vulnerabilities. They should also be trained on applicable laws and regulations, how crimes are investigated, and how crimes are prosecuted. This training can help eliminate the reluctance that organizations have about contacting law enforcement when security breaches occur or when crimes are committed.

Education for every level of practitioner can be found on the SANS (SysAdmin, Audit, Network, Security) Web site at http://www.sans.org/security-resources .php (Figure 1.2). The SANS Institute was established in 1989 as a cooperative research and education organization. Its programs are designed to educate security professionals, auditors, system administrators, network administrators, chief information security officers, and chief information officers.

Figure 1.2   SANS Security Resources Web site

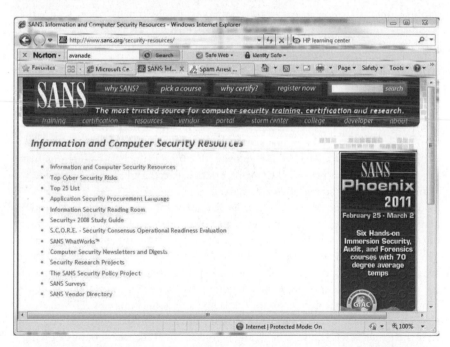

End Users

Legislation such as Sarbanes-Oxley will not change behaviors simply because it is the law. This is like speeding. Laws against driving over the speed limit do not stop some people from speeding: Many speeders are repeat offenders. Why? It's because certain behaviors are difficult to change. A person's behavior is based on their principles and values. People adopt new patterns of behavior only when their old ones are no longer effective.

The goal of training is to change behavior. An effective training program helps the workforce adopt an organization's principles and values. As already mentioned, management must be trained, buy in, and become an integral part of user education and the training process for everyone to take such training seriously. Only then will users adopt more secure behaviors.

WARNING

The hardest environment to control is the end user's environment. Training and education are vital to any organization with computer users and Internet access.

Security Awareness

malware
Another name for malicious code. This includes viruses, logic bombs (slag code or a delayed-action virus), and worms.

social engineering
A method of obtaining sensitive information about a company through exploitation of human nature.

A network is only as strong as its weakest link. We hear this phrase time and time again. Humans are considered to be the weakest link. No matter how secure the hardware and software are, if users aren't taught the dangers of social engineering, e-mail scams, and *malware*, the network can be jeopardized with a phone call or simple mouse click.

Social engineering plays on human nature to carry out an attack. Which is easier, getting an employee to give you a password or running password-cracking software? Obviously, getting an employee to give you a password eliminates a lot of effort on the part of a criminal. Social engineering is hard to detect because employers have very little influence over lack of common sense or ignorance on the part of employees. That said, employee education is the best counter against ignorance. Most business environments are fast-paced and service-oriented. Human nature is trusting and often naïve.

Take this scenario as an example. A vice president calls the help desk and states that he's in big trouble. He's trying to present a slideshow to an important client and has forgotten his password; therefore, he can't log onto the company Web site to make the presentation. He changed his password yesterday and can't remember the new one. He needs it right away because he has a room full of people waiting, and he's starting to look incompetent. The client is extremely important and could bring millions of dollars in revenue to the company. However, if the help desk staff member supplies the password as requested, without verifying that the caller is who he says he is, the help desk staff member could be giving access to an intruder.

If you think that this is an unlikely scenario, consider that in July 2010, a contest at the annual Defcon convention pitted social engineers against Fortune 500 companies. Participants in the contest had no problem getting data from Fortune 500 companies. Data that the contestants collected from employees included the operating system and service pack number they use, the e-mail client and antivirus software they use, and the name of their local wireless network.

Network World reported on this contest on July 30, 2010 (http://www.network world.com/news/2010/073110-how-to-steal-corporate-secrets.html). The first contestant, Wayne, was an Australian security consultant given the task to call a major U.S. company and get any data that could be used in a computer attack. From inside a soundproof booth in front of the audience, Wayne contacted an IT call center and talked with an employee. Wayne claimed to be a consultant from KPMG, an international firm that provides audit, tax, and advisory services, who was performing an audit and faced pressure from an approaching deadline. The call center employee was new and had only been with this employer for a month.

Ignoring the call center employee's request for his employee number, Wayne immediately launched into a routine about his boss being on his back, and how he really needed to wrap up this audit. Within a few minutes, the new worker appeared willing to give out whatever information Wayne requested. The call center employee even visited a fake web page for KPMG to which Wayne directed him. At the end of the call, Wayne asked the employee what beer he preferred and promised to buy him one.

When creating a security-awareness program, organizations should keep these goals in mind:

- ◆ Evaluate compelling issues.
- ◆ Know laws and policies for protecting data.
- ◆ Look at values and organizational culture.
- ◆ Set baseline knowledge requirements.
- ◆ Define best practices.
- ◆ Make lasting cultural and behavioral changes.
- ◆ Create positive approaches and methods.

For each topic in the awareness program, the two most important ideas to convey to end users and IT employees are what a potential incident looks like, and what the end user should do about it. If you need help putting together these policies, the National Institute of Standards and Technology (NIST) has some great information in its Computer Security Resource Center (CSRC) at http://csrc.nist.gov/groups/SMA/ate/ (Figure 1.3).

Figure 1.3   NIST Computer Security Resource Center Web site

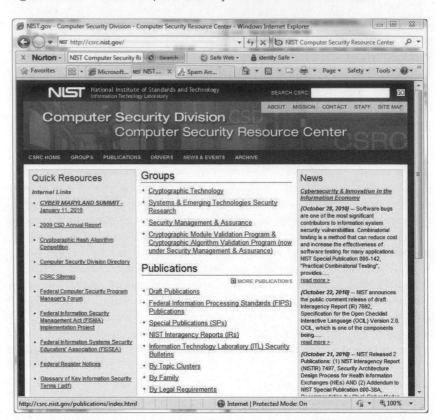

All organizations that rely on computer technology or use sensitive data should have a security awareness and training program. Such a program is required by various laws for specific industries, such as the Sarbanes-Oxley Act for all publically held companies, the Gram-Leach Bliley Act for financial institutions, and the Health Insurance Portability and Accountability Act for health-care entities. If you need more information on these federal security and privacy laws, see the "Corporate Concerns: Detection and Prevention" section earlier in this chapter. Many individual states also have laws that require businesses to protect sensitive personal and financial data, and to report data breaches. An effective awareness and training program can reduce an organization's risk profile, allow earlier identification of an attack or breach, and may even prevent loss of important forensic data when an attack occurs.

What Are Your Organization's Needs?

Each organization is different. As a professional, it is your job to assess your organization's specific needs.

Law enforcement professionals may determine that their caseloads are too extensive for the manpower they have. Maybe the equipment they are using is outdated. Perhaps they have issues with a particular type of software.

Corporate organizations may want to make sure they formulate security policies by assessing risk, threats, and their exposure to determine how best to keep their networking environment safe. Corporations can also have outdated equipment or applications, making their networks more vulnerable.

Because every organization is different, with different policies and requirements, there are no "one size fits all" rules that cover all the security bases. Training and education make a good start, but you must constantly update your knowledge of hardware, software, and threats. You should recognize how they affect your work and your organization so that you can continuously reassess your vulnerabilities. Remember, a computer forensic technician is a combination of a private eye and a computer scientist.

Security experts are able to monitor vast amounts of data. They can track Internet access, read employee e-mails, record phone calls, and monitor network access. How much you monitor depends on how much information you want to store. Remember that your monitoring plan should be clear-cut and built around specific goals and policies. Without proper planning and policies, you can quickly fill your log files and hard drives with useless or unused information. Here are some items to consider as you get ready to implement a monitoring policy.

- ◆ Identify potential resources at risk within your environment (for example, sensitive files, financial applications, and personnel files).

- ◆ After resources are identified, set up the policy. If a policy requires auditing large amounts of data, be sure the hardware has the necessary storage space, as well as sufficient processing power and memory.

- ◆ Make time to review the logs. The information in log files won't help protect against a system compromise if you don't read it for six months.

You can monitor as much or as little as you want, but if you don't read the logs, they cannot serve their intended purpose.

NOTE

Monitoring can be as simple or complex as you want to make it. Be consistent regardless of the plan you create. Many organizations monitor an extensive amount of information, while others, especially small ones, may monitor little or nothing. Just remember that it will be quite difficult to catch an intruder if you don't monitor anything.

Terms to Know

best practices	intrusion detection
computer forensics	malware
disaster recovery	security policies
electronic discovery	social engineering
incident	virus
incident response	worm
intrusion	

Review Questions

1. What is electronic discovery?

2. Name some examples of electronic discovery items.

3. The recovery of data focuses on what four factors?

4. Who works under more restrictive rules, law enforcement officials or corporate employees?

5. What is incident response?

6. Why is social engineering hard to prevent and detect?

7. Why aren't incidents reported in many corporate environments?

8. What law was passed to avoid future accounting scandals such as those involving Enron and WorldCom?

9. Name some factors that help to determine which criminal cases get priority.

10. Name a good resource for computer forensic training for law enforcement.

Chapter 2

Preparation—What to Do Before You Start

Be prepared! This motto is especially true for computer forensics. To do a thorough job, a computer forensic investigator should know the hardware, operating systems, file systems, and networking solutions associated with all equipment under investigation. Most organizations have incident response teams that can provide this information for forensic situations, or assist with its compilation.

As an investigator, you must know your legal limits and be familiar with local laws where the crime was committed or incident occurred. You'll also need to know the laws where perpetrators reside, to be sure that any case you build stands up in a court of law.

If you do most of the groundwork needed to build a case ahead of time, when that need arises you'll be able to complete the task more efficiently. This chapter guides you through the following processes.

Know Your Hardware

Information can be retrieved from many hardware devices, including internal and external hard drives, CD-ROMs, USB flash drives, Compact Flash devices, memory cards or sticks, and smartphones. Information stored on such devices is nonvolatile, and usually persists intact when such a device is powered off (and sometimes even after erasure).

By comparison, devices such as keyboards, monitors, and printers do not store data permanently (or at all). These devices are used to send data to and receive data from computers. After a computer is turned off, these devices do not truly store information. However, a trained computer forensic investigator who employs specialized techniques can often find data or evidence on these devices even when a system is powered off (as with printer buffers or onboard storage devices).

Because technology is constantly changing, keeping up-to-date on new devices and methods for communication is important. You must also determine which of these technologies and devices are permitted in an organization under investigation. That's because employees frequently use their own devices for convenience's sake, but intruders use them to gather information, often illicitly.

What I/O Devices Are Used?

Many of the terms used to describe computers or their components actually describe their capability, use, or size. Even though the word "computer" can apply to just about any device that contains a microprocessor, most of us think of a computer as a device that processes what we input using a keyboard or a mouse and then displays the results on a screen.

One of the first items on your planning agenda should be to list all types of *input/output (I/O)* devices used in the organization. This list will drive the selection of tools needed to analyze the information they contain. It will also give you a good idea of what areas could be susceptible to intrusion and might therefore need more monitoring.

input/output (I/O)
Data transfer that occurs between the thinking part of the computer, or CPU, and an external device or peripheral. For example, when you type on a keyboard, that device sends input to the computer. Usually software directs the computer to output what you type on a screen.

Servers

In the early days of computing, mainframes were the primary repositories for storing and processing data. These were huge computers that filled entire rooms. As the power of computers has increased, their size has decreased. Many mainframes have been replaced by enterprise servers—although you'll still find mainframes in use, particularly in large enterprises. Mainframes generally involve large, specialized, expensive hardware systems from vendors such as IBM, Hitachi, HP (NonStop systems), Fujitsu, and NEC. Older models use proprietary CPUs, memory, and bus architectures. Enterprise servers, on the other hand, are generally modular, rack-mounted computers built around stock Intel or AMD server processors (such as Xeon and Opteron, respectively), and use standard memory packages and bus architectures. Price is also a major differentiator: It's easy to spend millions on a mainframe installation, but difficult to spend more than $500,000 on an entire equipment rack stuffed with server blades, storage devices, high-speed interconnects, plus redundant power supplies.

Servers can play various roles. By identifying the role that each server plays, you can more easily determine which tools you'll need. Common server roles include application, file, web hosting, print, e-mail, Voice over Internet Protocol (VoIP) services and messaging, and File Transfer Protocol (FTP).

You should also determine where servers are situated. Are they accessed from the internal network only, from the external world (over the Internet), or both? This helps identify vulnerabilities, as well as protective measures that should be in place. This is important because, owing to the anonymity of networks and the Internet, attacks on all types of servers are increasing. The reasons for such attacks can be attributed to everything from simple curiosity to malicious intent.

Workstations

The term *workstation* used to refer to extremely powerful *desktop* computers most often used by research and development teams. Because technology has advanced so rapidly and a lot of processing power can be packed into a small machine, *workstation* is often used interchangeably with *personal computer (PC)* or *desktop*.

Although PCs and workstations can be used as stand-alone systems (for example, in a home environment), they are often linked together to form a local area network (LAN). Figure 2.1 shows the relationship between a server and workstations on a LAN.

Figure 2.1   Typical LAN setup

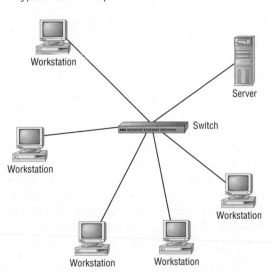

_____ **NOTE** _____

server
A computer with sufficient processing power and storage capacity to provide services to other computers over a network. Servers often include multiple processors, large amounts of memory, and many sizable hard drives. They also often incorporate two or more high-speed network interfaces (Gigabit Ethernet, also known as GbE, or better).

workstation
A high-end desktop computer that delivers enhanced processing power, significant memory capacity, and performs special functions, such as software or game development, CAD/CAM design, finite element analysis, and so forth.

personal computer (PC)
A personal computer intended for generic use by an individual. PCs were originally known as microcomputers because they were built on a smaller scale than the systems most businesses used at the time.

desktop
A PC designed to be set up in a permanent location because its components are too large or heavy to transport easily.

You should maintain an inventory of workstations on the premises. You should also know who connects to the network remotely.

In today's mobile society, telecommuting has become a way of life. Telecommuting saves overhead and energy costs. Many organizations hire contractors without providing them with work space on-site. This is an important factor to remember. Everyone has heard horror stories about people hacking into corporate networks through home computers. It can—and does—happen all the time!

John Deutch

One high-profile case is that of ex-CIA director John Deutch. He stored over 17,000 pages of classified documents on unsecured Macintosh computers in two of his homes. National security secrets were stored where almost anyone could access them. His computers, designated for unclassified use only, were connected to modems and regularly used to access the Internet and the Department of Defense (DoD). Family members were also allowed to use those same PCs.

Unsecured classified magnetic media were also found in Deutch's residences. A team of data recovery experts retrieved all data from Deutch's unclassified computers and magnetic media. The results of this inquiry were submitted to CIA senior management.

Deutch pled guilty to storing government secrets on unsecured home computers in exchange for receiving no prison time. Deutch was pardoned by President Bill Clinton hours before his presidency ended.

---

mobile device
A catch-all term that refers to any of a number of handheld computing and communications devices, including cell phones, smartphones, handheld computers, and even so-called personal digital assistants (PDAs). All of these handheld devices have some or all of the following capabilities: general computing including web access and compact local applications (called apps), wireless Internet and networking components, wireless telecommunications, global positioning systems (GPSes), e-mail access, and phone/address book capabilities. Mobile devices generally use flash memory instead of a hard drive for storage to keep them as light and small as possible.

Workstation security is too often overlooked and under-appreciated. Yet this is one target that proves irresistible to intruders because it is a path of least resistance when deploying an attack.

Mobile Devices and More

Mobile devices include ordinary cell phones as well as smartphones. Cell phone design puts a strong emphasis on phone use; smartphones include a strong emphasis on Internet access and applications as well. Cell phones are more compact, feature smaller screens and keyboards, and aim more at basic voice communication with limited text-handling. Smartphones are somewhat larger with bigger, higher-resolution screens and keyboards that more easily accommodate text-handling, and feature basic Internet access (Web, e-mail, Twitter, and so forth) along with voice communications. At the moment, the Apple iPhone is the must-have smartphone, though other models from LG, HTC, and Motorola also inspire strong "gadget lust."

Mobile devices also encompass handheld computers and PDAs, which may also be referred to as palmtops or pocket computers. The two major categories in this case are handheld and palm-sized. The differences between the two are size, display, and method of data entry. Handheld computers tend to be larger, with larger liquid crystal displays (LCDs), and might use a miniature keyboard in combination with touch-screen technology for data entry (the Apple iPad is an interesting and popular example of this type). Palm-sized computers are smaller and lighter, with smaller LCDs and stylus/touch-screen technology or handwriting recognition programs for data entry. They can also include voice recognition technologies. A typical PDA can function as a cell phone, fax, web browser, and personal organizer. Figure 2.2 shows some typical mobile devices, including a cell phone, a smartphone, and an iPad.

Figure 2.2   Samsung 2G cell phone (left) and Apple iPhone (right) on top of an Apple iPad

Smartphones, handheld PCs, and PDAs are often designed to work in conjunction with a desktop or laptop PC. Communication to synchronize the device and the computer typically occurs via a USB cable. Many mobile devices can rest in a cradle while hooked up to a PC. Besides communicating via cable, mobile devices can use infrared (IR) ports or various wireless methods (such as 802.11b, 802.11g, 802.11n, and Bluetooth) to transfer data.

All mobile devices are highly susceptible to theft because they are small, valuable, and frequently contain important or sensitive information. Many of them use wireless or infrared technology so that any data they transfer can be intercepted if it is not properly protected.

WARNING

Mobile devices, especially smartphones, remain some of the fastest selling consumer devices in history. You should know whether they are used on the network of the organization you're investigating because malicious individuals can use them to transfer sensitive information outside normal access controls, for later reuse or even resale.

Other Devices

CD/DVD-ROM/RW drive
A drive, either internal or external, that is used to read and/or write CDs and DVDs. A CD can store large amounts of digital information (650 MB to 750 MB) on a very small surface. Single-sided, single-layer DVDs hold 4.70 GB while double-sided double-layer DVDs hold more than 17 GB of digital information. CDs and DVDs are incredibly inexpensive to manufacture.

Many other devices can be used to transport or transmit data. They mainly consist of removable media. When you think of removable media, you probably think of floppy disks or CDs and DVDs, which are used in *floppy drives* and *CD/DVD-ROM/RW drives*, respectively. An increasing number of Blu-ray Disc devices (which can accommodate 50 GB of data per recordable media blank) are also showing up in the workplace.

In addition, you should be aware of other devices and determine if any of them are being used. For example, older storage media and devices are present in many workplaces. These include:

- **floppy disks**: There are several form factors called floppy disks. Capacities range from hundreds of kilobytes to a couple of megabytes. From most recent to oldest, they are:
  - 3.5-inch rotating magnetic media in rigid but compact plastic shells
  - 5.25-inch rotating magnetic media in flexible plastic shells
  - 8-inch rotating magnetic media in flexible plastic shells
- **zip disks**: These are somewhat larger than conventional floppies and store hundreds of megabytes of data.
- **Jaz disks**: Removable, single-platter hard disks packaged in special protective plastic shells. These devices, which can store hundreds of megabytes and up to 8 GB, are basically hard disks (the drive mechanism) with removable media (the Jaz disks themselves).

Remember that for any kind of removable media (and this includes all kinds of tape formats and other lesser-known removable media from days of yore) a matching drive must be found, and then a driver for a PC or other computer used to access media contents. Putting together all the pieces of this sometimes pesky puzzle can make life interesting during forensic investigations.

USB flash drives (UFDs) come in many sizes, from 1 GB to as high as 256 GB (older models in the 16 MB to 512 MB range are also still kicking around). USB flash drives can be used for exchanging large files with someone, running an alternate or repair system on another computer (such as a laptop computer), and keeping certain files separate from files on a hard disk (for example, hacking utilities).

USB flash drive (UFD)
A small, portable, high-capacity flash memory device that attaches to a computer or mobile device via a Universal Serial Bus (USB) port.

Figure 2.3 shows various UFDs, all of which are small enough to fit into a shirt or pants pocket with ease. Many UFDs include password and encryption utilities, and there are many utilities available to protect UFD contents from third parties as well. Secure UFDs from vendors like IronPort are also available. These not only protect their contents, but also permit access to be managed and controlled remotely and centrally, even to the point of destroying a UFD that has been lost or possibly stolen.

external hard drive
A hard disk in an external enclosure with its own power supply and data interface(s). Nearly all external hard disks support USB; many support higher-speed interfaces such as eSATA or FireWire (IEEE 1394).

At the time of this writing, modern *external hard drives* come in capacities from 160 GB to as high as 4 TB. Many include backup utilities, and some even include encryption plus protection and password management utilities as well. You will learn about passwords, encryption, and decryption in Chapter 7, "Passwords and Encryption."

Figure 2.3   UFDs, ranging in physical size (tiny blue model and large Survivor model with waterproof case both hold 8 GB of data)

External hard drives (see Figure 2.4) come in two primary form factors nowadays: smaller, more portable units (which can accommodate as much as 2 TB) incorporate 2.5-inch notebook drives; larger, less portable but more spacious units (which can accommodate as much as 4 TB right now) incorporate standard 3.5-inch desktop PC drives.

Figure 2.4   Two external hard disks: 160 FB 2.5" USB mini-jack type on top of 1.5 TB 3.5" USB Type B jack

 *Real World Scenario*

Tales from the Trenches: A Preparation War Story

Computer forensic experts should heed the Boy Scout motto: "Be prepared!"

While working with a group of computer forensic specialists who were preparing for a trip to a "far off land" to recover information of "interest to the nation," we organized a list of every item that might possibly be needed during an extended stay. This team was assembled based on each member's unique talents and skills. We brainstormed for days, running through every scenario we could imagine to determine how best to prepare for the upcoming mission.

Our team developed a list incorporating all typical items you would expect for such a trip, including strong, secure shipping containers, appropriate commercial forensic recovery tools, a collection of hard drives of various sizes, commercial hard drive duplication hardware, and adapters to read assorted forms of media. We collected a copy of each operating system we anticipated seeing in the field as well as an assortment of application CDs and a variety of other software.

We conducted intensive "ramp up" training to bring all team members "up to speed" and "on the same page" with policies and procedures for this mission. Each team member was instructed on legal limits and requirements for conducting searches and seizing evidence in this foreign location. Everyone was reminded that any evidence located might later be used in court proceedings. Everyone was ready to go. We had planned for every possible contingency.

With all the preparation completed and the equipment safely packed away, the team departed for their new assignment, confident they had the training, equipment, and resources necessary to accomplish their mission. The team arrived on-site and began to set up lab equipment in a safe and secure location to protect their gear and to preserve the integrity of any evidence they processed. Members of the team were assigned to test the equipment to ensure everything worked properly. Other team members were dispatched to locate potential evidence to bring back to the lab for analysis.

Within a few days the team had begun to locate items of interest and began conducting forensic analyses of computers and hard drives. Each case was documented fully, and each investigation appeared to be running smoothly. All our prior planning appeared to be paying off and every part of the operation was running nicely. And then, right on time, Mr. Murphy made his much-dreaded appearance!

With every plan, no matter how well-conceived or executed, something always seems to go wrong. Usually it is something minor—something that typically would cost only a little time and money to fix— had we considered it before the team left home. It is usually something so trivial no one anticipates its occurrence. Here, it was something so important that the team was stuck until the problem was solved.

Continues

In this part of the world, old 5 1/4-inch floppy disks are still in use; and the team located a large collection of such disks that very possibly contained evidence linked to the investigation. The team had no blank 5 1/4-inch media on which to corral the evidence and, of course, no 5 1/4-inch disk drives were installed in any of the lab PCs. Even our training had skipped this issue, so younger members of the team had to be instructed in proper techniques for write-protecting such disks to safeguard evidence. New 5 1/4-inch media had to be flown in from another country along with brand-new 5 1/4-inch disk drives. While this did not stop the team from ultimately accomplishing their mission, it did cause a minor delay in processing time-critical information.

What can you learn from this? No matter how much planning and preparation you undertake, something for which you are not prepared usually pops up. It certainly is nice when you can run down to a local computer superstore and buy whatever you need; but sometimes you just have to make do until proper supplies arrive. Planning is important, but so is another skill that the Scouts might just want to add to their list—an ability to improvise.

Networked printers, webcams, networked fax machines, and networked copiers also have vulnerabilities that can lead to data exposure or denial of service. They can be used as gateways for attacks on other systems. These types of I/O devices are often taken for granted, and their security is rarely questioned. Sometimes organizations use the same printers to print sensitive documents that they use to print public documents, such as announcements for company parties. Don't forget these devices as you inventory the environment.

Check for Unauthorized Hardware

Frequently, employees just assume that it's okay to install a device on the network or their PC. Unauthorized installations can present security issues to an organization. Once you have inventoried all approved devices in use in the organization you're investigating, it's time to look for installed hardware that isn't approved. You may be surprised at what you will find, if not astonished outright.

Modems

Modems are devices connected to a phone line that can be used to dial into a server or computer. Wireless modems convert digital data into radio signals and convert radio signals back into digital signals. Although modems are still in use in some geographic areas, they have been replaced (particularly in urban areas) by high-speed cable and digital subscriber line (DSL) solutions, which are faster than dial-up access.

modem
A shorthand version of the words modulator-demodulator. A modem is used to send digital data over a phone line. The sending modem converts digital data into a signal that is compatible with the phone line (modulation), and the receiving modem then converts that signal back into digital data (demodulation).

war dialing
Automated software that attempts to dial numbers within a given range of phone numbers to determine if any of those numbers are actually used by modems accepting dial-in requests.

Nevertheless, modems and modem pools or banks are still operational in corporations or SOHO (small office, home office) environments. Many companies still use modems so employees can dial into their networks and work from home. These modems are usually configured to be available to any incoming calls. *War dialing* takes advantage of these situations and targets connected modems set to receive calls without authentication.

NOTE

War dialing was extremely popular years ago. In fact, it figured into the popular 1983 movie *War Games* starring Mathew Broderick, who dialed into a military missile control system and nearly started a world war while thinking he was simply playing a strategy game. However, because newer technologies have replaced connected modems set to receive calls without authentication, war dialing may be an unlikely threat for a LAN. It depends on how advanced an organization's technology might be.

 Real World Scenario

Tales from the Trenches: The Case of the Missing Modems

Security audits can—and very often do—turn up all kinds of unexpected elements in an organization's IT infrastructure. One case in point was an audit, followed by a datacenter move, that I helped to conduct for a major U.S. banking and financial services company.

In the process of conducting the audit, we discovered that the datacenter continued to maintain an even dozen analog phone lines through its PBX system (such lines are normally digital, and analog lines in this environment usually point to the presence of a modem somewhere). But while we could find the lines, try as we might, searching high and low, we couldn't find the modems that went with them.

The mystery was solved when we started to disassemble the raised-floor area in the datacenter. (In many datacenters, cabling and power leads are generally routed under the floor, and related equipment such as servers, power conditioners, cooling units, and so forth, sit on top of the floor.) As we started moving servers, we had to disconnect their cables, which perforce meant lifting the floor tiles to get at the cables and wires. Directly under one dozen of the one-hundred-plus servers in that room, we found our missing modems. It turned out the company permitted project administrators to request and use special modems to dial into their project servers so that they could be remotely restarted after hours and on weekends. They used special interface devices called POST boot cards that can recycle the power to a server and support what's called a "cold start" when a machine needs to be completely reset. Over time, records for these devices were misplaced or lost. The lines were kept live, and the modems kept running, but nobody knew where they were, or even that they were still up and running.

Continues

This discovery underscores the importance of systematic phone number and extension checking when conducting security surveys. Whenever a live modem is found, it needs to be located and documented. Even more important, such modems should only remain online if there's no other equipment available to perform the tasks that they handle. In our datacenter, for example, a gradual switchover from Compaq to Dell servers meant that the Dell Remote Access Controller (DRAC) devices that the bank had purchased for their new servers could have taken over the role that those mysterious modems were meant to handle. When it comes to modems, the cardinal rule of security has to be "Don't use them, if you don't need them!"

Cable and DSL modems are more popular these days. These devices are not vulnerable to dial-up attacks, but they present a danger because they maintain always-on connections to the Internet. Cable modems enable Internet access through a shared cable medium and users are actually on a LAN with all subscribers in their area, which means everything that travels to or from a connected machine can be intercepted by other cable users if the security features in the hardware are compromised.

Real World Scenario

Former Employee of Hostgator.com Sentenced to Prison for Computer Attack

On January 26, 2009, Cliff L. Wade, a former support technician at Hostgator.com, a Houston-based Internet service provider, was sentenced in a Georgia federal court to eight months in prison and three years of supervised release, plus a fine of $100, in connection with a scheme to intentionally damage his former employer's network and business.

In early October 2007, Wade moved to Atlanta, GA, from Houston, TX, and started work for a competitor organization without notifying Hostgator of his departure or his changed employment situation. After this time, Wade accessed the Hostgator system and intentionally executed various command and code functions to impair the integrity of Hostgator's customer support network. Hostgator.com neither authorized nor was aware of Wade's activities, and Wade's intrusion caused the company to suffer financial damages in excess of $5,000. Hostgator.com incurred a significant reduction in revenues, and also lost money from resulting damage assessments and the costs involved in restoring damaged data and programs to their proper states.

In the course of the investigation, computer forensic analyses conducted by the FBI revealed that, although Wade had attempted to erase all electronic traces of his identity or presence, those attacks could be linked by certain computer records to other computers outside Hostgator that were in use or otherwise controlled by Wade.

Continues

As you can see from this case, knowing who has access to what machines is important. The fact that Wade remained able to access to the computers at Hostgator, even after going AWOL, is revealing and informative. In fact, cases have been documented where former employees are able to access networks *years* after their termination dates.

Key Loggers

key logger
Device that intercepts, records, and stores everything typed on a keyboard into a file. This includes all keystrokes, even passwords.

Key loggers record and retrieve everything typed, including e-mail messages, instant messages, and website addresses. To install a hardware key logger, you unplug the keyboard cable from the back of the PC, plug it into one end of a key logger, and then plug the other end into the PC. Figure 2.5 is a photo of the Keelog KeyDemon USB Hardware Keylogger.

Figure 2.5 The Keylog KeyDemon USB keylogger plugs in between the keyboard cable and the PC's USB port.

(Photograph Courtesy of Keelog, 2010, www.keelog.com)

Organizations use key loggers for the following reasons:

◆ As a tool for computer fraud investigations
◆ As a monitoring device to detect unauthorized access
◆ To prevent unacceptable use of company resources
◆ As a backup tool

So why are they on the list of unauthorized hardware? Simply put, anything can be used for bad intent, and unauthorized individuals can use key loggers to capture logins and passwords illicitly. Unless an organization uses them according to an explicit policy, key loggers should not be present on a network, or systems attached to a network.

Key logging is not restricted to hardware. Numerous key logging programs are readily available on the Internet.

NOTE

Software key loggers become easier to detect as time goes by because their log files grow. You'll eventually be able to tell when one is in use because available hard-drive space decreases markedly.

Real World Scenario

Key Logging Scam Targets Bank Users

On March 13, 2007, the U.S. Army website http://www.army.mil/NEWS/ reported from Fort Belvoir, VA, that soldiers, family members, and DoD civilians who use their home computers to access Thrift Savings Plan (TSP is a popular, widely used bank for military personnel, their families, and those who work for the military) could be vulnerable to information theft, and possibly theft of funds, as a result.

In the story, TSP officials indicated that they had identified numerous customers who had fallen victim to a key logging attack. The technique of keystroke logging was used in these cases to obtain TSP personal identification numbers and passwords, which in turn could provide access to identity information such as social security numbers (SSNs) in compromised accounts.

Michael Milner, Director of the U.S. Army Criminal Investigation Command (CIC) Computer Crime Investigative Unit, said that "personal information is increasingly available on 'keylogger' lists for sale through criminal networks and so far, all of the TSP cases involve the transfer of electronic funds, since criminals normally prefer the 'paperless' way to steal money." Milner also went on to say that users should take steps to protect themselves from key loggers and malware, and should promptly close their web browsers after visiting the TSP site. Even then, he also observed that "logging off a Web site does not clear a browser's memory, and subsequent users might be able to access the TSP account information."

According to the TSP, external penetration testing they conducted confirmed that TSP records had not been breached, but that personal information for those users whose keystrokes had been logged was compromised. The institution also identified some customers who had relatively small amounts withdrawn from their accounts. As a security precaution, TSP has discontinued making electronic payments for online transactions.

I/O Devices

Besides key loggers and modems, you may find lots of unapproved and potentially dangerous devices on an organization's network. The technologies behind many of them are discussed in the next section. Here is a list of some of these devices:

- Any UFD plugs into a USB port and saves up to 256 GB of data. Sizes vary, but these drives are affordable and no software is required to use them. These drives are also easily carried or concealed in pockets.

- Compact Flash drives (CFDs) and memory sticks of many kinds come in capacities up to 128 GB. These drives are also affordable and highly portable, and plug right into most notebook PCs and mobile devices.

- Secure Digital (SD) and miniature SD (miniSD) drives now come in capacities up to 64 GB (128 GB units are scheduled for release in 2011). Widely used in cell phones, cameras, and other portable devices, an increasing number of notebook PCs and portable devices now feature SD ports.

- A portable laptop drive can be only half an inch thick and weigh less than 4 ounces, yet it can store 1 TB.

The common factor in all of these devices is that they are small, hold a lot of data, and are easy to transport. Detecting that they are being used on a network can be challenging because they are easy to conceal, and their data transfer rates are fast. Corporate policy should address use of such devices.

USB Devices

In the early days of computing, each computer came with a limited number of ports to which you could attach devices. Printers connected to parallel printer ports, and most computers had only one port. Modems used the serial port, but so did Palm Pilots and digital cameras. Most computers had two serial ports. New technology was needed to support all of the I/O devices people wanted to attach to their computers.

Universal Serial Bus (USB)
A connectivity standard that allows for the connection of multiple devices without the need for software or hardware.

Today, all laptop and desktop computers come with two or more *Universal Serial Bus (USB)* connectors. USB connectors let you attach devices to your computer quickly and easily. Compared to other ways of connecting devices to your computer, USB devices are simple and straightforward. USB devices you can attach to your computer include printers, scanners, modems, and storage devices of all kinds and sizes.

You might need to attach more devices to a computer than you have USB ports. Purchasing an inexpensive USB hub enables you to connect additional USB devices to your computer. Figure 2.6 depicts a USB hub.

The USB standard supports up to 127 devices per port, and USB hubs are covered in that standard. A hub typically includes four or more ports. Just plug a hub into any USB port on your computer, and then plug devices into the hub.

You can add dozens of available USB ports to a single computer by chaining hubs together using USB cables.

Figure 2.6   USB hub

USB standard version 2, which was released in April 2000, can support data rates up to 480 megabits per second (Mbps). USB standard version 3, released in November 2008 (the first commercial devices that implemented USB 3 became available in January 2010), supports data rates up to 5 gigabits per second (Gbps). At the time of this writing, USB 3 devices are starting to be widely available, but Intel isn't expected to support the standard until 2011.

NOTE

USB devices are also *hot pluggable*. This means they can be attached to and unplugged from the computer without turning off the system. No special settings are necessary to unplug the USB devices without damaging device data. Many USB data storage devices are tiny. For example, many UFDs are small enough to fit on a key ring. Just plug a UFD into your USB port, and the operating system (OS) recognizes it immediately, allowing you to transfer files at your convenience. When you're done, simply eject the drive, plug it into another system, and transfer the files to that system.

hot pluggable
Also called "hot swappable," a computer device such as an external drive that you can connect without having to power down the computer first.

FireWire

FireWire was originally developed by Apple and is now an official IEEE 1394 standard (more than 60 vendors belong to the 1394 Trade Association). At 400 Mbps, FireWire 1394a has base bandwidth nearly on par with USB 2 (a higher bandwidth 1394b version, called Firewire 800, runs at 800 Mbps). FireWire is well-suited for transferring large data files, and supports up to 63 devices on a single bus. Connecting to a device is similar to using USB.

FireWire
An IEEE-1394 technology that implements a high-performance, external bus standard for rapid data transfer and streaming multimedia (such as video).

Just like USB, FireWire is plug-and-play compliant and hot swappable, so you can connect and disconnect devices without shutting down your computer.

TIP

Because this technology is well-suited for high-quality digital, video, and audio, FireWire is a good way to store pornography or proprietary company designs. It can also be used on a plug-in computer storage device, making it easy to copy and then remove tons of data.

Keep Up with I/O Trends

As new technologies emerge, so do ways for intruders to infiltrate networks. Because technology is always changing, you have to evaluate new technologies before those devices appear on your (or your clients') networks. You should spend some time reading about these new technologies as they are developed and marketed.

Everybody has become familiar with seeing people talking to themselves in public places, thanks to wireless in-ear headsets for mobile devices that are so small you can't even see them when a person's head is turned the wrong way. You have Bluetooth to thank for these moments of apparent lunacy, but as you'll see, Bluetooth provides a great deal more functionality than enabling wireless voice link-ups: Bluetooth also enables printer, network, and even data transfer links.

Bluetooth

Bluetooth
A standard developed to allow various types of electronic equipment to make their own connections by using a short-range (10 meter) frequency-hopping radio link between devices.

Bluetooth was named after Harald Bluetooth, the king of Denmark in the late 900s. It doesn't require any special equipment to work. The devices simply find one another and begin communicating.

──── *NOTE* ────

Bluetooth operates on a frequency of 2.45 GHz, which is the same radio frequency band as baby monitors, garage door openers, and newer cordless phones.

The design process makes sure that Bluetooth and other devices don't interfere with one another. Bluetooth uses a technique called "spread-spectrum frequency hopping." This means a device will use randomly chosen frequencies within a designated range and regularly hop or change from one range to another. Bluetooth transmitters change frequencies 1,600 times every second.

Bluetooth covers an astonishing array of products (more than 11,000 of them as we write this chapter, according to the product list at Bluetooth.com). They include audio/visual, phone and headset, automotive, networking, and widespread computer applications. Wireless mice, keyboards, speakers, printers, and even USB extenders are all available in Bluetooth versions.

eSATA

eSATA
External Serial Advanced Technology Attachment (eSATA) is an interface technology that permits external hard drives to use the same high-speed SATA interface that internal hard drives use.

To understand *eSATA*, you should first know that Serial Advanced Technology Attachment (SATA) was originally designed for high-speed internal connections for PC hard drives. Add an *e* for external on the front, and you get eSATA, a high-speed interface for external hard disks. As of 2009, modern PCs use SATA more or less exclusively for hard drives, and old-fashioned parallel interfaces serve only to support legacy devices.

SATA comes in three generations, so eSATA devices do, too:

◆ SATA 1.5 Gbps is the first generation and supports data rates up to 1.5 Gbps. It's also known as SATA 1.0.

◆ SATA 3.0 Gbps is the second generation and supports data rates up to 3.0 Gbps. This exceeds the capability of all but the fastest solid state disks (SSDs), serial attached SCSI (SAS), and flash drives currently available in today's marketplace. It's also known as SATA 2.0.

◆ SATA 6.0 Gbps is the third generation and is a relatively recent introduction to the computing world (the standard was approved in July 2008, but devices and computer interfaces that implement the standard didn't hit the market until late 2009). It's also known as SATA 3.0.

Most eSATA devices (and interfaces) available today implement SATA 1.0 or 2.0, with 3.0 eSATA devices starting to enter the marketplace at the time of this writing. Over time, the newer and faster technology will garner more presence. The SATA (and eSATA) technology supports data transfers as fast as modern storage technology can go, especially in its 2.0 and 3.0 versions.

TIP

Unlike FireWire and USB, eSATA devices cannot draw power through the PC interface. This means external power is required for eSATA, which makes it less convenient—and harder to conceal—than these other two interfaces. However, its astounding speed (and increasing availability of eSATA ports and flash drives) means security policies for external storage devices must mention eSATA.

When it comes to modern external storage, eSATA and USB 3.0 represent the current pinnacle for bandwidth. Thus, these technologies are even better-suited for high-quality digital, video, and audio than FireWire. These, too, are compelling ways to grab and go out the door with pornography or proprietary company designs.

Other Technologies

In addition to the technologies we have already discussed, a few others are worth mentioning, especially wireless ones. The world of wireless is rapidly expanding, and you may find yourself investigating issues that involve capturing data through wireless devices. Here are brief descriptions of some of those technologies:

◆ 802.1*x* is a standard developed for wireless local area networks (WLANs). It utilizes port-based network access control. Current standards range from 802.11a to 802.11n.

◆ IR transmissions use an invisible light spectrum range for device communication, so the devices have to be in direct line of sight with each other.

◆ I-Mode is NTT DoCoMo's mobile Internet access system that originated in Japan.

◆ BlackBerry is an end-to-end wireless solution developed by Research In Motion Limited.

These technologies make our lives easier, yet they can pose a threat to any network environment. A wireless device advertises that it is out there, making it easy for an intruder to pick up and monitor.

Know Your Operating System

Once you have a good inventory of the I/O devices on the network and have identified what kind of unapproved devices you might find, you must enumerate which operating systems (and versions) are in use throughout the organization.

It used to be that you would find only one type of operating system on a network. With the advent of mobile computing, Internet business, and corporate mergers, networks have become more complex and diverse. Typical computer examinations must adapt to the fast-changing and diverse world in which computer forensic science examiners work. Before you can begin a forensic investigation, you must be familiar with various operating systems you might encounter.

Commonly Encountered Operating Systems

operating system
Acts as a director and interpreter between the user and all the software and hardware on the computer.

Not only do various *operating systems* exist, but each operating system has multiple versions, such as server and workstation, and new releases. How you handle and extract information from a computer running Linux will be very different from how you handle and extract information from a Windows computer.

Windows

Although you probably won't find it in use anymore, Microsoft's first attempt at a graphical operating system was Microsoft Windows 1 in 1985. Many subsequent versions of Microsoft Windows have been released. Table 2.1 highlights a few of the better-known versions of Windows that you might encounter on older systems.

In 1995, Microsoft introduced Windows 95, which was a significant improvement over Windows 3.*x* and was Microsoft's first truly consumer-oriented graphical operating system for PCs. Windows NT came into its own with Windows NT 4: It was released in 1996 and became quite popular in the late 1990s. Then, along came Windows 98, followed by Windows 2000 and Windows Me (Millennium Edition). In 2001, Windows XP made its appearance, followed by Windows Server 2003. In

2006, Windows Vista was released, and two years later Windows Server 2008 came on the scene. Microsoft's latest release for workstations is Windows 7, and Windows Server 2008 R2 (Release 2) for servers. The most common Microsoft systems you will encounter are Windows XP, Windows Vista, and Windows 7.

Table 2.1   Early Windows Graphical Operating Systems

Version	Release date	Description
Windows 1	1985	Microsoft's first attempt at a graphical operating system
Windows 3.1	1992	Used in the early 1990s prior to creation of Windows 95
Windows 3.11	1993	Used in early 1990s prior to creation of Windows 95
Windows for Workgroups 3.11	1994	Allowed resource sharing between users without aid of a central authentication server
Windows NT	1994	NT stands for *New Technology*. It was specifically designed for the corporate environment and intended for use on high-powered servers and workstations
Windows 95	1995	Popular in late 1990s; more than a million copies were sold in the first four days after it was released

UNIX/Linux

The UNIX operating system was originally created at AT&T's Bell Laboratories and licensed freely to most universities and research facilities. UNIX was designed to allow a number of programmers to simultaneously access a single computer and share its resources. The operating system coordinates the use of the computer's resources, and it controls all of the commands from all of the keyboards and all of the data being generated. It permits each user to work as if he or she were the only person working on the computer.

Bell Labs distributed the operating system in its source language form. By the end of the1970s, dozens of different versions of UNIX were available. The success of the UNIX operating system has led to many technologies that are part of the IT environment today. Although UNIX is often installed on mainframes, versions of UNIX have found their way into the PC world. Some of the different versions available are BSD, HP-UX, SCO, IBX AIX, Sun Solaris, and Digital.

Linux is a UNIX-like operating system that was written by Linus Torvalds in 1991. Originally named Freax, it was hosted on the Minix operating system. Linux is an *open source* operating system, which means that its source code is readily and freely available online, and that users can either purchase commercial distributions at low cost, or "roll their own" at no cost, if they prefer.

open source
Code that the code creator makes available under a license that permits end users to freely redistribute, make modifications of, and create derivative works of the source code.

Ready availability has allowed thousands of people to contribute patches, fixes, and improvements. Installing Linux has become easier as the versions and products have evolved. The earlier versions were all text-based and, frequently, hardware support had to be compiled into the kernel. Newer versions have graphical-based installations, making the process much less complicated. Various versions of Linux are available. Some of the more popular ones are Mandrake, SuSE, Caldera, MkLinux, Debian, Slackware, and Red Hat. You will probably encounter Red Hat most often.

Macintosh and Mac OS

Apple introduced the Macintosh line of personal computers in 1984. The first Macintosh, or Mac for short, had 128 KB of memory and a unique design. The monitor and floppy disk drive were built into the same cabinet that housed its main circuitry. In 1994, Apple introduced the PowerMac. In 1998, the third generation of Macs was born with the release of the iMac.

Early versions of the Macintosh operating system were called System $x.x$, where $x.x$ was the version number. With the release of Mac OS 8, however, Apple dropped the word "System." Now the versions are simply known as Mac OS with a version number. The most current version is OS X (so called because X is the Roman numeral for 10), based on the UNIX BSD operating system. Macs are popular for high-end users and graphic or drawing applications, such as CAD. You might encounter Mac OS 8, 9, and X.

Other Operating Systems

The first operating system used on the earliest IBM PCs was called the Disk Operating System (DOS). Microsoft's version of DOS is the most common one and is called MS-DOS. Those of you who have been around the computing environment for a while might remember that IBM Corporation also produced a DOS product called PC-DOS. If you run into a DOS machine, you probably won't find a mouse and you certainly won't find a colorful screen. To run a DOS operating system, you issue commands at a prompt on the screen.

Freespire, formerly called Linspire (and originally, Lindows), is a full-featured operating system like Microsoft Windows 7 or Apple Mac OS. It runs Windows applications on top of Linux so they appear as they would in a native Windows environment. Various virtual machine environments are also available for Windows, Linux, UNIX, and Mac OS. These environments permit various different guest operating systems to run on top of those host OSes as well.

Mobile device operating systems (smartphones and such) are not as complex as those for PCs. Mobile devices run a variety of operating systems that include 3Com's Palm OS, Symbian, Google Android, Microsoft Windows Mobile, or iPhone OS (iOS). Windows Mobile (version 7 is now shipping) is a Microsoft product that supports color displays, graphics, Word, Excel, and built-in MP3 players or MPEG movie players. Other mobile OS offerings likewise support a broad range of screen resolutions, dynamic input areas, improved network communication, and Bluetooth. Of these, Google Android appears to be grabbing ever-increasing mind and market share.

Know Your Local File Systems

File systems enable an operating system to find files requested from a hard disk. The file system keeps a table of contents of the files on the disk. When a file is requested, the table of contents is searched to locate and access the file.

To understand this better, let's take a quick look at hard disks. The hard disk on which an operating system is installed is broken into large pieces called *clusters* or *allocation units*. Each cluster contains a number of sectors. A disk partition contains those sectors. Without additional support, each partition would be one large unit of data. Operating systems add a directory structure to assign names to each file and manage the free space available to create new files. The directory structure and method for organizing a partition is called a file system.

Different file systems reflect different operating system requirements. Some work better on small machines; others work better on large servers. The same hard disk can have partitions with file systems belonging to DOS, Windows, or Linux. When more than one file system type is installed on a hard drive, this is called a multiboot or dual-boot configuration.

FAT/NTFS

A file system keeps a table of contents (TOC) of files on a drive. When a file is requested, that TOC is searched to locate and access the file. One common file system is *File Allocation Table (FAT)*. Each cluster has an entry in the FAT that describes how it is used. The operating system uses FAT entries to chain together clusters that form files.

In the 1970s, PC file systems were designed to support floppy disks. Hard disk support came later. DOS uses the FAT file system, which is also supported by all other DOS- and Windows-based operating systems. Early versions of DOS used FAT12. The FAT system for later versions of DOS and older versions of Windows 95 is called FAT16. It is simple, reliable, and uses little storage. The FAT is stored at the beginning of the partition to act as the table of contents. To protect the partition, two copies of the FAT are kept in the event that one becomes damaged. The FAT structure doesn't have a lot of organization; files are given the first open location on the disk.

file system
An operating system's method for organizing, managing, and accessing files through logical structures on a hard drive.

cluster
Also referred to as an allocation unit, a unit of disk space that's allocated for files and directories.

File Allocation Table (FAT)
A simple file system used by DOS, but supported by later Microsoft (and other) operating systems. The FAT resides at the beginning of a disk partition and acts as a table of contents for stored data.

Virtual FAT (VFAT)
Also called FAT32, an enhanced version of the FAT file system that allows for names longer than the 8.3 convention and uses smaller allocation units on the disk.

Virtual FAT (VFAT) or FAT32, is an enhanced version of the FAT file system. It's available in Windows 95 and early versions of Windows NT. It allows files to have longer names than the 8.3 convention adopted by DOS. FAT32 also accommodates the use of smaller allocation units on a disk. The 8.3 convention is the original FAT file naming system, in which filenames could be up to eight characters long and files had three character extensions, or less, such as .txt, .doc, .ext, .bat, .bin, and so forth.

The *extended FAT (exFAT)* file system is an enhanced version of VFAT/FAT32. This file system is available in Windows Vista SP1, Windows 7, and Windows Server 2008 (and for embedded devices on Windows Embedded Compact 6.0—often referred to as Windows CE or Windows Embedded CE—and newer versions). It supports disk partitions of up to 64 zettabytes (ZB); 512 TB is the current recommended maximum. Individual files can be as large as 16 Exabytes, but are also subject to the 512 TB partition limit (or smaller). The exFAT file system also supports nearly 2.8 million files per directory (up from 65,535 in FAT32), and improved free space allocation and delete performance.

extended FAT (exFAT)
Sometimes (and incorrectly) called FAT64, this extended version of the FAT file system was developed to keep FAT working with the kinds of large hard disks (1 TB and larger) now so widely installed in modern desktop and notebook PCs.

The *New Technology File System (NTFS)* was developed expressly for versions of Windows NT and Windows 2000. Windows NT supports NTFS 4 and Windows 2000 and higher support NTFS 5. Windows Vista and Windows Server 2008 and higher support NTFS 6. Only Windows NT and higher Windows operating systems can use data on an NTFS volume. NTFS organizes files into directories, which are then sorted. It also keeps track of transactions against the file system, making it a recoverable file system. The following graphic shows a copy of the file structure on a Windows 7 computer.

New Technology File System (NTFS)
A file system supported by Windows NT and higher-level Windows operating systems, including Windows Server 2000, 2003, and 2008, and Windows XP, Vista, and 7.

Figure 2.7   Windows folder hierarchy structure is laid out clearly in this treemap listing from WinDirStat.

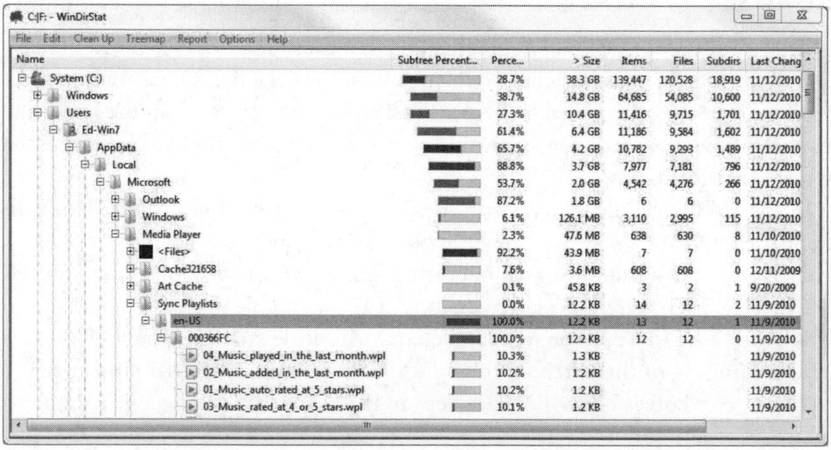

Notice the lines on the left side of the screen. Those lines indicate how many directories deep you are. In modern Windows versions file structures can go 20 or more levels deep.

Various UNIX/Linux File Systems

UNIX has been around for decades, making it the oldest of all file systems used on PC hardware. Also, UNIX file systems probably differ the most from other file systems used on PCs. The UNIX file system is organized as a hierarchy of directories starting from a single directory called root, which is represented by a slash (/).

UNIX looks at all disks and storage devices as part of one file system. Likewise, all Linux files are in one tree; there is no concept of drives such as A, B, C, and D. Storage devices are linked to the directory structure. In other words, a floppy disk may be accessed at /mnt/floppy and a CD-ROM on /cdrom. Any subdirectories that are created use the storage space assigned to their parent directory—unless they are assigned their own storage space. Filenames are case sensitive, so TEST and test are two different files.

The Linux operating system supports multiple and different file systems. To enable upper levels of the OS core to deal with these file systems, Linux defines an intermediary layer, known as the Virtual File System (VFS). Just as in UNIX, there are no drive letters in Linux. Instead, Linux creates a virtual file system, which makes all files on all devices appear to exist on one device. In Linux, as with UNIX, there is one root directory, and every file you can access is located under it.

Second/Third Extended Filesystems (ext2/ext3) are state-based file systems. This means the file system maintains state for all open files in memory—in other words, all open files have corresponding entries in data structures in memory.

Beginning with Red Hat Linux 7.2, the default file system changed from the ext2 format to the journaling ext3 file system. The ext3 file system is an enhanced version of the ext2 file system. It keeps logs and checkpoints for all transactions so that a file system check is no longer necessary after an unclean system shutdown. This way, if a system crashes, it can restore the file system using those logs.

The *Network File System (NFS)* was originally developed at Sun Microsystems in the 1980s to create a file system for diskless clients (networked computers with no local storage devices that rely upon servers for all their storage needs). NFS provides network access to shared file systems. The primary function of NFS is to mount directories to other computers. These directories can then be accessed as though they were local. This works the same way that mapped drives work in Microsoft networking.

Second/Third Extended Filesystems (ext2/ext3)
State-based filesystems used by the Linux operating system.

Network File System (NFS)
Provides remote access to shared file systems across networks. The primary function of NFS is to mount directories to other computers. These directories can then be accessed as though they were local.

Other File Systems

We've covered several file systems in this chapter; however, there are many other file systems available that are outside the scope of this book. The section "Tales from the Trenches: A Preparation War Story" presented earlier in this chapter warns that you can't always anticipate every possible contingency before you head into the field. We must also recognize that we can't arm you with information on every conceivable topic, nor every specific file system.

If you come across another file system that we don't mention here, remember that the Internet can be your biggest friend and ally. Other file systems we know about (and mentioned in the previous version of this book) include BFS (the BeOS File System designed for an alternative Power PC and PC operating system in the mid-1990s) and HPFS (the High Performance File System native to OS/2).

Indeed, other file systems abound, including the distributed Andrew File System (AFS), the Common Internet File System (CIFS), and even mainframe holdovers like the Hierarchical File System (or HFS). For less common file systems, you can use your favorite Internet search engine to learn more, or even to search for specific forensic tools if you should need them to capture and preserve data.

Maintain Tools and Procedures for Each Operating System and File System

The challenge for computer forensic scientists is to develop methods and techniques that provide valid and reliable results while preserving evidence and preventing harm to information. You need to have procedures and tools in place so that you can more easily collect the evidence you need.

What happens if a system is set up to log every event imaginable? The system's hard drive space will fill up, and someone will have to weed through all the collected information to figure out which events really can help an investigation. Having good procedures in place and conducting proper maintenance of your tools will help make the forensic process run more smoothly.

Preinstalled Tools Make Forensics Easier

For computer forensic science to be effective, it must be driven by information discovered during an investigation. Many systems currently include 500 GB or higher capacity hard disks. From a practical standpoint, it may be impossible to examine every file stored on a seized computer system. It could be equally difficult for law enforcement personnel to sort through, read, and comprehend the amount of information contained within files on today's huge systems. So, we'll take a look at some tools that can help you with this seemingly arduous task.

Eventually, you will work with a forensic toolkit. For now, let's look at the tools that are already installed on most operating systems. These are tools that you can readily take advantage of and use. All operating systems come with the ability to log events. Because Windows 7 is a popular operating system these days, we'll look at how it logs events. Event Viewer allows you to audit certain events. Event Viewer maintains three log files: one for system processes, one for security information, and one for applications. Figure 2.8 was captured on a Windows 7 computer. In Windows Server 2003 and 2008 versions, you will also find directory services, DNS server, and file replication logs, among many others.

Figure 2.8   The Windows 7 Event Viewer provides ready access to Windows audit logs and logged event detail.

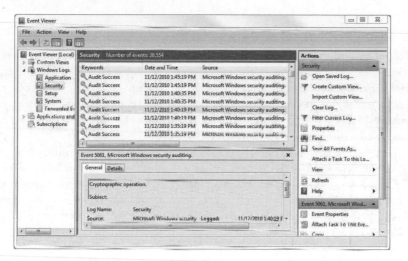

Auditing Users and File Access

Auditing is the process of tracking users and their actions on a network and its component systems. You should audit access use and rights changes to prevent unauthorized or unintentional access by a guest or restricted user account. This will stymie unauthorized access to sensitive or protected resources. How much you should audit depends on how much information you want to store. Keep in mind that auditing should be a clear-cut activity built around equally transparent goals and policies.

When deciding what to audit, first identify potential resources at risk within your networking environment. These resources might typically include sensitive files, financial applications, and personnel files. After those resources are identified, set up an audit policy using operating system tools. It can be useful to monitor successful as well as failed access attempts. Failure events allow you to identify attempts at unauthorized access; successful events can reveal accidental or intentional (but unwanted) escalations of access rights.

auditing
The process of tracking who's logging in and accessing what files.

Each operating system has its own methods to track and log access. Auditing is resource intensive and can easily add an additional 25 percent load to any server. Make time to view your logs. Log files can't help protect against a system compromise if an intrusion recorded in your logs isn't read for six months. Most operating systems produce log files in text file format, but viewing data graphically is much easier than interpreting text. If possible, import your log files into some type of database or log analysis tool.

TIP   Auditing can be as simple or as complex as you want to make it. Regardless of the auditing plan you devise, be consistent.

Tracking Incoming and Outgoing Computer Access

Most operating systems also include built-in utilities for tracking the address of a computer and tracing the route it takes to get to a destination on the Internet. Producing and recording such information can be quite important when internal users are engaging in malicious activity. With the advent of business-to-business activities, using tracking utilities is also a good way to know when employees are accessing the sites of business partners.

This section discussed tools that are already in place to track information traveling across a network. After you obtain this information, how can you use it? Can you accuse an employee of hacking based on the information that you have gathered? Such questions fall under the scope of knowing your legal limits, so let's move on and see what you can and cannot do with the information you gather, assemble, or produce as you conduct an investigation.

Know Your Limits

When an intrusion is detected, you must know to what lengths you can go to minimize the damage and also whether you can seize property. For example, let's say that you have determined that an employee has installed hacking tools on your network and he has hacked into a business partner's network. He then proceeded to steal passwords. Can you search his computer for evidence without a warrant? What about that UFD he carries on his keychain? Is that a work-related item or a personal item? These are the types of questions you'll need to answer before you act.

Legal Organizational Rights and Limits

Employers can be either public or private. This distinction is important because government employers are bound by the Fourth Amendment, as discussed in the next section. Not everything that passes through a business door can be considered part of the workplace. For example, the contents of an employee's purse or briefcase maintain their private character even though an employee brings them to work. Although circumstances might permit a supervisor to search an employee's desk for a work-related file, a supervisor must usually leave an employee's purse or briefcase alone.

When confronted with this issue, courts have analogized electronic storage devices to closed containers, and they have reasoned that accessing the information stored within an electronic storage device is akin to opening a closed container. Because individuals generally retain a reasonable expectation of privacy for the contents of closed containers, they also generally retain a reasonable expectation of privacy for data held within electronic storage devices.

Here are some cases to which you can refer for guidance:

◆ *United States v. Ross*, 456 U.S. 798, 822–23 (1982)

◆ *United States v. Barth*, 26 F. Supp. 2d 929, 936–37 (W.D. Tex. 1998)

◆ *United States v. Reyes*, 922 F. Supp. 818, 832–33 (S.D.N.Y. 1996)

◆ *United States v. Lynch*, 908 F. Supp. 284, 287 (D.V.I. 1995)

◆ *United States v. Chan*, 830 F. Supp. 531, 535 (N.D. Cal. 1993)

◆ *United States v. Blas*, 1990 WL 265179, at *21 (E.D. Wis. Dec. 4, 1990)

This analysis has interesting implications for items such as UFDs or external USB drives, which can be either work-related or private, depending on the circumstances. It is probably reasonable for employers to assume that UFDs found at an office are part of the workplace, but a court could treat a UFD that belongs to an employee as if it were a private, personal item.

Generally speaking, an employer may consent to a search of an employee's computer and peripherals if the employer has common authority over the equipment. There are currently no cases specifically addressing an employer's consent to search and seize an employee's computer and related items. However, cases exist that discuss searches of an employee's designated work area or desk.

In an electronic environment, employees do not know when a network administrator, supervisor, or anyone else accesses their data. As a practical matter, system administrators can, and sometimes do, look at data. But when they do, they leave no physical clues that would tell a user they have opened one of his files. Some users who are unfamiliar with computer technology may believe that their data is completely private. If an organization has published clear policies about privacy on the network, this effort would support the position that the user has granted implied consent to a search by working there under such a policy. However, if an organization or administration has not addressed these issues with its users and the situation remains ambiguous, the safest course is to obtain and exercise a warrant.

Search and Seizure Guidelines

The Fourth Amendment limits the ability of government agents to search for evidence without a warrant. It states "The right of the people to be secure in their persons, houses, papers, and effects, against unreasonable searches and seizures, shall not be violated, and no Warrants shall issue, but upon probable cause, supported by Oath or affirmation, and particularly describing the place to be searched, and the persons or things to be seized."

A warrantless search does not violate the Fourth Amendment if one of two conditions is met. Accordingly, investigators must consider two issues when asking if a government search of a computer requires a warrant:

1. Does the search violate a reasonable expectation of privacy?

2. If so, is the search nonetheless reasonable because it falls within an exception to the warrant requirement?

The most basic Fourth Amendment question in computer cases asks whether an individual enjoys a reasonable expectation of privacy in electronic information stored within computers or other electronic storage devices under that individual's control. For example, do individuals have a reasonable expectation of privacy in the contents of their laptop computers, floppy disks, or pagers? If the answer is yes, the government ordinarily must obtain a warrant before it accesses the information stored inside. A search is constitutional if it does not violate a person's "reasonable" or "legitimate" expectation of privacy [*Katz v. United States*, 389 U.S. 347, 362 (1967) (Harlan, J., concurring)]. In most cases, a defendant's subjective expectation of privacy focuses on whether the expectation of privacy was reasonable.

Recognizing that government agencies could not function properly if supervisors had to establish probable cause and obtain a warrant every time they needed to look for a file in an employee's office, in *O'Connor v. Ortega*, 480 U.S. 709 (1987), the Supreme Court held that two kinds of searches are exempt. Specifically, both (1) a non-investigatory, work-related intrusion and (2) an investigatory search for evidence of suspected work-related employee misfeasance are permissible without a warrant and should be judged by the standard of reasonableness (Id. at 725–26). These exemptions are stated under the Federal Guidelines for Searching and Seizing Computers. Access that document at http://www.knock-knock.com/federal_guidelines.htm.

Agents must evaluate whether a public employee retains a reasonable expectation of privacy in the workplace on a case-by-case basis, but written employment policies can simplify this task dramatically. See *O'Connor v. Orgeta*, 480 U.S. 709 at 717 (plurality). Courts have uniformly deferred to public employers' official policies that expressly authorize access to the employee's workspace, and they have relied on such policies when ruling that an employee cannot retain a reasonable expectation of privacy in the workplace. See the following cases:

◆ *American Postal Workers Union, Columbus Area Local AFL-CIO v. United States Postal Serv.*, 871 F.2d 556, 59–61 (6th Cir. 1989)

◆ *United States v. Bunkers*, 521 F.2d 1217, 1219–21 (9th Cir. 1975)

When planning to search a government computer in a government workplace, agents must look for official employment policies or "banners" to defeat a reasonable expectation of privacy.

Will This End Up in Court?

In the event that an incident is sufficiently serious, and the organizational policy is to prosecute, an investigation could end up in court. Courts require that information contained in the equipment (and not the equipment itself) be seized and that ample, unaltered information be presented in each case. Court compliance could require cooperative efforts between law enforcement officers and a computer forensic examiner to make sure that technical resources suffice to address both the scope and complexity of a search.

Computer forensic examiners can help prosecute a case with advice about how to present computer-related evidence in court. They can help prepare a case and anticipate and rebut defense claims. In addition, forensic examiners can assist prosecutors in complying with federal rules pertaining to expert witnesses. Under these rules, the government must provide, upon request, a written summary of expert testimony that it intends to use during its case. There is a reciprocal requirement for a summary of defense expert-witness testimony, as long as the defense has requested a summary from the government, and the government has complied.

Should this situation arise, make sure all evidence is processed properly. Good laboratory practices ensure the quality and integrity of evidence by dictating how examinations are planned, performed, monitored, recorded, and reported. Unless you work for law enforcement, you probably don't have a lab to process evidence; however, most large organizations do have a specially trained team to identify and collect evidence for any incidents that arise.

Often incidents occur that aren't actually crimes and require only internal investigation. The same specially trained team conducts those investigations and is also aware of what constitutes a crime that would require law enforcement involvement. Let's take a closer look at how such a team should be organized and how it works.

Develop Your Incident Response Team

Organizational policies and practices provide important guidance that applies to forensic examinations. They are designed to ensure quality and efficiency in the workplace. In an effort to properly preserve evidence, you must establish and make ready an *incident response team (IRT)*. That team needs to know how to handle workplace situations they will encounter when conducting investigations.

incident response team (IRT)
A team of individuals trained and prepared to recognize and immediately respond appropriately to any security incident.

Organize the Team

Incident response plans are needed so that you can intelligently react to intrusions, security breaches, or other identifiable incidents. More important is the issue of legal liability. You are potentially liable for damages caused by a hacker using your machines, so you will want to preserve any evidence you collect during an investigation.

incident response plan
The actions an organization takes when it detects an attack, whether ongoing or after the fact.

You must be able to prove to a court that you took reasonable measures to defend yourself from hackers. You must also present any evidence as clearly and concisely as possible. If a plan is not in place and duties not clearly assigned, your organization may wind up in a state of disarray. Failure to plan for security breaches and other incidents could result in a negative outcome in court.

The components of an incident response plan should include preparation, roles, rules, and procedures. Once a plan is prepared, appoint response team members. Note that this is not a full-time assignment; it is simply a group of people with obligations to act in a responsible manner when an incident occurs to which some response is warranted.

NOTE **Never underestimate the effect an incident has on employees. Disruptions in the workplace not only cause confusion, they also disturb employee schedules and diminish productivity.**

An incident response team is responsible for containing damage and getting systems back up and running properly. These steps include determination of the incident, formal notification to appropriate departments, and the recovering of essential network resources. With this in mind, the team should include the following personnel:

◆ Security and IT staff

◆ Someone to handle communication with management and employees

◆ Someone to handle communication with vendors, business partners, and the press

◆ Developers of in-house applications and interfaces

◆ Database managers

The entire team is responsible for successful incident handling. The entire team must remain in place until an incident is closed.

State Clear Processes

The basic premise of incident handling and response is that an organization needs a clear action plan to define procedures to be followed when an incident occurs. These procedures should include:

◆ Identifying initial infected resources by obtaining preliminary information about what kind of attack is underway, and what potential for damage exists.

◆ Notifying key personnel, such as the security department and the incident response team.

- Assembling the response team for duty assignments and selecting an incident lead.

- Diagnosing problems, identifying potential solutions, and setting priorities. The security response team must be clear about what to do, especially if potential damages are high.

- Escalating problems to additional teams if necessary. The key is to understand what actually happened and how severe any attack might be.

- Gathering all information learned about the incident up to its resolution, and storing it in a secure location on secure media, in case it may be needed for potential legal action.

- Communicating about the incident. This may include reporting it to law enforcement, IT security companies, or possibly customers and regulatory agencies.

If an event is newsworthy, expect media contact. Make sure someone is authorized—and prepared—to speak to the media.

NOTE

The team should prepare an incident report to determine and document incident causes and ultimate solutions. This report should be an internal document that puts everything, from the minute the incident was noticed until the minute service is restored, into perspective.

Coordinate with Local Law Enforcement

Local law enforcement relies on network administrators to report when their systems get hacked, but alas, intrusion victims are often reluctant to call the authorities. This reluctance is reflected in surveys conducted jointly by the Computer Security Institute and the FBI. Only 25 percent of respondents who experienced computer intrusions reported those incidents.

If organizations do not report incidents, law enforcement cannot provide an appropriate or effective response. Networks are getting more complex and more vulnerable to intrusions. Law enforcement agencies are familiar with computer crime investigations, view intrusions as important, and do respond appropriately. They are able to refer reports promptly to the proper agencies if they are not equipped to handle more complex cases.

Publicity is frequently an issue for victims of computer crime. Law enforcement is trained to be sensitive to victims' concerns about publicity and seizure of data. Many investigations also require information from the victim's incident response team.

Terms to Know

allocation unit	key logger
auditing	modem
Bluetooth	mobile device
CD/DVD-ROM/RW drive	Network File System (NFS)
cluster	New Technology File System (NTFS)
desktop	open source
extended FAT (exFAT)	operating system
external hard drive	personal computer (PC)
eSATA	Second/Third Extended Filesystems (ext2/ext3)
File Allocation Table (FAT)	server
file system	Universal Serial Bus (USB)
FireWire	USB Flash Drive (UFD)
incident response plan	Virtual FAT (VFAT)
incident response team (IRT)	war dialing
input/output (I/O)	workstation

Review Questions

1. What is the difference between a server and a PC?
2. How many devices can USB support?
3. Which has a faster transfer rate, eSATA or FireWire 800?
4. How does Bluetooth communicate?
5. What types of file systems can you find in the Windows environment?
6. What is the difference between NTFS and NFS?
7. What does an incident response team do?
8. Approximately what percentage of organizations report intrusions?
9. Can an employer search an employee's designated work area or desk?
10. Search and seizure laws are guided by which amendment?

Chapter 3

Computer Evidence

In this chapter, you learn about computer evidence—what it is and how it differs from conventional evidence. You'll also learn how to identify, collect, handle, and present computer evidence in and out of court.

Simply put, *evidence* is something that provides proof. You need evidence to prove that someone attacked your system. Without evidence, you only have a hunch. With evidence, you might have a case. Good, solid evidence answers several of the five Ws and the H for security violations: who, what, when, where, why, and how. You'll use the evidence you collect to further the discovery of the facts in an investigation. That same evidence might provide the proof necessary to result in a legal finding in your favor. Understanding computer evidence is the first step toward successfully investigating a security violation.

What Is Computer Evidence?

The main purpose of computer forensics is the proper identification and collection of computer evidence. It is both an art and a science. Computer evidence shares common characteristics with, but also differs from, conventional legal evidence. Forensic examiners need to understand the specifics of computer evidence so that they can properly collect it for later use.

Incidents and Computer Evidence

Computers may be involved in security violations in one of two ways. First, a computer can be used in the commission of crimes or violations of policy. Second, a computer can be the target for an attack. In the first situation, one or more computers are used to perform an inappropriate action. Such actions might be illegal (for example, fraud or identity theft) or simply disallowed under an organization's security policy (for example, participating in online auctions on company time).

Regardless of whether an action is a crime, any violation or intended violation of security policy is called a *security incident*. A company's security policy should outline an appropriate response for each type of incident. As covered in Chapter 2, "Preparation—What to Do Before You Start," most incidents that do not constitute crimes generally require only internal investigation. An organization's incident response team (IRT) normally carries out internal investigations. The IRT is specially trained to identify and collect evidence to document and categorize incidents. This team must also be cognizant when incidents are crimes and require law enforcement involvement.

In general, an incident response team deals with incidents where one or more computers serve as the target for an attack. Criminal investigations are frequently conducted to address the type of incident where a computer is used as a tool in committing a crime. In both situations, the computer forensic analysis produces evidence of activity carried out during an incident.

computer evidence
Any computer hardware, software, or data that can be used to prove one or more of the five Ws and the H for a security incident—namely, who, what, when, where, why, and how.

To investigate an incident properly and build a case that allows you to take action against a perpetrator, you'll need evidence to provide proof of the attacker's identity and actions. *Computer evidence* consists of files, along with their contents, that remain behind after an incident has occurred. In some cases, the files themselves—such as pictures or executable files—can provide evidence of an incident. In other cases, the contents of files such as logs or protocol traces provide necessary proof. Recognizing and identifying hardware, software, and data you can use is the first step in the evidence collection process.

Types of Evidence

Four basic types of evidence can be used in a court of law:

- ◆ Real evidence
- ◆ Documentary evidence
- ◆ Testimonial evidence
- ◆ Demonstrative evidence

Computer evidence generally falls into the first two categories.

Before you start looking for evidence, understand that most successful cases are based on several types of evidence. As you conduct an investigation, be aware of what types of evidence you can gather. Although computer forensics tends to focus on one or two types, a complete investigation should address all types of evidence available. In the following sections, we look more closely at each of these four types of evidence.

Real Evidence

The type of evidence most people already know about is *real evidence*. Real evidence is anything you can carry into a courtroom and place on a table in front of a jury. In effect, real evidence speaks for itself. It includes physical objects that relate to a case.

Of the four types of evidence, real evidence is the most tangible and easiest to understand. When presenting a case to a jury, real evidence can make a case seem more concrete. You may be asked to present real evidence, even when the most compelling evidence is not physical evidence at all.

Remember that most courtroom participants are not technically savvy. Consequently, any piece of pertinent tangible physical evidence will help a case. Without real evidence, in fact, a case may be perceived as weak or circumstantial.

In a murder trial, the case's real evidence might include the murder weapon. In the context of computer forensics, the actual computer used to commit a crime could be introduced as real evidence. If a suspect's fingerprints are found on that computer's keyboard, real evidence can be offered to prove that the suspect uses that machine. A hard drive from a suspect's computer or a mobile device might also constitute real evidence.

Sometimes real evidence that conclusively relates to a suspect (such as fingerprints or DNA) is called *hard evidence*.

real evidence
Any physical objects you can bring into court. Real evidence can be touched, held, or otherwise observed directly.

hard evidence
Real evidence conclusively associated with a suspect or activity.

Hot Java, Cold Jury

Cool Beans, Hot Java versus James T. Kirkpatrick is a fictitious case we'll use to illustrate the importance of real evidence. Kirkpatrick was charged with launching spam campaigns from a public terminal in the Cool Beans, Hot Java coffee shop. The Cool Beans network administrator provided ample proof that Kirkpatrick was in the shop during the alleged spam activity. Cool Beans provided security camera images of Kirkpatrick and accompanying computer access logs showing activity consistent with spam floods. Any technical person had to agree this case was a slam dunk.

However, the jury acquitted Kirkpatrick owing to the lack of compelling evidence. When questioned, jurors said that they found it difficult to convict a man based on little more than printed reports and pictures showing him in the shop. They wanted concrete evidence. Perhaps the actual computer Kirkpatrick used would have helped to convince the jury, or a network diagram showing how IP addresses are assigned, could have helped the jury make the jump from the virtual to the physical world.

Never overlook potential evidence when conducting an investigation. Other types of evidence may involve or refer to real evidence. For example, it is very common to use log file contents when arguing a case. The process of establishing the credibility and authenticity of such data is often easier when you start with the physical disk drive and/or computer from which you extracted the log file. In this example, real evidence supports the log file data and helps make proof more tangible.

Assume you have been asked to investigate a spammer. Because of the nature and volume of e-mails sent, local law enforcement has been called in to investigate and they have called on you to help out. You arrive on the scene to begin your investigation.

Before you touch anything, look around the scene and take pictures of everything. Digital pictures are inexpensive, but can be valuable later. As you work through the investigation, you'll frequently want to refer back to images of the crime scene as you originally found it. As an added bonus, it's not uncommon to find additional evidence in original pictures after extracting digital evidence from a suspect's machine.

After you photograph everything, start identifying all of the potentially pertinent real evidence that you have permission to search or seize. Notice that the suspect's computer has both a scanner and a mobile device cradle attached. That tells you to look for the mobile device and scanner source or target data. Mobile devices can be valuable sources for documentary evidence (which we discuss in the next section). Most people who use mobile devices store lots of personal data on them. Find the mobile device and make sure it has power. If you are authorized to seize a mobile device, be sure to take its power supply as well.

After looking for and securing the mobile device, look for any source documents (for example, printed hard copies) the suspect might have scanned. Also look for CD/DVD-ROMs the suspect may have used to store scanned images. Next, examine the physical computer and surrounding area for other signs of evidence. You should look for such items as:

- Handwritten notes. Even technically savvy people use notes. In fact, because handwritten notes are not stored on a computer, many people consider them to be more "secure."

- Any peripheral device that is, or can be, connected to the computer. This could include:
  - Storage devices
  - Communication devices
  - Input/output devices

- All removable media, such as:
  - Optical media (write-once or rewritable CDs, DVDs, or Blu-ray Discs)
  - Removable disks (floppies, ZIP disks, and so forth)
  - USB Flash Drives (UFDs) and other USB drives, plus eSATA or FireWire drives
  - Tapes and other magnetic media

This list is not exhaustive. It is simply a teaser to start you thinking about real evidence.

Looking for physical evidence is easy. Use your eyes and your brain. Look hard at the scene and think about how any physical device or object might provide evidence you need to prove your case, whether such evidence will be presented in a court of law or appear in an incident report.

After you acquire all the real evidence you can collect, it's time to consider other types of evidence that might be available. These types of evidence—documentary, testimonial, and demonstrative—are covered in the following sections.

Documentary Evidence

Much of the evidence you are likely to use in proving a case will be written documentation. Such evidence includes log files, database files, and incident-specific files and reports that supply information about what occurred. All evidence in written form, including computer-based file data, is called *documentary evidence*. All documentary evidence must be authenticated. Because anyone can create an arbitrary data file with specific content, you must prove that documentary evidence was collected appropriately and that the data it contains proves some fact.

Authenticating documentary evidence can be quite complex when you're trying to convince nontechnical jurors (or judges) that the contents of a file conclusively prove an attacker performed some specific action. Opposing attorneys are

documentary evidence
Written evidence, such as printed reports or data in log files. Such evidence cannot stand on its own and must be authenticated.

likely to attack the method of authenticating documentary evidence as well as the evidence itself. We have all heard of hard evidence thrown out of court because it was collected illegally. Computer evidence can be even more difficult to collect properly. We will cover admissibility in the section titled "Admissibility of Evidence in a Court of Law" later in this chapter.

Best Evidence Rule

best evidence rule
Whenever a document is presented as evidence, you must introduce the original document if at all possible. A copy may only be introduced if the original is not available.

In addition to basic rules that govern all computer evidence, you must consider one additional rule. Whenever you introduce documentary evidence, you must introduce an original document, not a copy. This is called the *best evidence rule*. The purpose of this rule is to protect evidence from tampering. If an original document is required, there is less opportunity for modification to occur during some copy operation. Of course, you'll have to convince the judge and jury that the document you bring into court is actually the original.

As you progress through an investigation, you will use utilities and tools to explore the contents of the computer and storage media. All files and file contents that support your case are considered documentary evidence. This is where you'll find the bulk of your evidence for many investigations.

Remember, most of your documentary evidence will come directly from items on the real evidence list (such as computers or mobile devices). Some documentary evidence will be supplied by third parties, such as access logs from an Internet service provider (ISP), but most will come from your own investigative activities.

You'll constantly be reminded to document each and every step in your investigation. Always document. There will be a test! Rest assured that if you testify in court, you'll be asked to justify your investigation and any and all actions you took to extract evidence.

After you get a handle on the physical evidence, you can start looking at the physical media's content for digital evidence. How do you look for digital evidence? You will use a collection of forensic tools to search for documentary evidence. Some of these tools are as simple as file listings or viewers, while others have been developed specifically for forensic investigations. Chapter 8, "Common Forensic Tools," covers frequently used forensic tools and their uses in an investigation. Until Chapter 8, we refer to tools designed to examine file system contents as *forensic tools*.

So, what are you looking for? Use forensic tools to look for any file or file contents that show what a suspect did while using the computer. This can include many types of log files and other activity files. For example, WS_FTP is a common File Transfer Protocol (FTP) client. When you use it to transfer files, the program lists all activity in a file named wsftp.log. Look for instances of this file. You'll be surprised how often people leave such audit trails lying around.

Here's a list of some of the steps you'll want to take while looking for documentary evidence:

◆ Catalog all programs installed on the target system.

◆ Harvest all audit and activity log files you can find that use default file-names. (To discover the default names for audit and log files, you might have to research each identified program. The program's web page is one place to start.)

◆ Examine operating system and application configuration files for recorded use of nonstandard audit or activity log filenames.

◆ Search for any files created as a result of using any identified program.

As with real evidence, experience will guide you in identifying and extracting documentary evidence. Be creative and persistent!

Testimonial Evidence

The testimony of a witness, either in verbal or written form, is called *testimonial evidence*. The most common form of testimonial evidence familiar to the general public is direct witness testimony in the courtroom. A witness is first sworn in, and then he or she presents testimony that directly relates knowledge of an incident. Testimonial evidence does not include opinions, just direct recollection from the witness.

A second common form of testimonial evidence is testimony delivered during a deposition. As with live testimony, during a deposition, the witness delivers testimony under oath. All testimony, as it is delivered, is recorded by a court reporter. A record of a deposition can be entered into evidence just like the testimony of a live witness in court. Each type of testimony has its advantages, but a deposition can often be taken much sooner, when events are fresh in a witness's mind.

You'll often need to use testimonial evidence to support and augment other types of evidence. For example, you may have a system administrator testify that your server keeps logs of all user accesses and has done so for the last two years. This testimony helps to validate the documentary evidence of access log contents taken from that server's hard disk drive (physical evidence).

When you first looked at the e-mail spammer scene in the fictitious Cool Beans, Hot Java versus James T. Kirkpatrick case, you contacted every possible witness, right? When investigating an incident, you'll want to talk with each person who has physical access to the suspect's computer, or who has substantive contact with that suspect. Interviewing witnesses is a task best left to law enforcement when dealing with criminal matters, but you should include their testimony in your investigation. Quite often, witness testimony provides extra information that leads you to additional documentary or physical evidence.

A witness could give you clues to hiding places for key storage media, or to the suspect's computer usage habits. If you have reason to believe a suspect carried out illegal activities during lunch, for example, this can help you limit the initial amount of data you must examine. Work with whoever is interviewing witnesses to get your questions presented. Those answers can save you a lot of work!

testimonial evidence
Evidence consisting of witness testimony, either in verbal or written form. Testimonial evidence may be presented in person by a witness in a court or in the form of a recorded deposition.

Demonstrative Evidence

Many types of computer evidence make sense to technical people but seem completely foreign to less technical folks. For judges and juries to understand the finer points of a case, it is often necessary to use visual aids and other illustrations to help explain some of the more technical details in the evidence. Any evidence that helps to explain, illustrate, or re-create other evidence is called *demonstrative evidence*. Demonstrative evidence does not stand on its own as do other types of evidence. It exists only to augment other evidence.

Let's assume you want to use a web server log file to show how an attacker exploited a new vulnerability. That attack crashed the server and caused substantial loss of business while the system was down. You can use charts, flowcharts, and other visual aids to help explain how web servers work in a way that is easy to understand. Demonstrative evidence is often essential to successful use of other types of evidence.

In many cases, you'll be called upon to explain highly technical concepts to nontechnical people. For example, in our e-mail spammer case, you'd have to explain what a spammer does. Although most people have heard of spam, not many understand how it originates and spreads. Further, you'd have to explain why it's so difficult to catch the originator of those messages, and why spam causes problems in the first place. It is always a good idea to start with the basics. Show how normal e-mail works and how a spammer causes problems by using excessive network bandwidth. Several illustrations are likely to help get this information across.

For example, you might want to start at the beginning. Building a complex technical argument from the ground up requires some basic education and background. Figure 3.1 is an illustration you might use to show how e-mail works.

Figure 3.1   Demonstrative evidence helps explain how e-mail works.

Where does your e-mail originate?

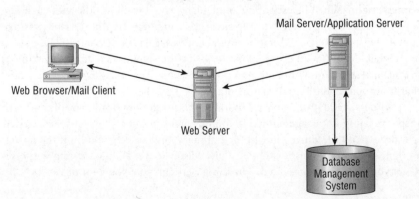

Developing the right visual aids normally comes after the bulk of other evidence has already been collected. Remember, demonstrative evidence is used to explain or demonstrate other evidence. Use it to make your points clear to a judge and jury.

Now that we have looked at the different types of evidence, let's see how you can obtain evidence legally.

Search and Seizure

You probably won't have unobstructed access to all evidence. Before you collect any evidence, make sure you have the right to either search or seize the evidence in question. This section briefly discusses options and restrictions that relate to searching and seizing evidence.

Voluntary Surrender

The easiest method of acquiring the legal right to search or seize computer equipment is through *voluntary surrender*. This type of consent occurs most often in cases where the primary owner is different from the suspect. In many cases, the equipment owner cooperates with the investigators by providing access to evidence. You might want to consider obtaining written consent to search prior to beginning your evidence collection activities.

Be aware that evidence you want might reside on a business-critical system. Although the equipment owner may be cooperative, you must be sensitive to the impact your requests for evidence may have on the owner's business. Although you might want to seize all the computers in the Human Resources department to analyze payroll activity, you can't put the whole department out of operation for long.

If your activities will alter the business functions of an organization, you may need to change your plans. For example, you could make arrangements to create images of each drive from the Human Resources department computers during off-business hours. If you can image each drive overnight, you could get what you need without impacting the normal flow of operations.

You would also have voluntary consent in cases in which an employee signed a search and seizure consent agreement as a condition of employment. Such prior consent relieves you from having to get additional permission to access evidence. As in any investigation, the value of evidence often diminishes over time. The sooner you collect evidence, the higher the likelihood that such evidence will be useful. If no such consent exists, you must get a court involved.

Never assume you have consent to search or seize computer equipment. Always ensure that you are in compliance with all policies and laws when conducting an

voluntary surrender
Permission granted by a computer equipment owner to search and/or seize equipment for investigative purposes.

investigation. Few things are more frustrating than having to throw out good evidence because it was acquired without proper consent.

Subpoena

In cases where you lack voluntary consent to search or seize evidence, you must ask permission from a court. The first option for using a court order is a *subpoena*. A subpoena compels the individual or organization that owns computer equipment to surrender it.

A subpoena is appropriate when it is unlikely that notifying the computer equipment owner will result in evidence being destroyed. A subpoena provides the owner ample time to take malicious action and remove sensitive information. Make sure you are confident a subpoena will not allow a suspect to destroy evidence.

One common use for a subpoena is when a nonsuspect equipment owner is unwilling to surrender evidence. An owner could have many reasons for being unwilling to release evidence. The evidence could contain sensitive information and company policy could require a court order to release this type of information. Many times, a court order is required by policy or regulation to document that sufficient authority exists to release such information. In any case, where cooperation is based on proper authority, a subpoena may provide access to evidence you need.

Search Warrant

When you need to search or seize computer equipment that belongs to a suspect in an investigation, it's possible that evidence may be damaged or rendered useless if the suspect knows of the investigation. You must have a court grant law enforcement officers permission to search and/or seize the identified computer equipment without giving the owner any prior notice.

A *search warrant* allows law enforcement officers to acquire evidence from a suspect's machine without giving a suspect any opportunity to taint the evidence. Resort to a search warrant only when a subpoena puts evidence at risk. If you are working as an independent investigator, you cannot execute a search warrant. This option is open only to law enforcement officials.

Because a search warrant is an extreme step, courts are reluctant to grant such a ruling without compelling reasons to do so. Make sure you are prepared to justify your request. If you are operating on a "hunch," you are likely to be refused. Before asking for a search warrant, gather some preliminary evidence that points to the suspect and his or her machine as a crucial part of the evidence chain.

Chain of Custody

After you understand how to identify computer evidence and you know what equipment you can access, you are ready to begin collecting evidence. The steps you take during the collection process determine whether that evidence will be useful once the investigation is completed. You must ensure that your evidence has been acquired properly and remains pristine. This section discusses several concepts necessary to ensure that collected evidence remains valid for later use.

Definition

All evidence presented in a court of law must exist in the same condition as it did when it was collected. Simply put, evidence cannot change at all once you collect it; in legal terms, the evidence must be in pristine condition. You'll be required to prove to the court that the evidence did not change during the investigation. That means you must provide your own evidence that all collected evidence exists, without changes, as it did when it was collected. The documentation that chronicles every move and access of evidence is called the *chain of custody*. The chain starts when you collect any piece of evidence.

The chain of custody is so named because evidence has the potential to change each time it is accessed. You can think of the path evidence takes to the courtroom as a chain in which each access is a link in the chain. If any link breaks (and thereby breaks the integrity of the evidence), the whole chain breaks at that point.

The court expects the chain of custody to be complete and without gaps. You demonstrate a complete chain of custody by providing an evidence log that shows every access to evidence, from the time of its collection to its appearance in court.

A complete chain of custody log also includes procedures that describe each step. For example, an entry might read "checked out hard disk drive serial number BR549 to create a primary analysis image." You should also include a description of what "creating a primary analysis image" means. The defense will examine the chain of custody documents, looking for gaps or inconsistencies. Any issue with the chain of custody has the real potential of causing the court to throw out the evidence in question. If that happens, any evidence you collect becomes useless and your credibility will be questioned.

chain of custody
Documentation of all steps that evidence has taken from the time it is located at a crime scene to the time it's introduced in a courtroom. All steps include collection, transportation, analysis, and storage processes. All accesses to the evidence must be documented as well.

Controls

Each step in the chain of custody must impose specific controls to maintain the integrity of the evidence. The first control could be to take pictures of the evidence's original state. This, of course, is only applicable for real evidence. Once you photograph and/or document the initial state of the entire scene, you can begin to collect evidence.

From the very first step, you must list all procedures you use during the collection process and be ready to justify all of your actions. For example, when you collect a disk drive for analysis, you must carefully follow standard practices regarding disk identification, removal, handling, storage, and analysis. Each step in the evidence collection and handling process must have at least one associated control that preserves the state of the evidence.

Continuing our disk drive evidence example, you must use proper handling techniques with disk drives, and you must also document each step in that process. Before you start, take precautions against disk drive damage. Such precautions include:

◆ Grounding to prevent static discharge

◆ Securing and padding the work surface to prevent physical shock

◆ Noting power requirements to protect against inadvertent power-related damage

You'll also need to implement and document all controls that prevent accidental changes to the evidence. These precautions include:

◆ Implementing a write blocker to prevent accidental writes to the media

◆ Generating a snapshot of the media using a hash or checksum before any analysis (Hash and checksums are discussed in more detail in Chapter 8.)

◆ Using analysis tools that have been verified to run using read-only access

Needless to say, you must plan each step along this path. At every step, make sure at least one control is present to ensure that the evidence stays pristine and unaltered. The section entitled "Leave No Trace," which appears later in this chapter, covers some specific controls; however, the preceding list illuminates the level of detail required to satisfy a court of law that evidence has not changed since it was collected.

The following steps illustrate how to handle a disk drive you suspect contains evidence:

1. After you have determined that you need to analyze a hard disk drive, the first step is to seize the drive. You must fully document the entire process, including:

   ◆ Seizure authority

   ◆ Seizure process

   ◆ Safety precautions

   ◆ Source location, time, and person who performed seizure actions

   ◆ Packing and transportation method

- Destination location, time, and person who transferred the item to secure storage
- Description of storage facilities, including procedures to ensure evidence security

2. After seizing the drive, mount it in read-only mode and make a copy of the drive for analysis. Make sure you:

- Document the process of mounting the device
- Describe the precautions taken to prevent changes to the media
- List all of the steps in the copy process

3. Compare your copy of the drive to the original to ensure that you have an exact copy. Make sure you:

- Describe the process and tools used to compare drive images

4. After making a clean copy of the original drive, you can begin your analysis of that copy.

Figure 3.2 illustrates the process.

Figure 3.2   Documenting chain of custody when seizing a disk drive as evidence

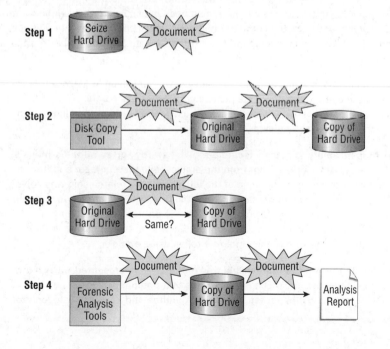

Real World Scenario

Tales from the Trenches: Computer Evidence

The computer forensic expert is often called on to save the day, even when that "day" occurred over a year and a half ago.

The statute of limitations for sexual harassment can range from as few as 30 days for federal employees to as long as three years in certain states. After being contacted by senior management for a small publicly traded company located in a state with an extended statute of limitations for this crime, I boarded a flight to see if I could help locate evidence that was more than 18 months old.

A senior manager for the company was being sued for sexual harassment by an employee who had left the company 18 months earlier. The employee had not made any allegations when leaving the company and had only recently filed suit. After speaking with the senior manager named in the suit, the company officials were hoping I might be able to locate proof that the romance was mutual and consensual and thus did not constitute sexual harassment.

As is the norm in a majority of businesses, when the complaining employee left the company, the employee's desktop computer hard disk had been reformatted, reloaded, and that computer reassigned to another employee. The company CIO was able to track down the computer and presented it to me to see what I could locate. By this time, the computer had been in use by another employee for almost 15 months. The senior manager's laptop computer had been lost six months ago. In addition, the company recently implemented a new installation of Microsoft Exchange and had no backup tapes from the old e-mail server.

I imaged the hard drive using the Image MASSter Solo 4 Forensic Portable Evidence Seizure Tool from Intelligent Computer Solutions and created a new case file using AccessData's Forensic Toolkit (FTK). I added the acquired image of the hard disk as evidence in the case file in FTK and then indexed the case. After this prep work, things happened quickly.

One of the strengths of FTK is its ability to quickly locate e-mails. I swiftly sorted all the e-mails by date and began reading a string of "love letters" sent from the employee to the manager and from the manager to the employee. It was obvious from the tone of the letters that the relationship was indeed mutual. Additionally, I was able to locate calendar entries from the employee's Outlook `.pst` file that listed planned meeting times and locations for the couple. I found one particularly humorous and potentially case-defeating file on the computer in an e-mail attachment sent from the employee to the manager. It was a self-photographed nude picture of the employee taken using a mirror.

I located more than enough data to show the relationship was mutual. When presented with all this evidence, the employee dropped the lawsuit. This case illustrates that potential evidence can be found on computers long after incidents occur, if an investigator takes the time and knows how to look for it.

Documentation

The first item in your hands when you enter a crime scene should be a camera, and the second item a pencil. The key to providing a chain of custody that a court will accept is meticulous documentation. You must enter notes into an evidence log, listing all information pertinent to accesses to the evidence.

Each and every time evidence is accessed (including initial collection) the evidence log should include at least the following items of information:

- Date and time of action
- Action type (choose one)
    - Initial evidence collection
    - Evidence location change
    - Remove evidence for analysis
    - Return evidence to storage
- Personnel collecting/accessing evidence
- Computer descriptive information
    - Computer make and model
    - Serial number(s)
    - Location
    - Additional ID information
    - BIOS settings specific to disk drives
- Disk drive descriptive information
    - Disk drive manufacturer, model number, and serial number
    - Drive parameters (heads, cylinders, sectors per track)
    - Jumper settings
    - Computer connection information (adapter, master/slave)
- Handling procedure
    - Preparation (static grounding, prevention of physical shock, etc.)
    - Contamination precautions taken
    - Step-by-step events within the events of each action
    - Inventory of supporting items created/acquired (e.g., hash or check-sum of drive/files)
- Complete description of action
    - Procedure used
    - Tools used
    - Description of each analysis step and its results

◆ Reason for action

◆ Notes

 ◆ Comments not specifically requested anywhere else in the log

 ◆ The notes section provides additional details as an investigation unfolds

This log provides the court with a chain that can be traced back to the point at which the evidence was collected. It provides the beginning of the assurance that the evidence has not changed from its original state. The next step in the process is to justify that each step in the chain was carried out according to industry best practices and standards. Once you establish that you have handled evidence in an appropriate manner and maintained the integrity of the evidence, you are ready to take it to court.

Figure 3.3 illustrates a minimal log format. This type of log usually needs supporting documents for each line item. The minimal log format gives a brief overview of evidence handling history, and the detailed description for each line item would provide the additional details mentioned previously.

Figure 3.3   Chain of custody log

Chain of Custody Log

Line	Item	Date	Time	Who	Description
1	Hard disk drive, ser #123456	7/15/04	10:15 AM	M. SOLOMON	Seized hard drive from scene, permission provided by business owner
2	Hard disk drive, ser #123456	7/15/04	10:45 AM	M. SOLOMON	Transported HDD to evidence locker in main office
3	Hard disk drive, ser #123456	7/16/04	7:30 AM	M. SOLOMON	Removed HDD to create analysis copy
4	Hard disk drive, ser #123456	7/16/04	9:15 AM	M. SOLOMON	Returned HDD to evidence locker

Before you take evidence to court, you need to ensure that it will be acceptable. In the next section, we cover the rules that govern what evidence is admissible in a court of law.

Admissibility of Evidence in a Court of Law

Not all evidence is appropriate for admission into a court. The court applies specific rules to evidence submitted. It's a waste of time and effort to analyze evidence that a court refuses to consider. Some evidence never has a chance of making it to court, and good evidence can be tainted by an investigator on its way to court, making it unacceptable.

Know what separates valid evidence from invalid evidence. It will save you substantial amounts of time, and it could make the difference between a successful and unsuccessful case.

Relevance and Admissibility

The courts apply two basic standards to all evidence. Any evidence you want to use in a court case must be relevant and admissible. *Relevant evidence* is any evidence that proves or disproves the facts in a case. If evidence does not serve to prove or disprove the facts in a case, it can be deemed irrelevant and, therefore, not allowed.

In addition to evidence being judged relevant, evidence must also be admissible. *Admissible evidence* is evidence that conforms to all regulations and statues governing the nature and the manner in which it was obtained and collected. Certain evidence may be relevant, but not admissible.

There are many reasons why evidence could be inadmissible. Unfortunately, investigators can contribute to inadmissibility of evidence. The two quickest ways to render good evidence inadmissible are to:

1. Collect evidence illegally.

2. Modify evidence after it is in your possession.

It is extremely important that investigators be diligent in all activities required to preserve all evidence in an admissible state. Inadmissible evidence weakens your case, and the effort you put into obtaining evidence that is deemed inadmissible is often wasted.

Make every effort to maintain the admissibility of evidence, starting from the beginning of your investigation. All too often, investigations start as internal incident response efforts that do not include law enforcement. During an investigation, you might determine that an incident involved criminal activity. At that point, it is time to involve law enforcement. This is why it is important to preserve evidence before criminal activity is discovered. IRT procedures should be consistent with court requirements for collecting and handling evidence. If not, valuable evidence might become inadmissible before a criminal investigation gets underway.

relevant evidence
Evidence that serves to prove or disprove facts in a case.

admissible evidence
Evidence that meets all regulatory and statutory requirements, and has been properly obtained and handled.

Techniques to Ensure Admissibility

Your main goal in an investigation is to ensure admissibility of evidence. The IRT is responsible for ensuring that damage from an incident has been contained and the organization's primary business functions can continue. As an investigator, you must operate with different goals in mind. In smaller organizations, separating these two responsibilities can be difficult.

Always remember the importance of preserving evidence. Make sure you collect and handle evidence properly at each step. The success of any court appearance depends on the quality of your part of the investigation.

Know the Rules

Before you ever participate in an investigation, you should know the rules surrounding evidence collection and handling. Each state imposes slightly different rules, so know your local laws and policies. There are also very different rules for different types of evidence. For example, analyzing a database that contains confidential personal medical information will have more stringent requirements than a database containing a parts inventory. Ask questions before engaging in evidence collection. In this case, forgiveness is far more difficult to obtain than permission.

The best place to start is by developing a relationship with local law enforcement agents. Call your local agency and ask for the computer forensic unit. Meet with them and take the time to learn how they approach investigations. Most of the time, law enforcement officers will gladly provide guidance and help you comply with their investigative requirements. Learning from them will save all of you substantial time and effort when an event occurs that requires law enforcement involvement.

Also spend some time with your own organization's legal staff. They can provide valuable input to guide your investigative efforts as well. The goal is to ensure that your processes comply with any statutes, regulations, and policies before any investigation starts.

Protect the Chain of Custody

Once you find yourself in the midst of an investigation, take every effort to protect the chain of custody. The best process is worthless if it is not followed and enforced. If your process requires that the evidence locker be physically locked at all times, never leave it unlocked while you "run a quick check." Even small deviations from published policy can render evidence inadmissible.

Be doggedly diligent in protecting evidence. You should allow only trained personnel near evidence. Make sure they are trained in the proper handling of evidence, and understand the importance of maintaining the chain of custody. The cost of training is far less than the cost of losing valuable evidence due to a single careless act. Defense attorneys look for such mistakes. Take great care to ensure that you don't make any mistakes, take any shortcuts, or otherwise taint your evidence.

Treat Each Incident as a Criminal Act

The single most important practice to enact is to treat every incident as a criminal act. Always assume that evidence you collect will be used in a court case. You'll go a long way to ensure that all collected evidence is admissible. It is a lot easier to loosen up the evidence collection standards, once you decide there will be no need for law enforcement involvement, than it is to fix a sloppy collection effort later in a criminal investigation.

Always assuming evidence will be used in court also tends to make you more diligent in adhering to evidence handling procedures. The belief that evidence is only for internal use can foster a more casual atmosphere that may lead to more mistakes. Take the high road and treat all evidence as though a judge will see it. It will increase the overall quality of your investigative work.

If you assume you will end up presenting your evidence in court, you must ensure that it is pristine. In the next section, we'll look at issues related to keeping evidence pure and unspoiled.

Leave No Trace

The Boy Scouts embrace a philosophy that protects our environment from the effects of hiking, camping, and other outdoor activities. It is called "Leave No Trace," and it affects most outdoor endeavors. The basic idea is that after engaging in an outdoor activity, there should be no trace that you were ever there. The reality is that most outdoor venues allow a more relaxed version, possibly called "Leave Almost No Trace."

In computer forensics, though, you must adhere to a strict "Leave No Trace" policy. You must prove that none of your analysis efforts left any trace on the evidence media. In fact, you'll have to prove that you never modified the evidence in any way.

There are several ways to ensure that evidence remains unmodified, but they are not equally convincing in a court of law. Decide which approach you'll take before the investigation starts (or at least before the analysis of a particular piece of evidence starts).

Read-Only Image

One method to ensure that no changes occur to media is through the use of read-only images. There are multiple ways to access media in read-only mode. One method is to mount the evidence volume in read-only mode. Although this is a safe option when performed properly, it is exceedingly difficult to convince a court that you used the correct options when mounting, or accessing, a volume.

Further, it is very easy to accidentally mount the volume using the wrong options and inadvertently write to the volume. This is a huge risk when working with the primary copy because writing anything to the primary copy makes the volume inadmissible.

If you decide to mount a suspect's volume in read-only mode, only mount the volume to make a full copy of the volume (or selected files). Be diligent in documenting and verifying the options you used. However, if another option exists (such as write-blocking devices), use it instead. You'll have an easier time convincing the court of the volume's integrity.

Software Write Blocker

software write blocker
Software that sits between the operating system and the disk driver that blocks all write requests.

One method to ensure that no writes impact a mounted volume is through the use of a *software write blocker*. A software write blocker is a layer of software that sits between the operating system and the actual device driver for the disk. All disk access requests that use standard operating system calls are prevented from writing to the disk.

Although this approach is generally safe, some software write blockers allow direct disk access in some cases. Be sure you do your homework and verify that the tool you use is secure in all cases. You also need to ensure that your tool of choice is updated to the latest version (so you need to keep track of the version you use for each investigation). If any vulnerability is detected in a version of the software you are using for an investigation, document its effect on your analysis.

Most vendors that produce computer forensic software and tools provide a software write blocker. Take a look at several tools and the utility they provide. Make sure their capabilities match your needs.

The last step in any media analysis is to run a checksum on the volume and compare it to the checksum run on the same volume prior to analysis. If the two do not match, the volume has changed. If this ever happens, there is clearly a problem with the software write blocker. (Checksums and hashes are discussed in Chapter 4, "Common Tasks.")

Hardware Write Blocker

Another method for preventing writes to media is through the use of a *hardware write blocker*. Some courts view hardware write blockers as more secure than software write blockers because a physical connection blocks any other paths to the disk. The concept behind a hardware write blocker is the same as for the software write blocker. Normal read access to the device is supported, but all write requests are blocked.

Several vendors sell hardware write blockers, from inline cable devices to full subsystems that support multiple interfaces. As with software write blockers, do your homework to validate manufacturer's claims. Any court will likely require that you provide independent proof that the device you chose performs as advertised.

hardware write blocker
A hardware device that is plugged in between the disk controller and the physical disk, and blocks any write requests.

Software and Hardware Write Blockers

Here are some products that block disk writes. Look at all of them and evaluate their features to decide which one is right for your use.

Write Block Software Tools

◆ PDBLOCK, by Digital Intelligence, Inc. (www.digitalintelligence.com)

◆ EnCase, by Guidance Software (www.guidancesoftware.com)

◆ Super DriveLock from Intelligent Computer Solutions, Inc. (www.ics-iq.com)

◆ Forensic Write Blockers from Tableau (www.tableau.com)

◆ Forensic UltraDock from WiebeTech (www.wiebetech.com)

Write Block Hardware Devices

◆ ACARD Write Block Kit, by ACARD Technology (www.acard.com)

◆ DriveLock and FastBloc, by Intelligent Computer Solutions (www.ics-iq.com)

◆ NoWrite, MyKey Technology, Inc. (www.mykeytech.com)

◆ UltraKit and UltraBlock, by Digital Intelligence, Inc. (www.digitalintelligence.com)

◆ FastBloc, Guidance Software (www.guidancesoftware.com)

Also look at the Computer Forensic Tool Testing (CFTT) Project Web site for further analysis of the tools listed previously (and more). You can visit the CFTT Web site at www.cftt.nist.gov.

Terms to Know

admissible evidence

best evidence rule

chain of custody

computer evidence

demonstrative evidence

documentary evidence

hard evidence

hardware write blocker

real evidence

relevant evidence

search warrant

software write blocker

subpoena

testimonial evidence

voluntary surrender

Review Questions

1. What are two general ways in which computers are involved in security violations?

2. What is computer evidence?

3. What is an incident response team?

4. What is real evidence?

5. What is documentary evidence?

6. What is demonstrative evidence?

7. What is a subpoena?

8. What is a search warrant?

9. What is the chain of custody?

10. What is admissible evidence?

Chapter 4

Common Tasks

The goal of computer forensics is to get to the truth of the matter. You get to the truth by identifying and acquiring sufficient evidence to prove the identity or the activities of a computer user. Items of interest to investigators and examiners are either the results of prohibited activity or those items that support other prohibited activity. This chapter looks at the entire forensic process from a common flow approach.

You will learn the basic tasks present in nearly all forensic investigations. When you first approach a crime scene, you must identify any and all pertinent evidence. After you have identified the evidence, you will collect it and handle it in a manner that preserves its pristine state. After you have custody of the evidence, you can analyze it and present your findings.

Evidence Identification

Your initial task in an investigation is to identify the evidence you need for your case. Remember, without evidence you don't really have much more than an opinion. Every case is different, so you will likely need different types of evidence for each case. Knowing what evidence you will need is an integral part of a successful investigation. One rule of thumb is to "take everything." Unfortunately, there are substantial legal and logistical issues involved in this approach. More realistically, you should take anything and everything that could be remotely related to your case. Religiously adhere to the chain of custody guidelines and label everything as it is removed.

Who Will Use the Evidence You Collect?

Treat every computer forensic investigation as if the case you build will end up in court. The case in question does not need to involve criminal activity to warrant such care. You may be surprised that even simple investigations can end up as prime evidence for lawsuits in the future. Don't take chances. Protect your organization's assets by providing evidence that can be admitted into a court of law, if need be.

---

distributed denial of service (DDoS) attack
An attack that uses one or more systems to flood another system with so much traffic that the targeted system is unable to respond to legitimate requests for service or access.

The facts surrounding the target of the investigation will determine the methods you employ. An investigation into how a server was used in a *distributed denial of service attack (DDoS)* is different from gathering evidence of illegal images stored on a laptop. Always understand the purpose of your investigation before you start.

Suppose you were called to investigate possible stolen credit cards. The law enforcement officers working on this case expect to find incriminating evidence on the suspect's home computer. They have interviewed some of the suspect's coworkers and found that she talked about a "database of valuable information at home." When you arrive at the suspect's home, where should you start? What type of evidence should you look for? Try to answer these questions by looking at some common guidelines for investigations.

site survey
Notes, photographs, drawings, and any other documentation that describe the state and condition of a scene.

When you enter a crime scene, look around carefully. Always document the scene by taking photographs, drawing sketches, and writing descriptions of what you see. The notes you take, together with photographs or drawings, form the initial *site survey*. As you progress in your investigation, you may find that looking back at the site survey gives you more contextual clues that show where or what to look at next.

Don't get too caught up in finding specific evidence. Rather, treat an investigation like a large puzzle. Avoid fixating on the picture (on the box cover); instead, look at the shapes and how the pieces fit together. Try to avoid looking only for evidence you expect to find. When you focus on the end product too much, you can miss important evidence that may lead you in a different direction. Be on the lookout for any evidence that could be of interest to your case.

TIP

Physical Hardware

You might expect that the primary focus of a computer forensic investigation is computer hardware; however, that's not always true. Often, much more evidence than just physical hardware can be found. However, hardware is one crucial type of evidence you must consider.

Take a look around your own office. How many types of computer hardware do you see? Chapter 2, "Preparation—What to Do Before You Start," covered different types of hardware and encouraged you to know what gets used in your organization. You probably use several different types of hardware on a daily basis.

Physical hardware is a great place to get fingerprints. If part of your case depends on proving a certain person used specific hardware, fingerprints may provide the evidence you need. If you want to get fingerprint evidence from computer hardware, the best way to do that is to check the equipment out to a police or licensed expert third-party fingerprint technician/expert to obtain the fingerprint evidence. That's a totally different kind of forensics and should be turned over to experts in that area of forensics. Think about the hardware you tend to touch on a routine basis:

◆ Keyboard

◆ Printers

◆ Mouse

◆ Touchpad

◆ CD-ROM/DVD drive

◆ Laptop case

◆ Scanner lids

◆ Mobile device cradle (especially its buttons and switches)

◆ Keyboard-video-monitor (KVM) switches (if your office has more computers than monitors)

◆ Game controller

◆ Media storage units (CD/DVDs, tape, floppy cases, and drawers)

And the list goes on. Your investigation may not require you to establish that a user touched specific hardware, but be prepared do so when necessary.

Beyond the appeal of fingerprints, physical hardware is vital because it holds the most common target of an investigation—data. Because all data resides on some type of hardware, you need access to hardware to get at the data. Ensure that you have the proper authority to either seize or search the hardware before you continue.

What Else Can Hardware Tell You?

Pay attention to all clues that hardware provides. If you find an expensive, high-speed scanner attached to a suspect's computer, you should probably expect to find a repository of scanned documents on the computer or some server. If you are investigating possible confidential information disclosure and you do not find many scanned documents on the computer in question, look elsewhere for the documents. Few people invest in an expensive scanner unless they plan to use it. Look in not-so-obvious places for the scanned documents.

After you have proper authorization, you need to start cataloging the physical evidence. Different people choose different starting points. Some examiners start with the most prominent computer, normally the one in the center of the workspace. Others choose a point of reference, such as the entry door, as a starting point.

Regardless of where you start, move through the scene carefully and document your actions as you proceed. Start where you are most comfortable. The goal is to consider all physical evidence. Choosing a starting point and moving through the scene in a methodical manner makes it less likely that you will miss important evidence. Don't forget to look up! And down! And *all* around. Computer forensic evidence has even been found inside walls.

wireless access point (WAP)
Network device that contains a radio transmitter/receiver that is connected to another network. A WAP provides wireless devices access to a regular wired network.

Follow all communications links. If a computer you are examining is connected to a network, follow the cable or scan for the *wireless access point (WAP)*. Know how this computer is connected to other computers. Your investigation might need to expand to other computers connected to the investigation target. Be careful to avoid unnecessarily expanding the scope of your investigation, though. You might not need to examine all of the computers to which the target is connected, but you do need to know about any network connections.

The crown jewels in most computer investigations are the computers' hard disk drives. By and large, most evidence lives on some hard drive. Issues surrounding hard disk drives are discussed later in this chapter in the section entitled "Evidence Preservation." However, remember that a hard disk drive is only one type of hardware. Take time to consider all types of hardware as you identify evidence for later analysis.

Let's apply our discussion to the real world. Suppose you arrive at the home of a suspected credit card thief. Local law enforcement officers have executed a search warrant and asked you to help in the investigation. You cannot seize anything, but you can search the computer and associated hardware. You take pictures and start looking around. You notice the normal hardware that surrounds computers, but there is one little black block that catches your eye. Closer inspection reveals a small credit card swipe device with a Universal Serial Bus (USB) cable. You know this could be the device used to read stolen credit cards. Great! Juries love things they can touch and see. Now you need to find where those stolen numbers are stored.

Removable Storage

Removable storage is commonly used for several purposes. You'll find files of all kinds lying around if you look. Refer to Chapter 2 for more detailed information about different types of hardware. Removable media are also common repositories for evidence.

Take some time to carefully inspect all removable or external media you find for possible use in your investigation. Think about how most people use such media. It generally serves these purposes:

◆ Data archival/backups

◆ Data transport

◆ Program installation

Real World Scenario

Tales from the Trenches: The Missing Man

Computer forensic examiners are sometimes called upon to locate missing individuals. One day I was contacted by the Chief Executive Officer of an Internet startup company and asked if I could come to his office to discuss a matter of some importance. Because his office was located only a few miles away, I said I would be there within the hour.

As soon as I arrived, the CEO greeted me, took me into his office, and closed the door. (This is always the sign that I am about to hear a really good story.) The CEO explained that the Vice President of Sales for the company had not reported to work in over a week. This was, to say the least, highly unusual. The CEO had contacted everyone he could think of, but he had been unable to locate the VP. He even drove to the VP's apartment and had the landlord check to see if everything was okay. When the landlord went inside, he found nothing, and I mean nothing. The entire apartment was empty. No clothing, no furniture, and of course, no VP.

Continues

The CEO asked me to examine the VP's desktop computer to see if I could locate any information as to where the VP might have gone and why he might have left. At this point, I asked the CEO if he had contacted the police yet. He said he had, but because there was no evidence of foul play, they only took a report and "would get back to him." The VP was not married and had no family, so there was really no one else looking for the VP besides the CEO. He went on to explain that the VP handled all the sales, marketing, and collections for the company, a large portion of running the business. Now, without him, the company was suffering.

The CEO escorted me to the VP's office and unlocked the door. I located the VP's desktop computer sitting on the desk and noted that it was powered off. I took digital photos of the office and the evidence and then I removed the hard drive from the computer so that I could take it back to my lab. Following normal procedures, I completed a chain of custody form and gave a receipt for the hard drive to the CEO. I let him know I would get back to him as soon as possible and inform him of what I found.

After creating a forensically sound image of the hard drive, I imported the image into a commercial forensic utility, the Forensic Toolkit from AccessData, and began looking for clues about what the VP had been doing prior to his disappearance. I located many graphics images of tropical beaches and real estate in Grand Cayman. I also located evidence that in the days just prior to his disappearance the VP had visited many Internet sites researching banking privacy laws in the Cayman Islands. Of course, I was beginning to suspect that the VP might have traveled to the Caymans. I located a copy of an online airline reservation for a one-way flight to the Island just over a week ago along with a hotel reservation for a two-week stay.

I had located the VP. Well, that was the good news. Now it was time to find out what the VP had been up to just prior to his departure and maybe figure out why he left. I reviewed a number of e-mail messages the VP had sent to and received from several of the company's clients. These messages said that these clients should send their payments for services rendered by the company to the company's new address and to please make all checks out to "Service Tech." He explained that this was a new division within the company that would be handling their accounts. I found that 18 different customers had received similar e-mails and responded to the VP acknowledging the change. I compiled my findings and made an appointment to speak with the CEO immediately.

Before I informed the CEO of my findings, I had to ask him a few questions. I let him know I thought I knew exactly where the VP was and why he left so quickly. I told him about the e-mail messages and asked him about the "Service Tech" division and the address change for billing. As I thought, the CEO had no idea what I was talking about. There was no "Service Tech" division and the billing address had been the same since the company was founded.

At that point I informed the CEO that it would be best if we contacted the police again, and he did so. The investigation ultimately found that the VP had opened a bank account in Grand Cayman in the name of "Service Tech" and deposited over $900,000 in checks from the company's customers. Law enforcement agents were able to locate the now ex-VP based on the information provided by my investigation, and most of the funds were eventually returned to the company.

This definitely isn't an example of a "normal day at the office," but it shows that the work computer forensic investigators do can be exciting and worthwhile.

The first two uses for removable or external storage are of the most interest to us. Although you may not be successful in finding evidence you need on a hard disk drive, always look for backups or other secondary copies. Be especially persistent when looking for historical evidence. Removable storage devices come in many shapes and sizes. In years past, the primary removable storage devices available to most users were floppy disks and magnetic tapes. Those days are long gone. You need to be on the lookout for other places to store evidence, including:

◆ Optical media, including CDs, DVDs, and Blu-ray Discs

◆ USB drives and storage devices

◆ eSATA and FireWire external hard disks

◆ Networked storage devices of all kinds (servers, NAS, SAN)

◆ Flash memory cards and UFDs

Generally, you will find two types of files on removable or external media: intentionally archived and transient.

Intentionally archived files are copied to removable media to keep as extra copies, or they are copied prior to deleting originals. If you find a system that looks like it has been cleansed of suspicious files, start looking for backups. In fact, the presence of software that cleanses systems, such as Evidence Eliminator or Window Washer, generally means a user may be hiding something. It is a good bet that some evidence was copied to removable media before the last cleansing cycle.

Many organizations that process large volumes of data often clear log files frequently. For example, many ISPs keep no activity logs longer than 30 days. You may find that an ISP archives old log files, but they may not. Don't depend on archived data. Removable storage is only one part of evidence collection.

Transient files are files, or file remnants, that have been temporarily copied onto removable media. Such media is often used to transport data from one computer to another. Although files are commonly deleted from the media after they have served their purpose, you might find lingering files. In any case, you will probably find files you can at least partially recover. Few people take the time to securely cleanse removable media, though they may do so for external media.

Removable and external media analysis is painstakingly slow. Most offices usually have a lot of such media lying around, and the devices used to read them can be far slower than most hard drives. Nevertheless, take your time and look at what is on each disk, tape, or device. Your rigor might pay off by producing evidence that cannot be found elsewhere.

TIP

The rule of thumb for removable and external media is to take all that you can legally find and seize. Subsequent analysis can be slow, but it can also yield evidence you won't find anywhere else.

Documents

The last type of common evidence is hard-copy documents. A hard-copy document is anything written that you can touch and hold. Evidence that consists of documents is called *documentary evidence.* Although this discussion is concerned with written evidence, recall from Chapter 3, "Computer Evidence," that data stored in computer files is also classified as documentary evidence. Printed reports, handwritten notes, cocktail napkins with drawings, and white boards are all examples of documentary evidence.

_____ **NOTE** _____ **The most important characteristic of documentary evidence is that it cannot stand on its own. It must be authenticated. When you find suspicious files on a hard drive (or removable media), you must prove that they are authentic. You must prove that the evidence came from the suspect's computer and has not been altered since it was collected. Refer to Chapter 3 for a discussion of evidence handling.**

Take pictures of all white boards and other writings. Carefully examine the crime scene for any documents that might be admissible as evidence. Look around the computer for sticky notes. It is amazing how many people keep passwords on sticky notes attached to the sides of their monitors. Also look around, behind, on top of, and under all hardware components. Another common place to hide notes is in, or under, desk drawers.

Back at the credit card investigation scene, you notice a white board on the wall during your site survey. It looks like it has been used a lot but it has been wiped clean. Fortunately for you, no one took the time to use cleaning fluid to clean the board. If you look closely, you can still read some of what was written and then erased. It looks like a list of filenames. You should (and do) write them down for later use.

Most people keep notes handy to jog their memories. Sit down at the subject's desk and look around carefully. Every scrap of paper is potential evidence. Look for written notes that contain either information directly related to the investigation or information that gives you some insight into the subject's activities. Look for any of these pieces of written information:

- ◆ Password
- ◆ Encryption key or pass code
- ◆ Uniform Resource Locator (URL)
- ◆ IP address

- E-mail address
- Telephone number
- Name
- Address
- Filename
- Upload/Download/Working directory

This list is just a sampler of information that could assist your investigation. Anything that helps point you toward or helps you access evidence is valuable. Most people write some things down so they can remember them. Look for those notes. They can help direct you to more evidence in a fraction of the time it would take to perform an exhaustive search.

Evidence Preservation

Before you can prove that you maintained the integrity of data you present as evidence, you must prove that you maintained the integrity of the hardware that contains the data. From the beginning of your investigation, you must take precautions, and document those precautions, to protect the hardware.

The main goal of evidence preservation is to ensure that absolutely no changes have taken place since the evidence was collected. Your collection and handling procedures will be examined. Take all necessary precautions to protect collected evidence from damage that might change its state. Static discharge is a significant concern. You must bring static protection devices with you to each investigation. Use them, and make notes to explain the steps you take to avoid inadvertent damage.

You will have to address several concerns throughout your investigation. Do not handle any evidence until you are absolutely sure you can legally acquire the evidence and that the collection and analysis process will not change that evidence. The following sections cover some of the general issues regarding evidence preservation.

Pull the Plug or Shut It Down?

One of the classic debates in computer forensic circles is the correct approach to handling a live system. If the computer system in question is operating when you approach it, should you turn it off? The question becomes more pronounced when you are brought in as part of an incident response team during an ongoing attack. Before you switch into investigator mode, you need to limit the extent of the damage. However, disconnecting the computer from the network or power supply can damage or destroy crucial evidence.

Let's assume you want to "freeze" the system as it is and immediately halt all processing. You can accomplish this by literally pulling the power plug out of the wall (or pull it from the back of the computer). Removing power immediately stops all disk writes, but it destroys anything in memory. Such an abrupt crash could also corrupt files on the disk. You may find that the very file you want to use as evidence has been corrupted by the forced crash.

One client once unknowingly tested their disaster recovery plan in a very real way. Early one morning, the UNIX computer that hosted the company's central database had the power cord pulled from the back of the computer. When power was restored, the file system detected one file that was hopelessly corrupted and promptly deleted it. Unfortunately, that file was a core database file, so the client lost their entire database. Fortunately, the backup process had been completed only 15 minutes prior to the crash, and no data had been entered afterward. Although newer operating systems tend to behave less destructively, be aware that a sudden loss of power can produce negative results.

On the other hand, you may want to perform a proper system shutdown. Although shutting a system down protects any files from accidental corruption, the shutdown process itself writes many entries to activity log files and changes the state of the evidence. Further, a suspect computer could run procedures that cleanse log files on shutdown. Thus, a proper shutdown might wipe out crucial evidence.

A third option is to leave the system up and running. Several of the popular computer forensic software suites support live forensics. With a small footprint, these tools allow you to take a snapshot of the entire system, including memory and disks, while it is still running. The easiest way to do this is to install the small monitor program on the computer prior to any incidents. Of course, this approach only works if you have a manageable number of workstations and you have the authority to install such programs. This is possible in an environment where the organization owns the hardware and can dictate what software is loaded. If you are fortunate enough to deploy forensic software on all of the computers in your organization, the forensics process can be greatly simplified.

You can still run live forensics even if you have had no previous access to the computer. One common way to do this is to carry the required forensic software on a USB drive. You can run the forensics directly from the USB drive, and save any output to that drive as well. This option gives you the ability to take a snapshot of the live system without changing its state. The availability of large-capacity USB drives that fit on a key ring makes it possible to carry your entire tool set with you inconspicuously wherever you go.

Returning to the credit card investigation scene, you need to look for the files that match the name found written on the white board. Because you carry your USB flash drive preloaded with the forensic program ProDiscover Incident Response from Technology Pathways (www.techpathways.com), all you have to do is plug in the USB drive, run the program, and begin examining the evidence.

NOTE   We haven't talked about specific forensic tools at this point, but stay tuned. We cover many of the most common hardware and software tools used in computer forensic investigations in Chapter 8, "Common Forensic Tools."

You immediately have access to the utility you need to search for the files in question. Because you can only search the suspect's computer and not seize it, you need to search the drive without copying it first. That may sound like a strange restriction, but you'll probably run into many interesting situations as an investigator. Now, search away!

Proving That a Forensic Tool Does Not Change the Evidence

If your investigation ends up in court, be prepared to provide evidence that the tools you use do not corrupt the evidence. That can be a tough sell if you try to prove this by yourself. An easier course is to use commercially available forensic tools that have already been accepted by courts. If in doubt, ask a local law enforcement contact which tools are accepted in local courts. If you use tools a judge has seen before, you are likely to avoid a lot of wasted time. Another valuable resource is the Computer Forensic Tool Testing (CFTT) Project from the National Institute of Standards and Technology or NIST (www.cftt.nist.gov).

Supply Power As Needed

Some types of evidence require uninterrupted power to maintain memory contents. The most common type of hardware in this category is the personal digital assistant (PDA) and some cell phones. PDAs and cell phones can contain valuable evidence. They also come in a variety of shapes and sizes. You can find traditional hand-held PDAs, as well as PDAs that are integrated into mobile devices, wireless phones, and even wristwatches. Regardless of their design, some cell phones and PDAs share a common trait: when the power runs out, the data is lost. (Note: smartphones usually include flash memory cards where they store information, so that running out of power or a dead battery doesn't result in data loss.)

Let's assume you find a gold mine of information on a suspect's PDA or cell phone. You extract the information and analyze it to find just what you were looking for. After a job well done, and after the self-congratulations, you lock up all the evidence in the evidence locker and await the assigned trial date. When your trial date arrives, you open the evidence locker and find that the battery has run out of juice. Your original evidence is gone. Well, your analysis report should still exist. You can proceed with documentation of your findings, but it would be a lot easier to show the device with the data still on it. Although you know what was there, it no longer corresponds to the device from which it was originally taken.

If you seize devices that require power to maintain data, seize their chargers as well. Make sure you either seize the charger or are prepared to buy a charger for that device. Also be prepared to explain your actions in court. Another interesting feature of PDAs is that their very operation changes the stored data. You may have to explain to a judge or jury how PDAs keep track of current time in order to notify the user of timed events. Be careful when asked if the data in the PDA has changed since it was seized; it has. It is also highly recommended to place mobile devices and cellular phones into a product like the StrongHold Bag from Paraben Corporation (http://www.paraben.com/stronghold-bag.html) to block electronic wireless signals from reaching the devices and further changing the evidence. You simply have to explain that the evidence in question did not change.

Provide Evidence of Initial State

So, you have the system you need to analyze. How do you poke around the data and convince a judge or jury that you didn't change anything in the process? If you're talking about a disk drive, the answer is really quite simple. Just take a snapshot of the contents of the drive before you touch anything, and then compare the snapshot to the drive after your analysis. If they are the same, you didn't change anything.

hash
A mathematical function that creates a fixed-length string from a message of any length. The result of a hash function is a hash value, sometimes called a message digest. Hash functions are one-way functions. That is, you can create a hash value from a message, but you cannot create a message from a hash value.

The most common method for performing a drive integrity check is to calculate a hash for the entire drive. A hash is a unique value generated for a collection of data. It is a "signature value," which means that if any single bit in the hashed data set changes, so also will the hash value. Most forensic tool sets include a utility to calculate some kind of hash value, usually a Message Digest 5 (MD5) or Secure Hashing Algorithm Version 1.0 (SHA-1) hash value. Although other valid methods exist to generate a single value for a file, or collection of files, MD5 and SHA-1 hash values are the most common. Both algorithms examine the input and generate a single value, but SHA-1 is considered to be stronger and more mathematically secure than MD5. For either algorithm, any change to the input (in this case, an entire drive's worth of content) will result in a different hash value.

After you ensure the physical integrity of the media (static electricity countermeasures, stable workspace, etc.) you can mount the media and access it in read-only mode. It is important that you explicitly separate suspect media from other media during any access to the data. The only safe way to ensure that nothing changes the data on the drive is to use trusted tools to access the original evidence media only once. The only reason to directly access suspect media is to copy it for later analysis.

Write Blockers

When available, use a write-blocking device to access suspect media. You can use software or hardware write blockers (see Chapter 3). Software write blockers prevent any operating system write operations from modifying the media. In essence, a software write blocker lives between the operating system and the device driver. Any requests for writes to the media are rejected.

Hardware write blockers are physical devices that sit between the drive itself and its controller card. The cable that transmits write instructions and data is physically altered to disallow any writes. The hardware write blocker is harder to bypass and is generally easier to explain in court, so you should use it instead of the software write blocker if you can.

If you have no access to either software or hardware write blockers, you can mount media in read-only mode. You will have to meticulously document the mount options you use to provide evidence to the judge or jury that you allowed no writes during analysis.

State Preservation Evidence

After you mount the suspect media, the first step you take is to create a hash. Use your own utility or a tool from your forensic tool set to create an SHA-1 or MD5 hash of the entire media. This provides a reference to the initial state of the media, and you will use this reference throughout your investigation to prove that any copies you make have the same content as the original media. After the volume is mounted and you have calculated the hash, you can create a bit-for-bit copy of the suspect media. You will perform all further actions on this copy, not on the original media.

That's all you do with the original media. After the copy operation, discontinue access to the original. It is important that you follow these steps with each media device you analyze:

1. Mount the suspect media in read-only mode (use a write blocker when possible).

2. Calculate an SHA-1 or MD5 hash for the entire device.

3. Create a bit-by-bit copy of the media.

4. Recalculate the SHA-1 or MD5 hash for the original and for the copy: both must be identical to the original SHA-1 or MD5 hash.

5. Unmount the media and return it to the evidence locker.

Take extra precautions to protect the original media and the initial hash. You will need both at the time of trial so that you can ensure that evidence you find is admissible. Even if your investigation does not go to court, being able to prove that your activities made no changes to a disk drive is helpful. You need the initial hash to substantiate that claim.

NOTE

The next step in the investigative process is the most time-consuming. After you have copies of the original media, it is time to start the analysis.

Evidence Analysis

Before you begin your media examination, create a hash of the copy you made of the original media. Does it agree with the hash of the original? If so, you may proceed. If not, find out why. Perhaps you mounted the copy and allowed some writes to occur. Or perhaps the copy process was flawed. In any case, don't start the analysis until you have a clean copy (an exact copy of the original media, with the same hash).

NOTE

---

checksum

Checksum or hash sum is a method to detect errors in transmission or storage of data to determine if data has been altered. A checksum or hash performs a mathematical calculation on the data involved before it is sent to calculate a unique value conditioned by the content of the data itself. This calculation is repeated following reception of the data and if the two values agree it's assumed that the received data is identical to the sent data (even a change in a single bit will cause the hash or checksum value to change).

Most computer forensic tool sets include utilities that create device copies and calculate checksums where appropriate. If you are using the UNIX operating system, you can obtain and use the md5sum utility to calculate checksums. Most Linux distributions include the md5sum utility as part of their command-line environment, but if yours is missing for some reason, check with the primary distribution download site for your Linux version to find a copy (thus, for example, you can download this utility through links on the ubuntu.com site at https://help.ubuntu.com/community/HowToMD5SUM). If you would like a Windows version of the utility, go to http://www.etree.org/md5com.html.

The next sections discuss how to approach media analysis. The actual analysis process is part science and part art. You must develop a sense of where to look first, and then possess the technical skills to extract the information. We'll focus on the high level overview here, as opposed to detailing specific actions you take with individual tools. Chapter 8 covers such tools, so we'll save those details and recommendations until then.

Knowing Where to Look

There is no easy answer to the question "Where do I look for evidence?" As with any investigation, not all evidence is clear or easily available. Some evidence is subtle, and some may be deliberately hidden or damaged. The specific type of evidence you are searching for depends on the goal of your investigation. If you are looking for evidence in a music CD pirating case, you will likely be searching for stored sound files. If you are gathering evidence in an e-mail fraud case, you will likely look at activity logs and e-mail-related files.

Let's get back to our credit card investigation example. Where should you look for credit card numbers? You know key credit card data includes the card number, expiration date, and possibly card owner information. That kind of information could be stored in a spreadsheet or a database. You search the hard disk for files that resemble the filenames you found on the white board. Unfortunately, you found nothing in the file system, deleted files, or in slack space. (The space on a hard disk where a file ends and the disk storage cluster ends is referred to as *slack space*, which is discussed in more detail in Chapter 6, "Extracting Information from Data".)

Where do you look next? In this investigation, you will look at removable and external media. We'll rejoin that investigation a little later.

You must be comfortable with the operating system running on the suspect computer. You might be using UNIX-based forensic tools, but if the suspect media is an image of the primary drive from a Windows computer, you'd better be comfortable with Windows as well. Default locations for files differ dramatically among various operating systems. In fact, file location defaults can even be different between releases in the same operating system family. Know the operating system with which you are working.

Activity logs and other standard files are commonly stored in default locations on many systems. Always look in those default locations for logs and configuration files. This step alone can tell you about the suspect. If all logs and configuration files live in the default locations, it is likely that the suspect did not implement security. On the other hand, if you find several applications using nonstandard paths and file storage locations, your suspect may have hidden incriminating files well.

Use every means at your disposal to understand what the suspect was trying to do with the computer. Consider all the supporting evidence uncovered so far. This is where documentary evidence you collect at the scene might be helpful. As you work through different types of evidence, your forensic tool set can help by flagging unusual data on the suspect media.

Good forensic tools help you by providing access to areas of a computer that can be used to hide data. But before you look for hidden data, look at the evidence that you can get to easily. Depending on what you are seeking, you might find it helpful to look where the suspect has been surfing on the Web. Look at the history and cache files for each web browser on the system, and then look at the cookies as well. Although web browsers allow you to look at some historical data, get a tool designed to explore web browser activity. Likewise, look into e-mail correspondence for each e-mail client installed on the computer.

NOTE

Make absolutely sure you have the legal authority to examine a system. You may be allowed to look for only certain type of files or activity. Do not exceed your authority.

As mentioned previously, we'll discuss specific forensic tools in Chapter 8. For now, let's look at a few of the different types of tools you'll need in the computer forensic process.

Viewers

File viewers provide small images of file contents. These programs scan a directory for files that match your criteria and show what is in those files. Viewers are great for finding pictures or movie files. Although most use a file's extension to

file viewer
A utility that provides thumbnail images of files. Such tools are useful for scanning a group of files visually.

identify graphics files, some more sophisticated tools can look at a file's header to identify it as a graphics file.

Some viewers also handle nongraphics file types, such as word processing files. The advantage of a viewer tool is that it provides visual representations for the files it finds. This can make scanning for inappropriate pictures far easier than looking at images individually.

Extension Checkers

extension checker
A utility that compares a file's extension to its header. If the two do not match, the discrepancy is reported.

Another useful forensic tool is an *extension checker*. This type of tool compares a file's extension with its actual data type. One favorite method for hiding data from casual users is to change the file extension. For example, if you want to hide the image file named `blueangels.jpg`, you could rename it to `blueangel.db`, or even something totally obscure, such as `br.549`. An extension checker utility looks at the extension and compares it to the file's actual header. Any discrepancies are reported as exceptions.

Unerase Tools

unerase tool
A utility that assists in recovering previously deleted files. In some cases, files can be completely recovered. At other times, only portions of a file can be recovered.

Most people are familiar with *unerase tools* to recover deleted files. These tools have been around the DOS and Windows worlds for years. On older Windows versions, a simple unerase tool can recover files easily. Newer operating systems complicate this process, but files placed in the Recycle Bin can often be recovered with the help of forensic utilities, even if the Recycle Bin has been emptied. File-recovery utilities, available for nearly all file systems in use today, help in identifying and restructuring deleted files.

Searching Tools

searching tool
A tool that searches for patterns (mostly string patterns) in large file collections.

Forensic examiners must often search large numbers of files for specific keywords or phrases. Several *searching tools* support such large-scale searches. An investigation may turn up certain words or phrases that can identify evidence. Searching for known IP addresses, e-mail addresses, or people's names can link bits of evidence together.

Wading through a Sea of Data

The first thing you will notice when you start to use the tools discussed in the previous section is the enormous volume of results that they return. No matter how narrowly you define the scope of your activities, you end up with more data than you can use. Your job is to sift through that data and to extract only pertinent information.

Log files provide great audit trails for system activity. They can tell you nearly every event that occurred within a specific scope. For example, web server log files can keep track of every request from and response to web clients. However, most applications allow for minimal logging to avoid performance impacts. Before you spend too much time looking through log files, be sure you understand what level of detail each application log contains.

A couple of tools can make analysis of log files easier:

Log file scanner   Log scanner utilities do little more than scan log files and extract events that match a requested event pattern. For text log files, a simple text search utility could provide a similar result in some cases. Most log file scanners make this process easier by allowing queries for specific times that involve certain events.

Log-based IDS   This type of intrusion detection system (IDS) provides a convenient method to analyze multiple log files. When searching for activity consistent with a network intrusion, let the IDS look at log files and highlight suspicious activity. This information is not helpful for every investigation, however.

In some cases, you can use tools to help analyze data. In other cases, you must physically examine all of that data yourself. In either case, one of the more difficult aspects of computer forensics is the process of separating the evidence that matters from everything else.

Sampling Data

Sometimes you will find that the volume of data is so large that there is no feasible way to examine it all. Some log files contain so much detail that it is nearly impossible to use it all. You might be able to process it, but the amount of useful evidence can be overwhelming.

Any time you have more data than is practical, consider taking samples of such data. You can use data sampling for input and output data. For example, suppose you are analyzing a large drive with more than a million photos. Your job is to find out if there are any images of classified equipment. One way to approach this task is to use a viewer utility on an arbitrary collection of pictures. Determine whether patterns exist. If you find from looking at samples of 25 pictures that files are organized by department, you can use this additional information to narrow your search.

On the other end of the spectrum, suppose your search yields 5,000 pictures of classified equipment. You would not want to submit all 5,000 pictures as evidence. Too much evidence can be overwhelming if presented all at once. Instead of submitting all 5,000 pictures, you may want to select a representative sample to submit, along with information describing the remaining pictures in that group.

All 5,000 pictures could be entered as evidence, but only the sample needs to be presented. The same approach applies to log file entries. Whenever a large volume of data or large number of redundant data exists, use a representative sample to present the whole data set.

Evidence Presentation

After analysis is complete, it's time to present results. The goal in any case is to persuade the audience using evidence. Your audience might be a judge, jury, or a group of managers meeting in a conference room. Your goal is to use the evidence you have collected to prove one or more facts. Even with great evidence, the success of a case often depends how effectively the evidence is presented.

This section covers some basic ideas to remember when presenting evidence. These ideas are simple and common in many presentations. Though simple, they are important and bear repeating.

Know Your Audience

Before presenting any topic, get to know as much about your audience as possible. Know why they are willing to listen to you and what they expect to learn from your presentation. A group of Information Services (IS) managers will have different expectations and motivations than a jury in a criminal trial. The more you know about them, the better you can deliver a convincing presentation.

Do Your Homework

When possible, find out who will be in your audience. If you are presenting evidence in a court of law, you will know quite a lot about the judge and the jurors. It may take more work to find out about your audience when presenting to other groups. Try to get as much basic demographic information about audience participants as possible.

For example, if you find you are presenting to a group of IS managers, your presentation will probably be different than if you were speaking to a group of auditors. Although the content will be the same, the tone and presentation style may differ. The better you know and understand the needs of your audience, the better your presentation will come across.

Another common presentation venue is a trade show or convention. You may be asked to present findings from an actual case you worked on. In this setting, there is a better chance that an audience will be more IS literate and technically minded. Organize your presentation to interest your audience. Take the time to do your homework, and develop the ability to speak to the needs and interests of your audience.

Read the Room

After you begin your presentation, attend carefully to the response you receive from your audience. Sometimes you will see rapt attention in their eyes as they hang on every word of your descriptions of the evidence. The other 98 percent of the time, though, the response is likely to be blank stares of mild interest. Seriously, always watch for signs of boredom. When you do see blank stares and fidgeting, change your pace, your tone, or even your approach. Remember: It is nearly impossible to bore someone into believing you.

Far too many presenters ignore their audiences. They might have a canned presentation, and they deliver it the same way regardless of the audience. You can't do that and be successful as a computer forensic examiner. You may or may not be called upon to present the evidence you uncovered, but you should be prepared nonetheless. Skilled presenters aren't necessarily less boring than anyone else—they simply know how to detect boredom early on and what to do about it. Many fine texts cover presentation techniques. Browse a few of them for some ideas on getting your point across.

Presenting facts is quite simple. Follow these basic steps:

1. Tell what you did.
2. Tell why you did it.
3. Tell how you did it.
4. Tell what you found.

Think about what you would want to hear if you were in the audience. The facts remain the same, but the delivery approach must change to appeal to each audience. For example, technical audiences like facts and "how-to" information. Managers tend to like higher-level pitches. For a group of managers, skip the gory details and talk more about the big picture. Although you focus on big-picture topics, be prepared to answer detailed questions when they arise.

Speaking and presentation books cover far more on reading an audience. Remember that boring someone does little more than tune them out. A persuasive argument is rarely boring. Watch the audience and react to them. You will connect more effectively, and have a better chance of persuading them to consider seriously the points you present.

Target the Points

When planning a presentation, write an outline of the points you want to make. Always start with an outline, no matter how rough. Use the evidence and the process of collecting it to support or explain your points. A random list of evidence is likely leave an audience more confused than convinced. Get organized, and stay on point!

Take the time to list each point you wish to make, and then expand the points with evidence. The core of your presentation is the evidence, so your evidence should dictate the flow of the presentation. Your points should specifically address each piece or type of evidence, and your evidence should support each point in the presentation. Although the relationship between presentation points and evidence seems circular, the actual points should be the target of your initial outline.

Add to your initial outline until you have a structure that brings out all of the evidence you choose to present. The next section discusses the organization of a presentation. But don't worry about organization until you are confident that you are able to address each of the important points in your presentation.

Your points can be either generic or specific to a particular case. A generic outline might look like this:

1. Initial site survey

2. Evidence collection

3. Evidence handling and storage

4. Initial site analysis

5. Data analysis

6. Findings

Your initial outline should reflect your own style and comfort level. The important thing is to ensure that your presentation is clear and concise. Spend your audience's time wisely; don't waste it. Include all the information you need to and nothing more.

TIP — **Start with a simple outline. You don't have to produce a final product in one sitting. You can be far more productive when you get something into an outline, then go back over the material to edit it. Treat your outline as a brainstorm session and get everything you can remember into an outline. This makes sure you don't overlook crucial ideas while wrestling with the details.**

Organization of Presentation

After you have an outline and a general flow, you need to consider how to organize your presentation. Although each presentation is different, you can use a few common rules of thumb. First, use a presentation method with which you are comfortable. If you are most comfortable drawing pictures as you go, set up a white board and dispense with the PowerPoint presentation. If you do use PowerPoint, plan for no more than 30 slides per hour. This guideline works well for general presentations. If you feel you need to spend more time on one topic, consider creating multiple slides for that topic. If you spend too much time on a single slide, it can become stale, and you risk losing your audience's attention.

Use what works best for your personality. Remember that the main purpose for your presentation is to present evidence you believe proves one or more facts in a case. Take the audience on a tour through the evidence trail that leads them to a conclusion about what happened that resulted in this case. Sometimes the presentation should take a chronological approach. At other times, a topical approach keeps consistency and cohesion.

Don't get locked into any particular type of organization. Think through what you want your audience to take away from your presentation. Use a flow and organization that makes sense to you and that leads the audience where you want them to go.

The outline approach works best for us. Whether we are writing a report or developing a presentation, we always work from an outline. As the outline grows and matures, we expand the content into the final format. For presentations, we frequently use PowerPoint. We generally move from an outline to PowerPoint only when we have each slide listed and the major points for each slide. Experiment and find a method that works well for your style.

TIP

Keep It Simple

Above all else, use the *KISS method* when presenting technical information to others (even other technical people). The KISS method stands for "Keep It Simple, Stupid." It's a silly reminder to us all that complexity breeds confusion. Part of the challenge in any presentation of evidence is to make the complex seem simple. Always use the simplest techniques you can think of to present evidence.

KISS method
KISS stands for "Keep It Simple, Stupid." This acronym reminds us to avoid making things more complicated than they need to be.

Whenever possible, use visual aids. The common saying "a picture is worth a thousand words," is truer today than ever before. Humans process visual images far more efficiently than written words. Whenever you can use a picture, drawing, or chart to convey a concept with just a few words, use it. The audience will remember a picture far longer than any words you use to describe it. Use pictures of the crime scene. If your audience is nontechnical, use a picture of a disk drive to explain the process of searching for hidden files. (See Figure 4.1.) Always look for opportunities to simplify the presentation.

Another decision you must make when planning a presentation is how much technology to use. Multimedia presentations with video and sound can be impressive, but they can also be distracting. Use technical props only when they simplify a presentation, not to impress your audience. Although some presenters use technology to add pizzazz to their presentations, this can come across as showy and insubstantial. In such cases, added technical features do not amplify the substance of the presentation.

Use technology when it enhances the audience's understanding. Don't use it when it merely adds complexity. A simple presentation allows an audience to concentrate on the evidence. Always remember to consider your audience as you develop your presentation. Don't make it too complex. Keep it simple, you-know-who!

Figure 4.1   Graphics convey concepts efficiently.

Disk Sector

Files are stored in sectors.

Terms to Know

checksum

distributed denial of service attack (DDoS)

extension checker

file viewer

hash

KISS method

searching tool

site survey

unerase tool

wireless access point (WAP)

Review Questions

1. What is the first common task when handling evidence?

2. Which type of hardware is seldom of interest to an investigation?

3. When attempting to prove that an individual used a computer, what clues might computer hardware provide?

4. In addition to hard disk drives, where else might data containing evidence reside?

5. Should handwritten notes be considered in a computer forensic investigation?

6. What is the primary concern in evidence collection and handling?

7. Can you analyze a system that is intact and running?

8. What happens when a PDA's battery runs down?

9. What device prohibits any changes to a hard disk drive?

10. How can you prove that you made no changes to a disk drive during analysis?

Chapter 5

Capturing the Data Image

It's time to look at what happens as an investigation begins. As with any other items of evidence, computer system components and other electronic devices must be handled correctly. An examiner must follow certain procedures to document their receipt and handling. Each computer examination is unique, and the investigator must consider the total effects of the circumstances as the investigation proceeds.

A forensic investigator must also be familiar with the types of evidence that may be encountered on a machine and how to properly preserve each type. Properly processing computer evidence is extremely important because information gathered may end up as evidence in a legal proceeding. Forensic investigators must start by capturing the data in the proper order. When you encounter a situation, should you immediately turn the machine off or should you leave it running and examine it quickly? What happens to the evidence when the machine is shut down? This chapter answers these questions and more as we explain how to extract the evidence once an investigation gets underway.

The Imaging Process

Part of your role as an investigator is to ensure that a nearly perfect snapshot of the system can be taken. The challenge is that nearly anything you do to a system can change it. For example, unplugging the network cable will change the system—but leaving the network plugged in will change it, too. Even if you decide to do nothing, the system will change because its clock will continue keeping time. It's easy to see the dilemma that a computer forensic investigator faces!

It's important to capture as accurate a representation of the system as possible and to document each step that you take along the way. Remember, any information gathered may end up in court so you need to be ready (and able) to defend your processes. At a minimum, make certain you document:

- ◆ What actions were performed
- ◆ Who performed those actions (This may be important to establish a chain of ownership, most commonly referred to as the Chain of Custody, of the evidence gathered.)
- ◆ When those actions were performed
- ◆ Why you chose a particular course of action

Simply copying all the potentially useful files from a system is probably not going to be sufficient for a complete forensic investigation. For example, if a suspect has deleted all file system–level clues, it would be difficult for a forensic investigator to fully piece together the incident using existing files alone.

imaging
The process of creating a complete copy of a disk drive where the disk is copied sector-by-sector.

One of the tools that helps the forensic investigator glean hidden information is imaging. *Imaging* is the process of creating a complete sector-by-sector copy of a disk drive. A forensic investigator frequently performs imaging as a part of the data collection process. Often, you will want (or need) to make a complete copy of a disk drive at the start of the investigation to preserve evidence and then do low-level analysis of the image at a later time.

Most computer users are unaware that the majority of operating systems do not overwrite the contents of sectors when information or files are deleted. Instead of deleting information, most operating systems simply unlink the sectors from the file system table and leave the data untouched until they need those sectors again for some other purpose. With a complete image of a disk drive, a computer forensic investigator may be able to locate useful information or evidence in the unallocated sectors on the hard drive. Analyzing a disk image allows a computer forensic investigator to dive deeper into a system's state and conduct a more complete investigation.

As a matter of best practice, a forensic investigator will image all disk drives that he finds as a part of his initial efforts. The cost of imaging a disk drive is nominal although today's huge hard drives can make imaging somewhat time-intensive. A number of hardware and software tools are available that make the entire imaging process much easier to conduct. Some of these tools are covered later in this chapter. Imaging disk drives is an endeavor well worth the time it takes—particularly if the payoff is information relevant to your investigation.

Evidence Collection Order

Before we get into imaging, let's go over the order in which you process evidence. The most volatile data is memory that is highly sensitive to system use, such as registers, memory, and cache. Such data is lost whenever a system is used. Because of the nature of this volatile data, it should always be collected first to minimize corruption or loss. *Request for Comments (RFC)* 3227, entitled "Guidelines for Evidence Collection and Archiving," illustrates the typical order of volatility on a normal system from more to less volatile as follows:

1. Registers, cache

2. Routing table, ARP cache, process table, kernel statistics

3. Memory

4. Temporary file systems

5. Disk

6. Remote logging and monitoring data that is relevant to the system in question

7. Physical configuration, network topology

8. Archival media

We cover the collection of certain specific items later in the chapter. In the meantime, let's go over some procedures you should avoid.

Request for Comments (RFC)
Started in 1969, RFCs are a series of notes about the Internet. An Internet document can be submitted to the Internet Engineering Task Force (IETF) by anyone, but the IETF decides when and if a document becomes an RFC. Each RFC is designated by an RFC number. Once published, an RFC never changes. Modifications to an original RFC are assigned a new RFC number.

Evidence Collection Methods to Avoid

An individual who uses the suspect system itself to search for evidence often jeopardizes the investigation. An example of this would be an investigator who used the built-in search capabilities of a Windows computer under analysis to search for and open files. By opening a file to review the file's properties, the access date changes, as illustrated in Figure 5.1. Note that the dates may differ. The "created" date is the date and time the file was created. The "modified" date is the last date the file's contents were modified. The "accessed" date is the last date the file was opened for reading or writing.

Figure 5.1 On Windows, viewing a file's properties changes the access date.

Eula.txt Properties	

General | Security | Details | Previous Versions

Eula.txt

Type of file:	Text Document (.txt)
Opens with:	Notepad [Change...]
Location:	C:\Util
Size:	6.84 KB (7,005 bytes)
Size on disk:	8.00 KB (8,192 bytes)
Created:	Tuesday, September 07, 2010, 6:03:39 PM
Modified:	Saturday, September 04, 2010, 3:42:53 PM
Accessed:	Tuesday, September 07, 2010, 6:03:39 PM
Attributes:	☐ Read-only ☐ Hidden [Advanced...]

[OK] [Cancel] [Apply]

Real World Scenario

Tales from the Trenches: Don't Touch That Data!

Here's an example of a how a suspect compromised his own defense. A man who left his employer admitted that he took documents with him that shouldn't have taken. A year later, the man stated that since he left the company he'd done nothing with those documents. Since he had not even looked at them, he claimed that no damage had been done.

The man agreed to turn over his computer to me for forensic examination. I would be able to image the drive and check the last access date for the files, supporting his claim that he had not looked at them. Unfortunately, the night before the man was to provide the computer for evaluation, he opened all of the files "so that he could be sure that he knew what was in them." By doing so, he destroyed his defense. Because the computer only maintains the last access date and not each access date, this man compromised the evidence that could have supported his case.

Preparing Media and Tools

Use properly prepared media when making forensic copies to ensure that there is no commingling of data from different cases. Consider using solid-state disks to store collected data. Solid-state disks are currently more expensive than electromechanical disks, but they offer forensic investigators some advantages over electromechanical disks. First, solid-state disks experience fewer failures during repetitive and long read/write streams. Since some of the hard drives you examine may be rather large, you don't want to waste time unnecessarily by having to restart a task owing to mechanical failure. Secondly, solid-state disks provide faster access time to the data, which can reduce your analysis time. These advantages, coupled with the falling prices of solid-state disks, can make them a viable alternative to electromechanical disks.

Sanitize all media that is to be used in the examination process. If you cannot afford new media for each case, be sure that all previously used media has been properly sanitized. The media must not contain any viruses or other contaminants.

To properly sanitize a drive, all data must be removed and overwritten. The sanitization process overwrites all data on the drive (active and inactive file space, space between the end of a file and the end of a block or sector, file allocation tables, directories, block maps, and so forth) multiple times to ensure the drive is clean before evidence is added to it.

The U.S. Department of Defense, in its clearing and sanitizing standard DoD 5220.22-M, recommends overwriting all addressable locations on writable media with a character, its complement, a random character, and then verifying that random character. (However, this method is *not* approved for media containing top secret information.) To sanitize your media using this method, overwrite first with a certain byte value, such as 00000000 (0x00), and then with 11111111 (0xFF), and finally with a randomly chosen byte value. Of course, you'll need to record the randomly chosen value you used for the third pass. The verification pass ensures that you read back the same value you wrote in the third pass.

During the sanitization process, document your steps. You can sanitize and document the process in several different ways. Software sanitizing programs (such as the open source program Darik's Boot and Nuke, or DBAN, Ontrack DataEraser, and WinHex) are available for this purpose. All of them work by overwriting the entire disk, usually several times, in a way designed to destroy all traces of preexisting information.

Besides software programs, some companies have equipment designed specifically for this process. The device shown in Figure 5.2—the Image MASSter Solo-4—can make multiple copies and sanitizes at full SATA-2 speed, conforms to U.S. Department of Defense Standard DoD 5220.22-M, and gives you a forensic audit printout after wiping each drive.

Figure 5.2 Image MASSter Solo-4 disk sanitizing equipment

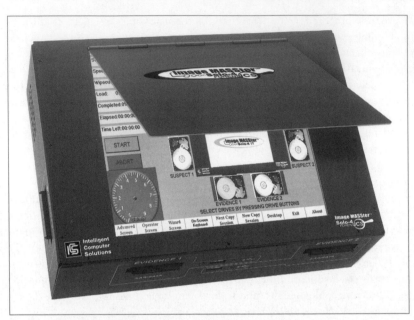

(Photograph Courtesy of Intelligent Computer Solutions, Inc. 2010)

Next, check to make sure that all forensic software tools are properly licensed for use and that all lab equipment is in working order. Several companies offer forensic imaging tools.

Forensic kits are also available. A kit includes additional tools that you may need for capturing data. The kit shown in Figure 5.3 includes tools made for seizing data from computers that cannot be opened in the field. High-speed data transfers can be performed between any suspect hard drives through the computer's SATA, eSATA, Fast SCSI, FireWire A/B, Express Memory Card, or Universal Serial Bus (USB) ports. The kit includes a bootable CD to start up the suspect's computer and run the acquisition program.

Collecting the Volatile Data

In some cases, evidence that is relevant to a case may only exist temporarily. Evidence can be lost when a computer is powered down. As a matter of practice, if the computer system is off when you first locate it, leave it shut down when you seize the computer to avoid further potential loss of data. If the computer system is still powered on, the forensic investigator faces a dilemma because powering down the computer to seize it may result in loss of data valuable to the investigation. When faced with this scenario (and you will be at some point during your career as a forensic investigator), you'll need to assess the risk of losing data and then decide how and when to shut down the system. You can somewhat reduce the effects of potentially losing volatile data by collecting a snapshot of the physical memory prior to shutting the computer down.

This is why the "Guidelines for Evidence Collection" (RFC 3227) lists the volatile data as the first kind of data you should try to capture. By capturing the volatile data before unplugging the computer, you get a snapshot of the system at the time you arrived on the scene. The following information should be collected:

◆ System date and time

◆ Current network connections

◆ Current open ports and applications listening on those ports

◆ Applications currently running

To capture this information, you may choose to conduct a live acquisition.

Figure 5.3   Image MASSter Forensic Toolkit

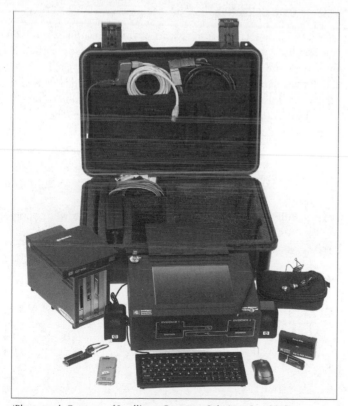

(Photograph Courtesy of Intelligent Computer Solutions, Inc. 2010)

Live acquisitions should only be performed by a properly trained forensic examiner, because any action taken on a live system may change the evidence.

In a live acquisition, goal is to collect the information without impacting the data on the system. The two most practical ways to do this are

◆ Saving the information to a remote forensic system

◆ Saving the information to a removable drive

To save the information to a remote system, you can use a tool called Netcat, which is a free tool used to create a reliable TCP connection between the target system and the forensic workstation. Using Netcat allows you to get on and off the target system in a relatively short amount of time. You can then analyze the data you have collected at a later time. You can also use Cryptcat, which is an encrypted version of Netcat. With Cryptcat, the traffic is encrypted between the target system and the forensic workstation. By using this type of process, the risk of data contamination or compromise is nearly eliminated.

Tools for Volatile Data Collection

Address Resolution Protocol (ARP)
A protocol used on the Internet to map computer network addresses to hardware addresses.

Let's look at how you can gather some pieces of information with individual tools, starting with volatile components first. One of the first places to capture information is from the *Address Resolution Protocol (ARP)* cache. The ARP cache is a table that maintains a mapping of each physical address and its corresponding network address. This information tells you to which other computers the computer you are working with is connected. The ARP cache indicates their network and hardware addresses, as shown in Figure 5.4.

You can see that the computer maintains a listing of addresses for two additional computers. This information can be especially useful for a forensic situation in which a company may have been attacked from the inside (internally).

Figure 5.4   ARP cache indicating the network and hardware addresses

```
Command Prompt

C:\XCOPY>arp -a

Interface: 10.0.2.15 --- 0xb
  Internet Address      Physical Address      Type
  10.0.2.2              52-54-00-12-35-02     dynamic
  10.0.2.255            ff-ff-ff-ff-ff-ff     static
  224.0.0.22            01-00-5e-00-00-16     static
  224.0.0.251           01-00-5e-00-00-fb     static
  224.0.0.252           01-00-5e-00-00-fc     static
  239.255.255.250       01-00-5e-7f-ff-fa     static
  255.255.255.255       ff-ff-ff-ff-ff-ff     static

C:\XCOPY>
```

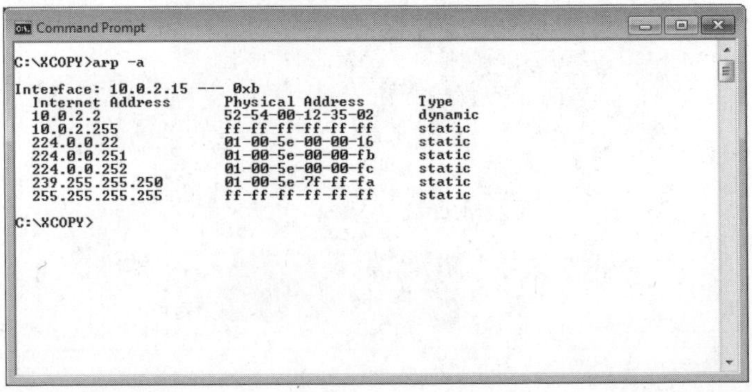

The information in the ARP cache is held for a maximum of 10 minutes, and then its entries are deleted.

Another useful piece of information is the output of the *traceroute* command. Originally developed for the UNIX operating system, traceroute (or tracert on Windows) is used for many operating systems and most routers. You use traceroute to track the path a packet takes to get to its destination. For example, if you need to request records from service providers in regard to a case, the information contained in the traceroute output tells you through which company's routers the data traveled.

Many firewalls do not issue error messages, so the traceroute client might time out. This means that it may stop at a certain point owing to firewall restrictions or router rules.

Figure 5.5 shows an example of tracert command output.

You can see that the path a packet took from our computer to the final destination passed through the following companies:

◆ ATT

◆ TeliaSonera

◆ Global Net Access

When tracing the route of a particular packet, the trace should go to the point where the packet originated and where it terminated. If the packet originated from a suspect's own computer, the suspect might notice the trace. In cases where a bot is used by the suspect, the trace won't go to the suspect's computer. (Bots are a particularly malicious type of malware. Intruders using bots are able to gain complete control over the subject's computer.)

traceroute/tracert
A command used to see where a network packet is being sent and received in addition to all the places it goes along the way to its destination. (It's traceroute for UNIX and tracert for Windows.)

WARNING

Figure 5.5   Output of tracert command

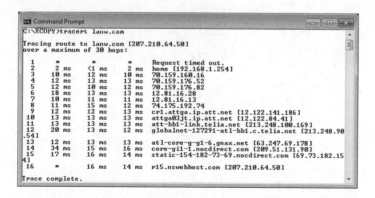

Next, an investigator may choose to collect a list of running services. Figure 5.6 shows the file output of a program called PsService, which we used to capture this data.

Figure 5.6   PsService output shows running processes (also called services).

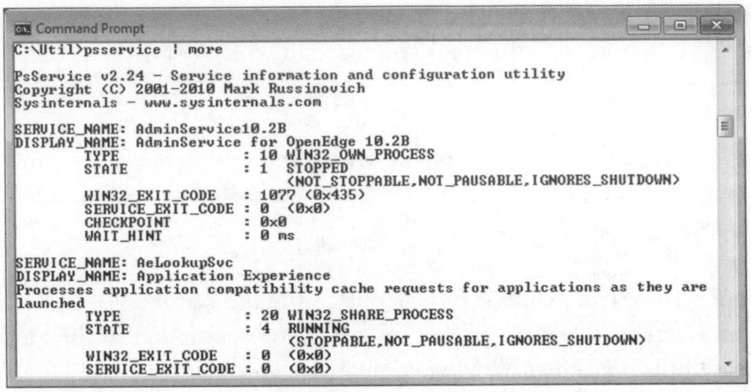

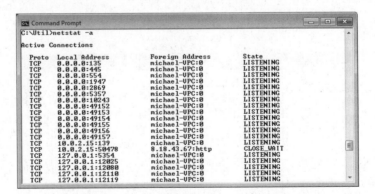

NOTE

PsService is not native to the Windows environment. It's obtained from the SysInternals site at `http://technet.microsoft.com`.

Netstat

A utility that displays the active port connections on which the computer is listening.

The *Netstat* utility (Figure 5.7) displays all active computer connections. This information provides the investigator with a list of what protocols are running and what ports are open.

Figure 5.7   Netstat output shows active connections.

The Shutdown Dilemma

After you've collected all the volatile data from the computer system at the scene, you may need to decide how to shut the system down for transport. Do you pull the plug? Or, would an orderly shutdown process be the better practice? Each situation is different and deciding how to shut down the system can be a difficult call. As the forensic investigator, people will look to you for guidance. You'll need to carefully weigh the risks involved in both methods and balance the risks against how to maintain the integrity of the original evidence. Some things to consider when making your decision include:

Normal shutdown process   If you elect to shut down the computer through the normal shutdown method, then file systems as well as individual files are more likely to be intact. On the other hand, each file written to the system during the shutdown process can result in fewer recoverable deleted files. It's also important to remember that there are destructive programs designed to delete data during a normal shutdown. It's always possible that a suspect may be running such programs. Also, a normal, orderly system shutdown clears space on the disk used for virtual memory, possibly taking valuable evidence along with it.

Disconnecting the power cord   Sometimes, depending on the evidence and information you have going into an incident scene, you may want to simply disconnect the computer system directly—that is, unplug it from the wall. If you decide to take this path, exercise caution. You run the risk of losing data, depending on the system the suspect computer is using. For example, there is an increased risk of losing data if the suspect system is running UNIX.

Forensic investigators should know the type of system that the suspect computer is using prior to disconnecting power to minimize the potential for lost data. Pulling the plug on a machine with an electromechanical disk causes any volatile data that you haven't already collected to be lost, including open files or data that hasn't been flushed from the cache to the disk. This makes collecting volatile data first even more important.

One scenario not yet discussed is live systems using encrypted files. If you are working with a live system that uses encrypted files that are mounted, you'll need to collect the evidence with a live acquisition. For more information, see "Collecting the Volatile Data," earlier in this chapter.

Remember, there are pros and cons for each shutdown method. It's easy to lose data (which may very well be valuable evidence) regardless of the method used so do your homework when making your decision!

Creating a Duplicate Hard Disk

Disk evidence is the foundation of computer forensics. Judges and juries can understand digital evidence on a disk as being analogous to files in folders or a filing cabinet. In a legal environment, the completeness and accuracy of digital evidence collection is often questioned. For this reason, careful collection of evidence is critical to forensic investigators. It's necessary to create a copy of the original disk for analysis because of the volatility of the data on a disk and the potential that evidence could be destroyed during handling and analysis. To be complete and accurate, the copy should be a bit-for-bit clone of the original disk, commonly called a bit stream image, or forensic image.

Whether you choose to literally pull the power plug (which immediately stops all disk writes) or properly shut down the computer, after the system is off, you can begin the process of creating a duplicate hard disk. An original method for creating hard drive images consisted of booting from a floppy boot disk and then creating a bit stream backup of the hard disk. A *bit stream backup* is a recording of every single bit of data that resides on a storage device. Using a bit stream method to make your backup copy not only copies working files (which any conventional backup utility automatically finds) but also copies hidden, erased, fragmented, corrupted, temporary, and special attribute files which may not be easily found otherwise. For example, temporary files might contain data from a document that was worked on but never saved to disk. This type of data can be recovered using a bit stream backup. AccessData's FTK and EnCase are two widely used tools for making forensic images that every forensic investigator should consider including in their investigative toolkit. (Forensic tools are discussed in more detail in Chapter 8, "Common Forensic Tools.")

Drive imaging can be performed in several ways:

♦ Disk–to–disk image, which is mainly used to test booting

♦ Disk–to–image file, which results in faster searches and is compressible

♦ Image file–to–disk, which is used to restore an image

bit stream backup
Bit stream backups (also known as mirror image or evidence grade backups) are used to create an exact replica of a storage device.

WARNING

Disk imaging is not the same as using backup software. Backup software programs generally copy data only, while imaging software makes a full, exact copy of the hard drive, including the operating system, software, file organization, as well as the data.

Among network administrators, tools such as Norton Ghost are popular for disk imaging. However, this type of software might not be suitable for forensic investigations. Ghost does not create an exact duplicate of the disk by default. It recreates the partition information and the file contents. A hash of the image will almost always result in a value different from the original disk. The validity of the evidence might be challenged, because the rules of evidence generally require that any copy be an exact duplicate of the original. If you have no other disk-imaging options available, however, use Ghost. It is better than having no image at all. A white paper on the use of Ghost as a forensic tool is available on the SANS Web site (www.sans.org).

Regardless of whether the examiner performs a direct device-to-device copy of the media or creates forensic evidence copies for examination or restoration, the copy process should be *forensically sound* and the examination of media should be conducted in a forensically sound environment. A forensically sound environment is one in which the investigator has complete control. No procedures are permitted without the investigator approving them. The use of physical write-blocking devices or software write-blocking devices can ensure that no writes impact the original media. These devices operate between the operating system and disk driver device or are plugged in between the disk controller and the physical disk to block any write requests. Nonforensic software can write to the drive, so using a write-blocking device eliminates this issue. (Hardware and software write blocking and proper documentation are discussed in Chapter 3, "Computer Evidence.")

forensically sound
Procedures whereby absolutely no alteration is caused to stored data. All evidence is preserved and protected from all contamination.

Understanding Full-Volume Copying

Moving on, let's define some terms and features in regard to making full-volume copies of data:

The first step in the forensic examination of a computer hard drive is to create the bit stream copy or *forensic duplicate*. This bit stream image of the original media is then used for analysis. Bit stream images capture not only the existing files but also the slack and unallocated space so deleted files and file fragments can be recovered.

Forensic duplicates can be created by using a hardware duplicator, such as the Image MASSter Solo-4 Forensic unit or the Forensic MD5 unit.

Many of the common tools used for obtaining a forensic duplicate are built into the software accompanying tools such as the Image MASSter Solo-4 Forensic unit. For example, Figure 5.8 shows this process using WinHex. (WinHex is a universal hexadecimal editor used in computer forensics, data recovery, low-level data processing, and IT security.)

forensic duplicate
A process used to copy an entire hard drive that includes all bits of information from the source drive stored in a raw bit stream format.

Figure 5.8   WinHex clone disk copy

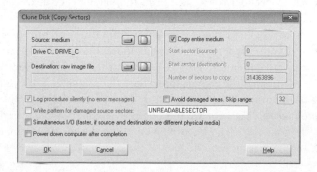

Creating a forensic image of the suspect drive, and using only the image for investigation and analysis, ensures the integrity of the original drive. The integrity of the original media must be maintained throughout the entire investigation. In a computer investigation, therefore, there is no substitute for properly obtaining a good working copy. An investigator must duplicate a disk using sound practices before performing any analysis; otherwise, the investigation can be jeopardized. If not done properly, your analysis will almost certainly alter file access times. Examinations should be conducted on a forensic duplicate of the original evidence, or via forensic evidence files. Using unsound tools can make it more to difficult get evidence admitted in court.

forensic compression
The compacting of an image file by compressing redundant sectors to reduce the amount of space it takes up.

As explained previously, forensic duplicating includes copying every bit of information on the disk regardless of whether or not it is part of the live data. This image provides a way for an investigator to do an in-depth analysis without altering the original evidence. Keep in mind that the speed of the duplication process varies greatly based on the physical state of the media, processor, and type of connection used for data transfer. In addition, some forensic tool kits offer forensic compression and spanning options. *Forensic compression* reduces image file size by compressing redundant sectors. *Spanning across multiple discs* is used when target media is smaller than the image file. For example, say that you are imaging or cloning a 500 GB drive and the drives you are using only hold 160 GB. You will need four drives to copy all the data. Spanning automatically breaks up the image into several smaller files (some programs let you preset file sizes).

spanning across multiple discs
Breaks the image file into chunks of a certain size so the image file can be backed up onto multiple CDs or other media.

After an image is made, you need to verify that it was made correctly. Verification confirms that the original media did not change during the copy procedure. How can you be sure that the copy is identical to the original? Programs that perform a *cyclic redundancy check (CRC)*, including CrCheck.exe, and CRC32, are available to do this job quite nicely for smaller storage devices. Larger storage devices require the use of a mathematical algorithm, such as the "fingerprint checker" Message Digest 5 (MD5) to show if a file or an entire hard drive image is the same or different. Secure Hash Algorithm SHA-1 and SHA-2 are more secure replacements for MD5. SHA-1 It's SHA-1and SHA-2 were designed by the National Security Agency (NSA) and are two of a number of cryptographic hash functions published by the National Institute of Standards and Technology as a U.S. Federal Information Processing Standard.

cyclic redundancy check (CRC)
A common technique for detecting data transmission errors. Each transmitted message carries a numerical value based on the number of set bits in the message. The receiving device then applies the same formula to the message and checks to make sure the accompanying numerical value is the same, thereby verifying data integrity.

The original suspect drive is hashed prior to imaging. The next step is to hash the image and see if they match.

These types of programs all use a checksum or hashing algorithm that holds up in court, verifying that a copy made using these tools is accurate and reliable.

Both the cyclic redundancy check (CRC) and the *Message Digest 5 (MD5)* confirmation ensure that the copying procedure did not corrupt the data. When MD5 is used, a change to even one bit of information on a large drive packed with data produces a different message digest. By comparing the original disks and copies, these methods can be used in computer forensic examinations to ensure that an image is an exact replica of the original.

Message Digest 5 (MD5)
MD5 is a one-way hash function, meaning that it takes a message and converts it into a fixed string of digits, which is then used to verify that the message hasn't been altered.

Tools for Imaging the Hard Drive

When you need to make an exact image of the hard drive, you should have a variety of tools in your lab. Each tool has its own strengths and weaknesses. You should work with as many tools as you can, and you should become familiar with them so that you know their strong points and how to apply each of them.

When choosing tools, one important consideration should be whether a tool can detect the presence of a *host protected area (HPA)*. These areas are created specifically to allow manufacturers to hide diagnostic and recovery tools. In essence, a portion of the disk is set aside and can't be used by the operating system. Neither the *Basic Input Output System (BIOS)* nor the operating system can see this hidden area. Companies such as Phoenix Technologies have developed products that can use this protected space to hold utilities for diagnostics, virus protection, emergency Internet access, and remote desktop rebuilds, but these products also allow consumers to use this area to hide data. Technically savvy criminals may conceal their activity in this area.

Full imaging will copy each sector of the original media, including data that is hidden, partially erased, encrypted, data contained in space that was swapped out of memory, and all of the unused space. A full image copy provides a wealth of information to the forensic investigator. When working with a suspect computer and making the image, remember these points:

◆ Record the time and date reported in the BIOS. This can be important, especially when time zones come into play.

◆ Remove the storage media (such as hard drives, etc.) before powering on the PC to check the BIOS.

◆ Do not boot a suspect machine's operating system, as booting it can destroy evidence.

◆ When making a bit stream image, be sure to document how that image was created. This includes recording the date, time, examiner, and tools used.

When making the image, make sure that the tool you use does not access the file system of the target media containing the evidence.

◆ Use tools that do not make any writes or change the file access time for any file on the evidence media.

After the image is made, the original evidence media should be sealed in an electrostatic-safe container, cataloged, and initialed on the seal. The container should then be locked in a safe room. Anyone who comes in contact with the container should initial it as well. Consider making a second bit stream image of your first image, especially if the seized machine was used in a workplace. The employer may want to put the machine back into service.

host protected area (HPA)
Area of a hard drive created specifically to allow manufacturers to hide diagnostic and recovery tools. (Sometimes referred to as hidden protected area or hardware protected area.)

Basic Input Output System (BIOS)
Responsible for booting the computer by providing a basic set of instructions.

WARNING

Extracting Data from Personal Portable Devices

In addition to extracting images from hard drives, you can use tools for memory imaging and forensic acquisition of data from personal portable devices such as cell phones, iPads, iPods, GPS devices, and personal digital assistants (PDAs).

Obtaining a bit-for-bit image of the selected memory region can properly preserve evidence. During this process, no data is modified on the target device, and the data retrieval is not detectable by the device user. The memory image of the device includes all user applications and databases, passwords, and various other pieces of information that may be useful in a forensic investigation.

One such tool, Device Seizure from Paraben, enables you to acquire a wealth of data, including:

◆ SMS history (text messages)

◆ Deleted SMS (text messages)

◆ Phonebook (both stored in the memory of the phone and on the SIM card)

◆ Call history

    ◆ Received calls

    ◆ Dialed numbers

    ◆ Missed calls

    ◆ Call dates and durations

◆ Datebook

◆ Scheduler

◆ Calendar

◆ To-do list

◆ File system (physical memory dumps)

    ◆ System files

    ◆ Multimedia files (images, videos, etc.)

    ◆ Java files

    ◆ Deleted data

    ◆ Quicknotes

◆ GPS waypoints, tracks, routes, etc.

◆ RAM/ROM

◆ PDA databases

◆ E-mail

◆ Registry (Windows mobile devices)

In these devices, just as on a hard disk, you can hide databases, data between the application and file partitions, and data in unused file system space. A hacker can write a program that accesses a database upon synchronization of the device. The normal user or untrained investigator will have no idea it is there. Mobile forensic software will enable you to capture a bit-for-bit image of the memory and dump the contents into a file that can be examined by a hex editor.

Image and Tool Documentation

Chapter 3 briefly described the evidence log documentation necessary to present a good case. Let's go into a little more detail here and specify some particular items of interest to document when you examine a system and make an image of its drive or memory contents:

- Collect the system date and time from the BIOS. Compare it to a reliable, known time source and note any differences.
- Record the drive parameters and boot order, along with the system serial numbers, component serial numbers, hardware component hashes, etc.
- On hard drives, record the number and types of partitions.
- On CDs, record the number of sessions.
- Note all operating and file systems used on the media.
- Document installed applications.

As an investigator, you must be prepared to prove your methods and documentation. The case of *United States v. Zacarias Moussaoui*, Criminal No. 01–00455-A, is a good example in which a defendant's attorney disputed the authentication of hard drives submitted as evidence in discovery. The response explains that the FBI used three methods to image the drives. Page 2 of the response refers to methods approved by National Institute of Standards and Technologies (NIST). This brings up an interesting point. NIST does not approve imaging software. It tests the imaging software using internally accepted standards and publishes the results. Since all testing is done using standard methodologies, forensic investigators can easily compare tool sets and choose the ones that meet their requirements. The Web site for the Computer Forensic Tool Testing (CFTT) Project is http://www.cftt.nist.gov/. The "Imaging/Capture Tools" section references these tests for some of the tools.

To read the whole story about the drives in *United States v. Zacarias Moussaoui*, go to news."ndlaw.com/hdocs/docs/terrorism/usmouss90402grsp.pdf **or** notablecases.vaed.uscourts.gov/1:01-cr-00455/docs/67282/0.pdf.

NOTE

Many of today's tools can capture all information needed for an investigation. But as the size of hard drives increases, so does the time it takes to sort through the volume of data acquired. When a case needs to move swiftly or disk space is limited, what do you do? In the next section, we'll cover partial volume images and capturing individual types of information rather than doing a full volume image.

Partial Volume Images

Thanks to inexpensive storage, the ability to store large amounts of data and information is now commonplace. A 500 GB hard drive is no longer expensive, and even 1 TB drives are reasonably affordable. Larger hard drives and more storage space can cause issues for an investigator who might be working onsite or during emergency cases. Although some utilities include newer technology to speed up the imaging process, there are times when creating a full volume image simply isn't possible, for example when data is stored on a mainframe computer.

Evidence is found primarily in files stored on hard drives, storage devices, and media, so there may be instances in which you don't necessarily want or need the entire operating system. If your suspected criminal is not particularly techno-savvy, you might only want the user-created files. Address books and database files can be used to prove criminal association, pictures can produce evidence of illegal activity such as counterfeiting, e-mail or documents can contain communications between criminals, and spreadsheets often contain drug deal lists. In such cases, copying only directories or files pertinent to your case may be more efficient than copying an entire drive.

Remember that full imaging copies each sector of the original media, including hidden data, partially erased data, encrypted data, and unused space. A full image copy also takes longer to make, and uses more space. The full imaging process is less efficient in terms of bandwidth than partial imaging because no matter how small the difference between the source (the system to be copied) and destination (where the new copy is located), the entire disk is copied. A partial image is quicker to copy and easier to work with and search. However, by using a partial image, you run the risk of missing valuable data. If you do not image the whole drive, be sure you record its partition data.

 Real World Scenario

Tales from the Trenches: Imaging

From time to time, I am called upon to image hard drives away from the comfort and security of my lab.

I have had to image hard drives at 2 o'clock in the morning. The reasons for the nocturnal timetables were simple: The employers needed to collect evidence of employee wrongdoing without the employees learning that the bosses were on to them.

Continues

Although this exercise might seem extreme, it actually occurs often. CEOs and board chairmen have asked me to investigate senior-level executives when they thought those executives were embezzling or violating Security and Exchange Commission (SEC) regulations.

The procedure to follow for acquiring evidence surreptitiously is straightforward: Don't get caught! For your career's sake, you must also check the company's policy to make sure that you have the legal authority to go into the office and that the company has a policy that establishes that the employee has "no expectation of privacy" on his company computer.

Typically, I arrive at the corporate offices in the middle of the night and am met by the director of security, who escorts me to the executive's office and unlocks the door. Usually, I take a couple of "digital photos" of the office and desk to make certain that I leave the room exactly as I found it. I also begin my chain of custody by taking photographs of the computer, including the serial numbers on the case and the hard drive.

I then open up the executive's computer and image the hard drive using a portable forensic acquisition device known as the Image MASSter Solo-4 from Intelligent Computer Solutions. Of course, if the computer is turned on, I must power it off before I remove the hard drive from the PC. After performing the forensic imaging, I then put the computer back together and leave the office exactly as I found it.

This method of forensic imaging requires that you "get it right" the first time. Make certain that you obtain an MD5 hash from the original drive and the forensic image, and that the two hash values match. Unlike performing a forensic image in your lab, you get only one chance to acquire the image successfully when you're in the field. If you don't capture the image successfully the first time, you might not get another chance to do so.

Don't attempt this type of forensic acquisition until you have some experience under your belt and you understand everything that can go wrong while imaging a computer.

When deciding which method to use, evaluate which of the following types of information you may need:

- Text documents, spreadsheets, databases, financial data, electronic mail, digital photographs, sound, and other multimedia files
- Previously deleted data, deleted folders, slack space data, and intentionally placed data
- Extra tracks or sectors on a floppy disk, or an HPA on a hard drive
- User settings and functionality of the hardware or software
- Boot files, registry files, swap files, temporary files, cache files, history files, and log files

Working with Virtual Machines

A virtual machine (VM) is a software application that acts like a computer and runs its own self-contained operating system, complete with applications inside the physical host machine. A single host machine can support one or more guest virtual machines at the same time, on different operating systems.

If you're in the forensic investigation business long enough, you're going to end up working with virtual machines sooner or later. As the use of virtual machines on personal computers grows, forensic investigators are more likely to find virtual machines as the subject of an investigation. In addition to being the subject of an investigation, virtual machines can be a benefit to the forensic investigator and you can also use them as part of your forensic tool box. Virtual machines allow you to do a physical to virtual (P2V) migration of the suspect system. Essentially, P2V enables you to clone the suspect machine and put the cloned image inside a virtual machine. Slick, isn't it?

Lots of tools are available to help you use virtual machines in your forensic investigations. Virtualization products include such tools as Live View, VMware, Microsoft VirtualServer / Virtual PC (free virtualization products from Microsoft), QEmu, and VirtualBox. There isn't enough space in this book to discuss all of these tools in detail but a brief overview of Live View should suggest what's available to forensic investigators.

Live View is a Java-based graphical forensic tool developed by CERT, Software Engineering Institute. It creates a VMware virtual machine from a physical disk or raw disk image. A forensic investigator can then "boot up" that image to get an interactive user's perspective on the environment without changing the underlying image or disk. Any changes made to the disk are written to a separate file, so you can easily maintain the original state of the disk. This helps you as a forensic investigator because you don't need to create extra copies of a disk or image to set up the virtual machine.

VMware is another product you may want in your forensic toolkit. VMware offers a commercial VMware Workstation <agree>product as well as a free VMware Server product.

Virtual environments are not without their limitations and caution should be exercised when gathering evidence from this type of environment. For example, virtual environments created by VMware are often considerably different from the original computer image, which will limit the admissibility in court of evidence gathered (or at the very least make it subject to challenges by the opposing counsel).

Even though the copied image of the target computer is exactly the same as the original, if the copied image is booted on a machine with a different hardware configuration from the original, the operating system will try to recreate the original image in its entirety and will attempt to install missing drivers during the boot-up process. This results in new data being written to the system—which, of course, modifies the image. In other words, you no longer have an exact duplicate of the original image of the suspect computer. Any seasoned attorney will challenge the authenticity and admissibility of modified images in court.

In addition, forensic investigators may find that some of the installed software products refuse to start, installed services may not work, and the computer itself might not boot. Virtual environments are a useful tool for forensic investigations but the limitations inherent to virtual environments may make the evidence gleaned inadmissible in court.

Virtual machines are often used to reduce analysis time in an investigation. Using virtual machines, investigators can take a parallel approach to searching for evidence—two examiners can work simultaneously on two separate images. This enables the investigative team to shorten the time necessary to search for and extract evidence using traditional investigative techniques and processes. This approach enables one investigator to do a "quick-and-dirty" search of the evidence using the virtual machine copy without the normal worries about invalidating the integrity of the acquired image. To protect the evidence, the second investigator works with proper computer forensic techniques and processes to validate the findings of the quick-and-dirty evidence search.

Remember, while using a virtual image to search for evidence can save valuable time, you must still follow traditional investigative processes and conduct a forensically sound (and well-documented) search on the nonvirtual machine image to collect evidence and have it stand up in court. Virtual images are also an extremely effective way to present and display evidence to the judge and jury at the time of trial. Using virtual images allows them to view the evidence exactly as it appeared to the suspect. This creates a great visual impact for the judge and jury in helping them to understand the details of the case.

In the next section, we'll briefly describe some of the imaging capture tools available to forensic investigators. You'll encounter these again in more depth in Chapter 8, which also introduces other tools available for capturing memory and disk images.

Imaging/Capture Tools

Just as with every other step along the way, you need to document any forensic software used during the examination. You should record its version and use it in accordance with the vendor's licensing agreement. The software you use should be properly tested and validated for forensic use. Several papers are available that document NIST and Department of Justice testing of various tools. You can find these papers on the NIST Web site at http://www.cftt.nist.gov/ and the Department of Justice's Office of Justice Programs Web site at http://www.ojp.usdoj.gov.

You also need to document all standard procedures and processes that you use, as well as any variations to or deviations from standard procedures. To analyze any system reliably, you must use unmodified, authentic tools. Remember, you should be prepared to testify to the authenticity and reliability of the tools that you use.

Be sure you have the proper tools to perform your investigation, including programs to collect evidence and perform forensic exams. Your set of tools should include the following:

◆ Programs for examining processes and services running

◆ Programs for examining the system state

◆ Scripts or programs to automate evidence collection

◆ A program for doing bit-to-bit copies

◆ Programs for generating checksums to verify the image

Your tools should be on read-only media, such as a CD-R. In addition, make sure to have a set of tools for every operating system.

Forensic tools come in many different shapes and sizes. Besides programs and scripts of capturing data, there are handheld forensic imaging tools such as the Image MASSter Solo 4 shown previously in this chapter. The successful use of forensic tools stems from being able to identify which are the most appropriate for your environment and becoming familiar with them before the need for an investigation arises.

Utilities

The *dd utility* is one of the original UNIX utilities; it's now used in Linux and Windows as well. It has been around since the 1970s and is probably in every forensic investigator's tool box. The free dd utility can make exact copies of disks suitable for forensic analysis, and it can be used as a means to build an evidence file.

Because dd is a command-line tool, it requires a sound knowledge of UNIX/ Linux and Windows command-line syntax to be used properly. You can use dd to copy and convert magnetic tape formats, convert between *ASCII* and *EBCDIC*, swap bytes, and force to uppercase and lowercase. Modified versions of dd intended specifically for forensic use are also available. The dd copy command supports special flags that make it suitable for copying devices such as tapes.

WinHex is a universal hexadecimal editor for Windows 95/98/Me/NT/2000/XP. WinHex has minimal system requirements, operates very fast, and consumes little memory. It is an advanced tool for inspecting and editing various types of files, and recovering deleted files or lost data from hard drives or from digital camera cards. The disk and memory imaging features include:

◆ Disk editor for both logical and physical disks, including hard disks, floppy disks, CD-ROM, DVD, Zip disks, and Compact Flash

◆ Supports FAT16, FAT32, NTFS, and CDFS file systems

dd utility
Copy and convert utility. Originally included with most versions of UNIX and Linux, versions now exist for Windows as well.

ASCII
American Standard Code for Information Interchange. A single-byte character encoding scheme used for text-based data.

EBCDIC
Extended Binary Coded Decimal Interchange Code. A character encoding set used by IBM mainframes. Most computer systems use a variant of ASCII, but IBM mainframes and midrange systems, such as the AS/400, use this character set primarily designed for ease of use on punched cards.

- RAM editor used to edit other processes' virtual memory
- Disk cloning
- Drive images that can be compressed or split into 650 MB archives

Grave-Robber is part of The Coroner's Toolkit (TCT), a set of tools used for collecting and analyzing forensic data on a UNIX system. Grave-Robber is a program that controls a number of other tools, all of which work to capture as much information as possible about a potentially compromised system and its files. Grave-Robber collects evidence in an automated way. It gathers data in the following order:

1. Memory
2. Unallocated file system
3. Netstat, ARP, route
4. Process data
5. Statistics and MD5 on all files and strings on directories
6. Configurations and logs

NOTE

Courts often accept evidence collected by tools that have been used in past trials. Tools such as The Coroner's Toolkit and commercially available forensic software are significant because the data collected by these tools is trusted and can be used as evidence.

Incident Response Collection Report (IRCR) is similar to TCT. The program is a collection of tools that gathers and analyzes forensic data on Windows systems. Like TCT, most of the tools within IRCR are oriented toward data collection rather than analysis. IRCR is simple enough that anyone can run the program and forward the output to a forensic investigator for further analysis.

Commercial Software

You should evaluate the following commercial software for your forensic needs:

Access Data's FTK Imager lets you take a snapshot of the entire disk drive and then copies every bit for analysis. The Forensic Toolkit (FTK) allows you to analyze the images made using the FTK Imager. These tools assist the forensic examiner in conducting a complete and thorough computer forensic examination of computer disk drives. Supported file systems include FAT 12/16/32, NTFS, NTFS compressed, and Linux ext2 and ext3. Like EnCase, it is a full suite of forensic applications.

EnCase is a commercial software package that enables an investigator to image and examine data from hard disks, removable media, and some PDAs. It enables examiners to acquire and analyze volatile data and image drives, verify the copy is exact using MD5 and CRC, and mount evidence files of hard drives and CD-ROMs as local drives. It also includes the ability to boot the mounted drive in VMware. Many law enforcement groups throughout the world use EnCase. If an investigation might be handed over to the police or used in a court of law, you should consider using EnCase.

Technology Pathways' ProDiscover Incident Response (IR) provides traditional and network forensic capabilities. This software has a remote agent with the ability to run in stealth mode, reducing the chance that the target will be alerted to the presence of the software. The deployed agent allows forensic investigators to collect and analyze a variety of data. It also has the ability to acquire a full image of the target. The live analysis supports capturing RAM in Windows Vista and Windows Server 2008. It also allows forensic investigators to search for pattern matches using wildcards.

ProDiscover IR contains a guide to assist users in programming the ProScript interface. This feature allows investigators to rapidly start common tasks.

ProDiscover IR is at the high end of the price range for forensic software and support is provided on a fee basis. The ProDiscover IR Web site contains forums, documentation, and downloads.

X-Ways Forensics (XWF) is a computer forensic environment that runs under Windows 2000/XP/2003/Vista*/2008*/7*, in 32 Bit and 64 Bit modes. Based on the WinHex hex and disk editor, XWF is able to run from external devices such as flash or external drives. It's also useful for collaboration with forensic investigators using X-Ways Investigator. X-Ways Forensics' features include, but are not limited to:

- ◆ Disk cloning and imaging
- ◆ Reading and partitioning file system structures inside raw (.dd) image files, ISO and VHD images
- ◆ Access to disks, RAIDs, and images more than 2 TB in size (more than 232 sectors) with sector sizes up to 4 KB
- ◆ Built-in interpretation of JBOD, RAID 0 and RAID 5 systems and dynamic disks
- ◆ Native support for a variety of file systems including FAT12, FAT16, FAT32, exFAT, TFAT, NTFS, ext2, ext3, Ext4, Next3, CDFS/ISO9660/Joliet, and UDF
- ◆ The ability to view and dump physical RAM and the virtual memory of running processes
- ◆ Several data recovery and file carving techniques

PDA, Mobile Phone, and Portable Device Tools

Mobile device forensics is concerned with recovering digital evidence from portable devices—mobile phones, BlackBerry devices, iPads, iPod Touch, and others—in a forensically sound manner. A mobile device is a digital device with internal memory that can communicate. Mobile devices may contain text and e-mail messages, contacts, locations, call records, photos, calendars, notes, and other types of personal information, or evidence. Such devices often possess several kinds of memory including volatile and nonvolatile memory, such as flash. They also have proprietary or custom interfaces, so the forensic process with such devices differs from computer forensics.

Device Seizure from Paraben acquires and analyzes cell phone, PDA, and GPS device data. Device Seizure supports a wide variety of cell phones and PDAs using the following Operating Systems: Palm through 6, Windows CE/Pocket PC/Mobile 4.x and earlier, BlackBerry 4.x and earlier, and Symbian 6.0. It also supports Garmin GPS devices.

Palm dd (pdd) is a Windows-based tool for Palm OS memory-imaging and forensic analysis. The Palm OS Console mode is used to capture memory card information and to create a bit-for-bit image of the selected memory region.

BitPim is a program that allows you to view and manipulate data on many CDMA phones from LG, Samsung, Sanyo, and other manufacturers. This includes most Qualcomm CDMA chipset-based phones.

Oxygen Forensic Suite 2010 is a mobile forensic software that supports over 1,800 devices and goes beyond standard logical analysis of cell phones, smartphones, and PDAs, enabling forensic investigators to extract more information and other data that is generally able to be retrieved using other mobile forensic tools.

Mobilyze was designed to forensically analyze iPhone, iPod Touch, and iPad devices. The product is capable of analyzing multiple devices simultaneously.

Zdziarski's Forensics Guide for the iPhone provides a way to make a bit-by-bit copy of the original media. By analyzing the image this method provides, an examiner can discover a wealth of information that other tools can't provide. Site access is freely available to full-time, active-duty law enforcement or military personnel tasked with mobile forensic imaging as part of their duties.

This is simply a list of the most common tools used to capture data for analysis. Remember that forensic tools come in many different shapes and sizes. Successful use of these tools stems from identifying the most appropriate tool for your environment, and becoming familiar with your tools before the need for an investigation arises.

Terms to Know

Address Resolution Protocol (ARP)

ASCII

Basic Input Output System (BIOS)

bit stream backup

cyclic redundancy check (CRC)

dd utility

EBCDIC

forensic compression

forensic duplicate

forensically sound

host protected area (HPA)

imaging

Message Digest 5 (MD5)

Netstat

Request for Comments (RFC)

spanning across multiple discs

traceroute/tracert

Review Questions

1. Why do you need to be careful about the utilities you choose to use for disk imaging?

2. What is an HPA?

3. Name some limitations of virtual environments when used for forensics:

4. How can you verify that in imaging the source media, the original media is unchanged?

5. Name a tool that can be used to image the data in the memory of a cell phone.

6. What does the Netstat utility do?

7. When collecting evidence, which do you want to extract first: the information in memory or on the hard drive?

8. Why can choosing the method used to shut down a suspect computer be a difficult decision to make?

9. If you need to boot a suspect computer to make an image copy, how should you do it?

10. Name three programs or utilities that can be used to collect forensic images.

Chapter 6

Extracting Information from Data

After you capture a data image, what should you look for? How do you figure out what portion of the captured data image is useful to your investigation? What happens if you can't find what you are looking for? These are some of the questions that run through the mind of every forensic investigator.

Criminals or intruders can (and do) use programs to delete e-mail, pictures, and documents that might provide proof of their activities. Trained forensic investigators must have tools available that will help them not only recover this information, but help them prepare the evidence for presentation to corporate executives, law enforcement officials, or the court.

In this chapter, you'll look at the process of divining the information you need from the data you have captured. You'll learn to analyze the information you have gathered and organize it into a usable format. You'll understand when to grab the low hanging fruit and when to dig deeper for data that may or may not exist. You'll study the types of hidden and trace evidence you're likely to encounter. Finally, you'll move on to learning best practices for preparing and presenting evidence.

Real World Scenario

Tales from the Trenches: Check That Evidence!

It's important for investigators to make certain that evidence makes sense before performing an in-depth analysis. With blood evidence, an investigator would ensure that the blood sample is human before processing a DNA match. The same common sense approach applies when working with computer forensic evidence. As a forensic investigator, you will need to examine much more than what the hiring client asks you to examine. There are three things Neil Broom always checks: the registered owner, the operating system install date, and external USB connections.

In one case, a defendant swore that no external hard drive had been used. However, the preliminary analysis showed that an external Seagate hard drive had been connected and that backup software had been used. In another case, the forensic investigators were asked to examine ten computers. A routine check of the operating system install date in the Windows registry revealed that five of those computers had operating systems which had been installed two weeks previously. Those computers were in operation for three years but their hard drives had been reformatted and older data reinstalled afterward. Because criminals often try to hide their behaviors and obscure evidence, it's wise to authenticate the evidence prior to analyzing it.

What Are You Looking For?

The variety of operating systems, application programs, and storage methods available today means that when it comes to looking for evidence there are a multitude of places to look. Digital evidence can be found in numerous sources, including stored data, applications used to create data, and the computer system that produced the activity. Systems can be huge and complex, and they can change rapidly. Data can be hidden in many different locations and formats. After you find such data, you may have to process it to make it readable by people.

Discovering Evidence Using Connectors

connector
The part of a cable that plugs into a port or interface to connect devices. Male connectors are identified by exposed pins. Female connectors are identified by holes into which the male connector can be inserted.

In recent years, manufacturers have developed branded forensic workstations that provide external native connectors for a variety of media, such as Serial ATA (SATA), SCSI (Small Computer System Interface), flash media, and the older IDE (Integrated Drive Electronics) drives. SATA hard drives are more commonly used by individuals, while SCSI hard drives are more likely to be found in a corporate environment.) As a forensic investigator, you will encounter and work with many different types of media. You may also encounter connectors that hook up

FireWire to SATA, SCSI, or IDE, and that hook up USB to SATA, SCSI, or IDE. A forensic investigator will determine what media the suspect has been using to store data and will have a variety of connectors on hand to aid the investigation.

The general discovery process is the same whether you are working with a SATA, SCSI, or IDE drive. You should adapt your techniques to suit the hardware you encounter.

To begin the discovery process for a drive, copy the image file onto your forensic workstation and then process it using one or several different forensic tools such as FTK, Encase, or ProDiscover.

Network Activity Files

Let's use an example case that involves the Internet and pictures. During your career as a forensic investigator, you may be called upon to investigate situations where an employee has illegally accessed and downloaded pictures of proprietary designs from a competitor's internal Web site and then used these designs in his or her own work.

After the forensic image has been added to your forensic computer, open your forensic software and start a case. Figure 6.1 shows the New Case Wizard from the AccessData Forensic Toolkit (FTK).

Figure 6.1   AccessData's Forensic Toolkit New Case Wizard

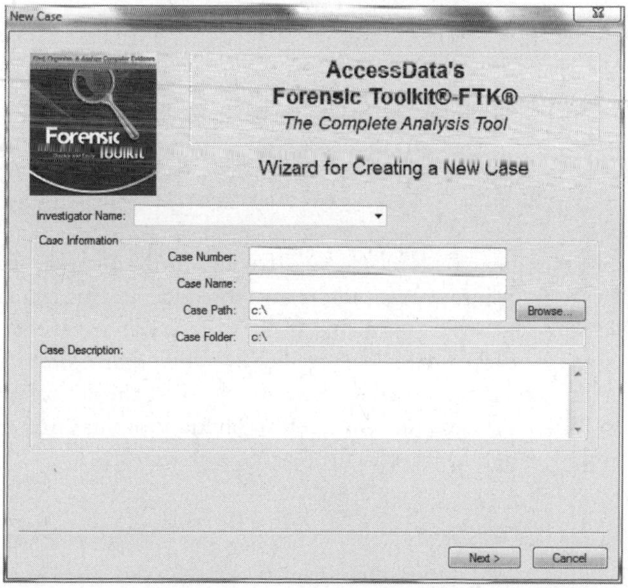

When a user logs on to a Windows XP, Vista, or Windows 7 system for the first time, a directory structure is created to hold that individual user's files and settings. This structure is called the profile. The profile creates a directory that has the same name as the user, along with various other folders and files.

Because this case involves searching for images that were downloaded from the Internet, the forensic investigation can begin by adding the entire image of the suspect computer to the FTK case. The image can then be preprocessed and evidence from the entire hard drive reviewed. Evidence from the folders where these files may be stored can be added to the case, as illustrated in Figure 6.2.

Figure 6.2   Adding evidence to a case in FTK

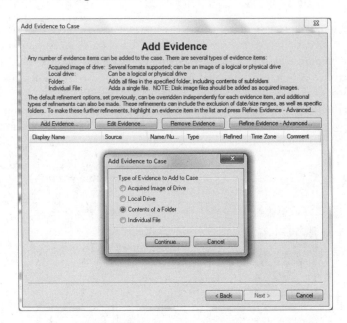

cache
Space on a hard disk used to improve performance speed by storing recently accessed data so that future requests for that data can be served faster locally.

temporary Internet files
Copies of all HTML, GIF, JPG, and other files associated with the sites a user has visited on the Internet.

Before a browser downloads a web page, it looks in the Temporary Internet Files folder to see if the information is already stored there. This increases the speed at which the page will load. Web browsers *cache* web pages that the user visited recently. This cached data is referred to as a *temporary Internet file,* and it is stored in a folder on the user's hard drive. All of the HTML pages and images are stored on the computer for a certain amount of time, and they are deleted when the temporary Internet file reaches a certain size.

Sometimes, while a user is viewing web pages, files can be written to the user's hard disk without the user's knowledge. For example, many sites contain *Trojan horse programs* that automatically download objectionable material (files) to a user's computer without the user's knowledge.

When working with web pages, it's important to keep in mind that a web page is not usually a single graphics file. A web page is a collection of multiple photos and graphics files that are displayed together as a single web page. Forensic investigators see each element that makes up a web page. This can be very important when reviewing graphics information, because the investigator needs to put the evidence into context. The user may have visited a single web page, yet the forensic application may show dozens and dozens of photographs in the Internet History. An untrained person might think the user had downloaded dozens of individual photos, yet the truth is only a single web page was visited.

Figure 6.3 shows how the information in the Temporary Internet Files folder can be viewed using forensic software.

Trojan horse program
In computers, a type of program or code that appears to be legitimate or harmless, but contains malicious or harmful instructions that may allow unauthorized users access to the victim's computer system.

Figure 6.3   FTK displaying information found in the Temporary Internet Files folder

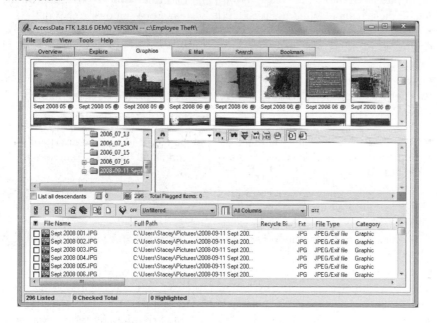

Information found in the Temporary Internet Files folder could have been unintentionally downloaded by the suspect. For example, some courts have determined that the existence of files automatically stored in a cache is not sufficient to convict a defendant of possessing or procuring child pornography. Other circumstances need to be evaluated to distinguish between unintentional and intentional acts. Such evaluations should consider the history of the files, their origin and use, and the control that the defendant had over the files.

In Firefox for Windows, the directory storing temporary Internet files is called Cache and is found in the following location:

```
C:\Documents and Settings\username\Application Data\Mozilla\Firefox\
Profiles\random_characters.default\Cache
```

In the path above, *username* is the Windows username of the suspect computer. *random_characters* is a series of random characters. The Application Data folder is hidden by default. To view this folder, go to Tools ➢ Folder Options, select the View tab, and then mark "Show Hidden Files And Folders" before proceeding.

In Internet Explorer, the location for temporary Internet files varies depending on the version of Windows used on the system. For Windows 7 or Windows Vista, the Temporary Internet Files directory resides in:

```
C:\Users\username\AppData\Local\Microsoft\Windows\Temporary Internet
Files\
```

or

```
C:\Users\username\AppData\Local\Microsoft\Windows\Temporary Internet
Files\Low\
```

Note that on PCs, Temporary Internet Files may be located on hard drivers other than the C drive. Forensic investigators should search all drives for Temporary Internet Files.

For systems that use Windows XP or Windows 2000, the Temporary Internet Files directory is located in:

```
C:\Documents and Settings\username\Local Settings\Temporary Internet
Files\
```

Forensic investigators may also find evidence in the browser's History folder. The History folder contains a list of links to web pages that the user visited. Figure 6.4 shows an example of data contained in the History folder. It also shows why this file may contain little or no data. The Internet Options dialog box in Internet Explorer includes Browsing history settings. The user can specify how long the list of visited Web sites should be kept. The default setting is generally 20 days. Computer users can change this setting to a shorter period, or set the browser to erase the entire history when the browser is closed.

Figure 6.4   Internet Explorer History list and Internet Options Browsing history settings

The Cookies folder is similar to the History folder. It holds *cookies*—information stored by Internet sites that were visited by the user. A number of utilities work with forensic software to display the contents of a cookie in an easily readable format. One such utility is DCode, which you can download from http://www.digital-detective.co.uk/downloads.asp

Flash cookies (also called Local Shared Objects, or LSOs) are files placed on your computer by a Flash plugin. These cookies are stored in central system folders and are protected from deletion. Cookie deletion settings in the browser don't affect LSOs. LSOs are used like standard browser cookies. The primary differences are that Flash cookies hold 25 times more data than standard browser cookies and never expire. Flash cookies are easily identifiable by their .sol file extension. The default storage location for LSO files is operating system-dependent. LSO files may be stored at: \Users*username*\AppData\Roaming\Macromedia\Flash Player\#SharedObjects\.

Unfortunately, conventional forensic software used to analyze Internet history may not find these files, and the forensic investigator may have to dig deeper to recover Flash cookie data. Once recovered, you can parse .sol files into a more readable form using the SharedObject Reader plugin, which can be downloaded from http://code.google.com/. From this web page, search for "SharedObject Reader" to locate the plugin.

Many applications create temporary files when the application is installed and when a file is created. These files are supposed to be deleted after installation is finished or when a document is closed—but sometimes this doesn't happen. For example, each time you create a document in Microsoft Word, the software creates a temporary file (with a .tmp extension) like those shown in Figure 6.5. The Properties dialog box indicates that the tmp7201.tmp file was created on September 09, 2010. Temporary files may provide useful evidence.

cookie
Small text file placed on a computer's hard drive as users browse Web sites. Each cookie file contains a unique number that identifies users to the Web site's computers upon the user's return to the site.

Figure 6.5   Temporary file listing and properties

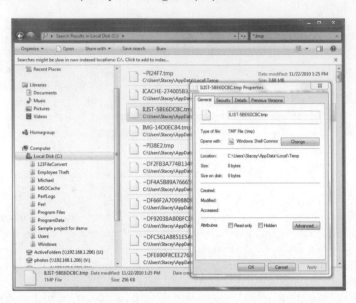

If, during your examination of the computer, you find no history files, temporary Internet files, or temporary files in the expected folders, the data has likely been stored somewhere else, so you'll need to dig deeper to uncover any hidden evidence.

Some additional file types that you may want to look for during a forensic investigation include:

◆ Files in strange locations

◆ Files with strange names

◆ Files that start with a period (.) and contain spaces

◆ Files that have changed recently

MAC time
Set of time stamps associated with a file. The time stamps describe the last time the file was modified (mtime), accessed (atime), and created (ctime).

MAC time attributes are extremely useful to the forensic investigator and assist in investigating and understanding system behavior, as well as following user activity with regard to a certain file. These time attributes are attached to any file or directory in UNIX, Windows, and other file systems. Microsoft, depending on the version of the operating system, calls these time attributes LastWriteTime, LastAccessTime, and CreationTime, or Created, Modified, and Accessed, as shown in Figure 6.5.

Various other available tools provide similar types of information. For example, you can use X-Ways Trace (available from X-Ways Software Technology AG at http://www.x-ways.net/trace/) to analyze a drive to locate information about Internet-related files. Such tools can be useful in gathering evidence regarding sites visited, last date visited, and cache filenames.

Activity Log Files

A device's log files contain the primary records of a user's activities on a system or network and can provide valuable information to the forensic investigator. For example, authentication logs document accounts related to a particular event, along with the IP address of the authenticated user. These files also contain date and time stamps, username, and the IP address where the request originated. Application logs may also yield valuable evidence to the forensic investigation because they record the time, date, and application identifier. When an application is used, it produces a text file on the desktop system containing the application identifier, the date and time the application was started, and how long the application was in use.

Operating systems logs may also reveal vital evidence. Logs from operating systems document system related events, such as types of devices used, errors, reboots, and much, much more. As a forensic investigator, you'll want to analyze operating system logs to identify patterns of activity along with any unusual patterns or events. Network device logs, such as firewall and router logs, should also be examined as a part of any forensic investigation. These logs may provide vital information or evidence about the user's activities on the network. The information gathered from network device logs can also be used to support the evidence gathered from logs provided by other systems.

One of the most important pieces of information that a log file may reveal is how an attacker entered a network and the source of illicit activities. For example, log files from servers and Windows security event logs on domain controllers can attribute activities to a specific user account.

E-mail Headers

E-mail headers are another source that forensic investigators should examine during the investigative process. Consider the following example. Several employees in a company report that they received e-mail messages from the support team requesting information to update a database. The e-mail instructs the user to send his logon and password information back to the sender. Because IT staff would never request such information from users, you suspect this is an attempt by an intruder to gain sensitive information. In this instance, one of the first items you may want to look at is the e-mail header. Figure 6.6 shows an example of an e-mail header.

The e-mail header shows the path the message took from its first communication point of origin until it reached the recipient. The first point is the *IP address* of the e-mail sender as assigned by his or her Internet service provider (ISP). Analyzing an e-mail header can provide valuable information to the forensic investigator regarding the source of the illicit request. In the following sections, we'll analyze the lines in the e-mail header to illustrate how to read and interpret this data.

e-mail header
Data at the beginning of an electronic message that contains information about the message.

IP address
A unique identifier for a computer or device on a TCP/IP network.

Figure 6.6   E-mail header

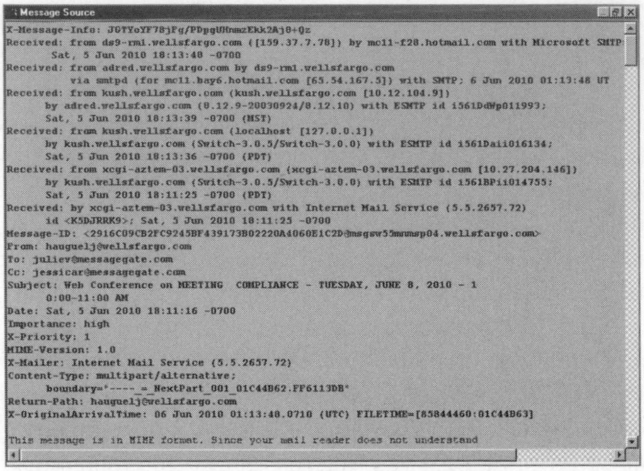

protocol
A set of rules and conventions that govern how computers exchange information over a network medium.

Transmission Control Protocol/ Internet Protocol (TCP/IP) network
A network that uses the TCP/IP protocol.

packet
Unit of information routed between an origin and a destination. A file is divided into efficient-size packets for transmission.

router
Device (or software) that determines the next network point to which a packet should be forwarded on the way to its destination.

Before communication can begin, a software or device driver must be installed on the computer and a common method of communication or *protocol* determined. In simple terms, a protocol is the language that computers use to talk to each other. For example, if I speak and understand only English and you speak and understand only French, communication isn't going to be very effective because neither of us knows what the other is saying or how to effectively talk to each other. The same holds true for computers.

Computers need addresses and protocols to communicate. An IP address is an identifier for a computer or device on a *TCP/IP network*. Networks using the TCP/IP protocol route messages based on the IP address of the destination.

IP addresses come in two kinds: IPv4 and IPv6 (older and newer versions of the same TCP/IP protocol). An IPv4 address is 32 bits, or 4 bytes, long and is a decimal number between 0 and 255, which is expressed as four octets in dotted decimal notation. For example, 192.00.132.25 is a valid IPv4 address. An IPv6 address is 128 bits, or 16 bytes, long represented using 16 hexadecimal digits (numbers 0 through 9, and letters *A* through *E* or *a* through *e*). FE80:3043:3B5B:B0D9:B388 is a valid IPv6 address.

Because of its routing ability, TCP/IP is the standard protocol of choice for most networks. TCP/IP breaks data into smaller units called *packets*. Devices called *routers* then pass the packets across the networks by reading the headers to determine if each packet belongs to the router's network or if it should be passed on to another network. This is similar to sending a letter, where the zip code indicates the letter's final destination. For example, when a person sends a letter from California to New York, the letter may be transported to various post offices before it actually arrives in New York. If the zip code on the letter does not match the zip code for the area in which it arrives, the letter is forwarded on until it reaches its final destination.

As a forensic investigator, you should also be familiar with e-mail and web protocols other than TCP/IP. Each part of the TCP/IP protocol suite contains important information for investigators. For example, within a network, an investigator can map an IP address to the Media Access Control (MAC) address. The MAC address identifies a specific piece of hardware, such as an individual network card. Criminals can use special software to change the MAC address of hardware to pretend to send or receive messages using a fake address (or the real address of some other hardware). Also, criminals can use low-level custom code to send messages over different paths and in different sequences (for example using UDP datagrams) that are reassembled at the recipient's end. A working knowledge of the TCP/IP stack and various protocols is required for a forensic investigator to be able to intercept and reassemble this type of message. Following is a list of the most common web protocols that you're likely to encounter.

UDP datagram
A message sent using the User Datagram Protocol (UDP), a network protocol used on the Internet. UDP allows applications to send datagrams to other hosts on an Internet Protocol (IP) network without requiring prior communications to set up special transmission channels or data paths.

Domain Name Service (DNS) resolves the names that users type into a web browser to their proper network addresses. DNS is most commonly used by applications to translate domain names of hosts to IP addresses.

File Transfer Protocol (FTP) performs basic interactive file transfers between hosts, allowing files to be uploaded and downloaded.

Simple Mail Transfer Protocol (SMTP) supports basic message delivery services between mail servers.

Post Office Protocol (POP) is used to retrieve e-mail from a mail server. It downloads the messages to the client, where they are then stored.

Internet Message Access Protocol (IMAP) allows e-mail to be accessed from computers at various locations (for example, home, office, while traveling, and so forth) without the need to transfer messages or files back and forth between computers.

HyperText Transfer Protocol (HTTP) is a low-overhead web browser service protocol that supports the transport of files containing text and graphics.

Multimedia Internet Message Extensions (MIME) is a type of communications protocol that supports binary, audio, and video data transmission.

The above information is a lot to absorb but it's necessary to understand for an investigator to make sense of the e-mail header (Figure 6.7).

When a user sends an e-mail message, the message is transmitted to a forwarding server or an ISP's mail server. The mail server adds a `Received:` field to the header of the e-mail message. The message will then be passed through additional mail servers before reaching its final destination. As the message is transferred from server to server, each mail server adds its own `Received:` field to the message header on top of the one from the last server. The e-mail message shown in Figure 6.7 has six `Received:` fields, meaning that it passed through six e-mail servers before reaching the recipient.

Figure 6.7   E-mail header

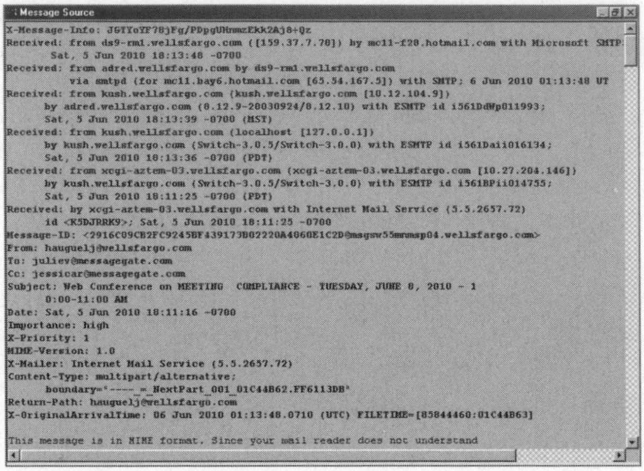

Reading the header from the bottom up, the information on the bottom line starts with an X. This entry is added by the sender's mail server, which records the time (in coordinated universal time, or UTC) the message was received by the mail server from the sender: 06 Jun 2010 01:13:40.0710 (UTC). Moving up in the header, the next X entry shows Internet Mail Service and an ID (`5.5.2657.72`). This information indicates that the sender's mail server uses Internet Mail Service and assigned a unique ID to the message. The `Received:` entry, found several lines above, shows when the next server in the relay received the message. As you follow the information up through the message header, you can trace the path the message traveled through the mail servers (in this case, at wellsfargo.com). The entry at the top was inserted by the last server in the relay before the message was delivered to its destination.

This header comes from Microsoft Outlook 2010. To view header information:

1. Open the e-mail (the e-mail opens on the message tab).

2. Click on the File tab.

3. Click on Properties.

You should now see the header as shown in Figure 6.8. (Note: the process may be different depending on which version of Microsoft Outlook you're using.)

Figure 6.8   Microsoft Outlook E-mail message Properties dialog box

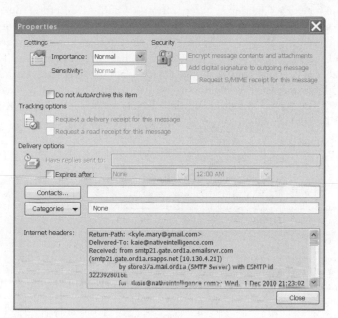

E-mail addresses and messages are stored in a file within the mail program's folder. These types of files usually have a `.pst` or `.pab` extension. Depending on your e-mail software, the steps may vary on how to expose the e-mail header. The following link offers instructions for some of the more popular programs: `http://www.spamcop.net/fom-serve/cache/19.html`

Deleted Files

The Recycle Bin, present in Windows operating systems, is another place where forensic investigators may find useful data. Many users do not realize that files sent to the Recycle Bin are not automatically deleted. In reality, the Recycle Bin acts as a halfway house for deleted files, so that files can be undeleted by a user upon demand. The Recycle Bin includes information such as the original location of files before they were deleted and date and time of deletion. When the Recycle Bin is emptied, this information record is deleted along with the other files. Forensic investigators may still be able to recover a deleted file's contents if they have not been overwritten.

Many people mistakenly believe that when they delete something from their computers, they actually erase all the information in the file. This is not necessarily true. When a file is deleted, the first character of the filename is changed to a hex E5. Chapter 2, "Preparation—What to Do Before You Start," discusses file systems and explains that a file system keeps a table of contents of the files on the disk. When a file is requested, the table of contents is searched to locate and access the file. When a user deletes a file, the actual file is still there, but the table of contents ignores it. The Davory data recovery utility is a great tool that allows forensic investigators to recover deleted files from a drive (see Figure 6.9). The Davory data recovery is available for download from X-Ways Software Technology AG at http://www.x-ways.net/davory/.

Figure 6.9   Davory data recovery

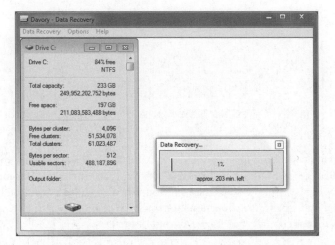

As you can see, the Davory utility recovered 3,905 files that were supposedly deleted. This example illustrates that with a little careful digging, you can find information about a file (and sometimes even the file itself), even when that file has been deleted or moved.

TIP

Remember, the data in deleted files isn't actually erased from the disk. When a file is deleted, the operating system deletes the pointers to the file and shows the space occupied by the file's data as available, but the data is still there, until other files begin to overwrite it.

Attempts at Password Cracking

As a forensic investigator, you should know what to look for when a system has been hacked. Let's examine a scenario that involves password cracking to access systems.

Passwords are used for many purposes. Many users don't create complex passwords, or have trouble remembering more than one. Thus, many users create one easy-to-remember password and use it for everything.

Often, an attacker captures the password file before cracking it. On a computer running early Windows versions, passwords are stored in a file with a .pwl extension and one is created automatically for each user. On a computer running Windows XP, Vista, Windows Server 2003, or Windows Server 2008, the password file is stored in a database called the Security Accounts Manager (SAM). On a Windows 7 computer, the password file is stored in the Credentials Manager. A popular way of obtaining passwords is to use a method called a *brute force attack*. Several programs use this method to obtain passwords. Some of the popular brute force programs include L0phtCrack, Crack, and John the Ripper. If you search the Internet for password-cracking tools, you might be amazed at how much information you can find. So, where do you find evidence on a computer that's been hacked or otherwise compromised? The log files are always a great place to start a forensic examination.

All operating systems come with the ability to audit and log events. In Figure 6.10, a Windows computer has been set up to log successful and failed attempts at logons.

NOTE

brute force attack
An attack that systematically tries every conceivable combination until a password is found, or until all possible combinations have been exhausted.

Figure 6.10   Event Properties dialog box for a Logon Failure attempt

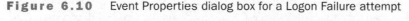
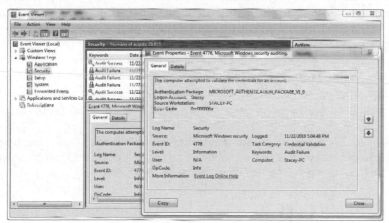

By examining the log, you can clearly observe that there were several failed attempts to log on an administrator made within one minute. As a forensic investigator, seeing this many failed attempts in such a short time period should alert you that someone could be trying to crack the password. Administrators frequently set the lockout threshold at three to five failed attempts. At the threshold point, the account locks and will thwart further attempts to crack it.

────── *NOTE* ──────

Password-cracking programs have legitimate uses. For example, when a network administrator suddenly quits, is fired, or dies, a password-cracking program can allow an authorized person access to the Administrator account.

In addition to those named above, there are several other logs you can review to aid your investigation and find evidence of a computer's activity. On older Windows operating systems, most of these logs are stored in the `C:\Windows\Security\Logs` directory. On Windows Vista and Windows 7 computers, the logs are stored in the `c:\Windows\Logs` directory. In Linux, the security logs are located in the `/Var/Log/` directory. This directory contains a record of all root access allowed and all denied access. Other logs are stored in `/Var/Adm/Syslog`, `/Var/Admmessages`, and `/Var/Adm/Kernel`.

Log files also reside on routers and intrusion prevention and detection systems, so you should be prepared to examine all of these files as a part of a forensic investigation. Telltale signs often appear in logs, offering strong indications that something is amiss. When you are examining security logs to trace an attempt to crack the Administrator password, look for long entries of random characters, password changes, and repeated occurrences of three dots (. . .). These are all suspicious items and should raise a flag to forensic investigators to dig deeper. Look through all log files to make sure you understand what has happened to a system.

port scanner
Program that attempts to connect to a list of computer ports or a range of IP addresses.

Often perpetrators use tools such as *port scanners* to find open ports on a system and then upload a remote access program to take control of that system. The longer they remain undetected, the longer a hijacked system can be used as a conduit. When this happens, you may find evidence of illicit activity in the log files.

As a forensic investigator, you should educate yourself about recent exploit scripts and newly discovered vulnerabilities. Remaining current helps you identify popular means of attack. Become familiar with how systems work, what services are running, when log entries are created, and what those log entries represent. Evidence is frequently found in these files, so you'll use them often during your career.

────── *TIP* ──────

In forensics, we're also concerned with how to crack passwords that a user placed on a system or documents on a system (e.g., a password-protected Word document). This topic is covered in Chapter 7, "Passwords and Encryption."

How People Think

When searching for the evidence you need, understanding how people think can be helpful. A powerful tool available to the forensic investigator is the ability to understand motives—that is, the reasons a suspect committed a crime. Understanding how criminals think makes it possible for you to discover, analyze, and reconstruct the events leading to a crime.

According to experts, criminal behavior often emerges from a combination of environmental, psychological, and biological factors. Certain characteristics (such as short attention span, lack of impulse control, and poor home life) may predict future criminal behavior. Although most crimes are committed by young men in their teens and twenties, this is not always true where computer crimes are concerned.

So, what motivates criminal activity?

Financial Gain   Many cybercriminals are motivated by financial gain. Identity theft, theft of trade secrets, credit card fraud, medical insurance fraud, and extortion are generally motivated by greed. In the United States, the poor economy owing to the recession that started in 2008 has been blamed for increases in criminal offenses.

Anger or Revenge   Anger, jealousy, and resentment are powerful motives. Disgruntled or dishonest employees as well as former employees, saboteurs, and extortionists often commit crimes of revenge. Revenge is also often cited as a motive in cyberbullying. For example, Lori Drew, a Missouri mother, was convicted in a landmark cyberbullying case. Prosecutors said that Drew's actions were motivated by a desire to humiliate 13-year-old Megan Meier for saying "mean things" about Drew's teenage daughter. Meier committed suicide shortly after a cyberbullying incident.

Power   Activists may want to force a course of action that suits their agenda. To accomplish this, they may deliberately cause damage—for example, by mounting a denial of service (DoS) attack—simply to garner attention or notoriety. DoS attacks can completely shut down and paralyze a network. High-profile sites are frequently targets for DoS attacks. Nation-states and terrorists may try to weaken the economy or digital infrastructure of a country in order to render its defenses less effective against physical attacks. In December 2009, a sophisticated, coordinated cyberattack was launched against 34 companies, including powerhouses such as Google, Adobe, and Northrup Grumman. Two independent, anonymous sources pointed to China as the source for these attacks.

Addiction, Curiosity, Boredom, Thrill-Seeking, Intellectual Gain, and Recognition   Many people who create viruses or worms are highly intelligent and are simply seeking an intellectual challenge. Other hackers who have committed computer intrusions report they were motivated by a desire to test a computer's security. Still others report that they were interested in earning a reputation for their skills and becoming well known. Regardless of the motivation, these activities are still illegal and may cause immeasurable damage to the systems they affect.

Sexual Impulses   Active and passive pedophiles, serial rapists, and serial killers might commit cybercrimes.

Psychiatric Illness   Personality disorders such as schizophrenia, bipolar disorder, aggression, and depression can motivate a person to hide their illness online, where they can interact without physical contact. Personality theorists have suggested that cyber criminals exhibit characteristics of psychiatric illnesses such as narcissism and antisocial personality disorder.

signature analysis
Technique that uses a filter to analyze both the header and the contents of the datagram, usually referred to as the packet payload.

When searching for data, forensic investigators must realize that users who want to store data and hide its actual content from others may do so in many ways. One of the most common methods is to hide data by changing the filename and the extension associated with a file so that it doesn't look suspicious. Although it can be difficult to determine if an original filename has been changed, most forensic software can detect a change made to the file extension. An altered file extension is detectable through a method called *signature analysis*. Although searching for text strings is the main method for obtaining digital evidence, using various types of forensic software, you can search on the evidence and perform signature analysis at the same time. Basically, signature analysis computes any hash value discrepancies between a file's extension and the file's header. When these two do not match, it's generally an indication that you should analyze the file in more detail. For example, those seeking to hide child pornography might change the extensions of such pictures from `.jpg` to `.txt` in an attempt to hide the content. Signature analysis can be used to identify such files.

Picking the Low-Hanging Fruit

The concept of low-hanging fruit comes from the idea that it is easier to go after information that is readily available than to dig for deeply rooted information. Cybercriminals may walk away from a system that is too hard to break or takes too long to get into. In some instances, grabbing the low-hanging fruit for the cybercriminal may be nothing more than choosing the easiest part of the system to deal with at the time.

The cybersecurity field is rife with low-hanging fruit. When a company doesn't install patches for operating systems, or enforce sound password and logoff policies, it leaves its systems vulnerable to attack. Some people (generally those with less than honorable intentions) believe that if you leave your system unprotected, you deserve to be hacked. And it will happen, because low-hanging fruit is the easiest to grab. More employees will attempt to access a network folder called `private` than a folder named `data`.

As a forensic investigator, you'll have to determine whether the low-hanging fruit provides enough evidence for your case. Let's start with an area that might provide the evidence you need without an extreme amount of investigative work.

This is evidence that is readily available, such as computer and log files, especially when dealing with unsophisticated criminals. People tend to treat their work computers as their own private storage facilities despite the fact that they are merely the company's computers that they're assigned to use. What people keep in their computers can be incredible—everything from their sexual preferences to evidence of crimes.

Although you should strive to have more than enough evidence, you might be able to use low-hanging fruit to get the information you need. It is at least a good place to start.

Hidden Evidence

In the first section of this chapter, we explored the types of evidence you can look for on a computer. What happens when you can't find any evidence but you know it's there? Chances are it's either hidden, or somewhere in the trace evidence. (We cover trace evidence in the next section.)

Metadata

There are various types of hidden evidence, starting with document *metadata*. Virtually all applications produce some type of evidence that ordinary users don't know about. For example, as a Microsoft Word document is written and changed, changes are normally tracked. To view this information, simply click the file and then choose Properties (see Figure 6.11).

metadata
Data component that describes other data. In other words, it's data about data.

Figure 6.11   Metadata for a Microsoft Word document

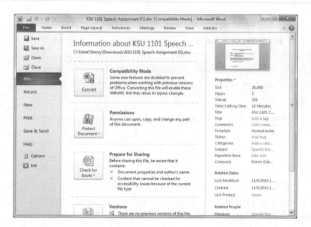

The information in the Properties dialog box can be especially useful to a forensic investigator. For example, let's say you are dealing with a situation in which a system was compromised and intellectual property was stolen. If a criminal is unsophisticated, you could very well end up with a good lead just by looking at the properties of the new documents. Metadata can be found in most Word, Excel, and PowerPoint documents. However, because metadata has become a known issue, there are ways to delete it. Microsoft released a tool that removes personal or hidden data that might not be immediately apparent when you view a document in a Microsoft Office XP or 2003 application. This tool is called `rhdtool.exe`, and resides at `http://www.microsoft.com/downloads/`. Note that this add-in is not compatible with 2007 and 2010 Office systems. The Document Inspector feature in the 2007 and 2010 Office systems replaces this add-in.

Although some metadata is readily accessible through the user interface in each Microsoft Office program, other metadata is accessible only through extraordinary means (for example, opening a document in a low-level, binary file editor such as HexEditor).

Metadata Tips

A criminal might try to hide information by backdating a document created in Microsoft Word—setting the system clock back and then saving the document. Upon a closer look, a forensic investigator can easily uncover the truth. When looking at file directory details, watch for discrepancies between the creation or modified date shown in Windows and time/date stamps in the metadata. For example, Windows might show a Last Modified Date of March 18, 2008, while metadata embedded in the document itself may show a later date. The metadata might also show a different author.

Metadata also tracks total editing time for each document. When a document is surreptitiously backdated, total editing time indicated can be unusually high and indicate that a document was edited for months or even years instead of the hours or days you would normally expect to see. Unusually high editing time is a red flag to a forensic investigator, and may indicate that a document has been tampered with or is a forgery.

Steganography

steganography
Process of passing information in a manner that hides the existence of one message inside another file or message.

The next method for hiding data we look at is *steganography*. Steganography is a special kind of cryptography that makes the presence of secret data undetectable. It encrypts an original plaintext message into a digital file. The least significant bit of each byte in the image or other data is replaced with bits from the secret message. Such a message can be hidden in a sound file, a graphics file, or in unused spaces on a hard disk. Someone who saves pornography to a hard disk may choose to hide evidence using this method. In some instances, steganography can be used as a means for covert communication among terrorists. Three of the more popular steganography programs include Hide and Seek, Stealth (both of which run on Windows-based systems), and Steganographic File System (SFS), which works on UNIX file systems.

HTML Documents

You can readily view all the code for a web page simply by opening a web page and choosing the View Source option from the View menu on the toolbar (or right-click anywhere on the web page and choose View Source). Figure 6.12 shows the source code for http://www.msn.com/index.html.

Figure 6.12   Source code for the home page on www.msn.com

Most web pages are written in HTML. Figure 6.12 gives you an idea how easy it would be to hide messages or data in web page coding. For example, say a perpetrator was stealing company secrets and wanted to allow a competitor company to access them. The perpetrator could set up his or her own Web site and hide the information in the source code. The competitor could then easily retrieve that information.

Hiding Documents by Changing Names, Properties, or Locations

Most operating systems allow users to hide files based on extensions. Using this feature is as simple as changing the properties of a directory to Hidden on the General tab in the properties in Windows. An untrained eye might never see system files or even the extensions associated with files if the user chose to hide them.

You can hide UNIX directories by putting them in existing directories that have many files, such as in the /dev directory on a UNIX implementation, or by making a directory that starts with three dots (...) instead of the normal single or double dot. To superficially hide files on a UNIX computer, put one dot in front of the file (for example, .myfile). This prevents the file from showing up in the output of a file listing. To see all hidden files, use the ls command with the -a parameter, like this: ls -a.

Hidden Disk Partitions

multiboot system
System that can boot, or start, and then run more than one operating system (though only one at a time).

Data can be concealed in hidden disk partitions. We'll use the example of a *multiboot system*, in which, essentially, one operating system is hidden from another. One of our laptops (Computer A) is set up for dual booting (two operating systems). It can boot to either Windows Vista or SuSE Linux. When you view the system in Windows, the Linux partition doesn't show up, mainly because Windows doesn't understand the Linux file system. So, Windows acts as though the Linux system isn't there. If a bootloader is set up to recognize the other operating system, you are given a choice of which operating system to use after a computer boots. This lets you know that more than one operating system is installed. However, some operating systems allow you to choose which operating system to boot to without user interaction. Simply choose the default operating system to boot when you do the setup. For example, another one of our computers (Computer B) dual boots either Windows 7 or Windows Server 2008. An ordinary user would not know that Windows Server 2008 is installed because we configured the system not to display the operating systems at boot time. This is another example where an untrained person might have no idea that hidden data exists. So, we can store files on the Windows 7 drive while booted to Windows Server 2008, and hide the directory so other users have no clue the files are even there. In this instance, the evidence you may be looking for as a forensic investigator could be stored partially on one partition and partially on another partition. If space allows, users seeking to hide could actually install more than two operating systems.

Covert Channels and Other Hiding Places

covert channel
Method whereby an entity receives information in an unauthorized and obscure manner.

Several other methods, such as *covert channels*, can be used to hide data. A tool such as Loki can transmit valuable data in seemingly normal network traffic. Loki is a Trojan horse that looks like a stream of pings but instead provides a back door to the computer on which the client is installed. After the client is installed, it allows communication to occur without being controlled by a security mechanism.

Suspects can also hide data in white space in documents, behind graphics in documents, and in host protected areas (HPAs) on drives. These areas on a hard drive are created specifically to allow manufacturers to hide diagnostic and recovery tools, but computer savvy people can use them to hide data as well.

 **Real World Scenario**

Tales from the Trenches: Hidden Evidence

While many technical methods exist for hiding data (examples include steganography, encryption, and digital watermarking), some cases that you work will involve data that was hidden using techniques so simple that any average Microsoft Office user could use them.

I once worked on a case involving two coworkers who transferred information to each other by embedding short messages at the end of Word documents. They changed the color of the text to white so that the message was white text on a white background and remained invisible to anyone who saw the document.

Another simple technique is to use a nonstandard font to write a Word document. The person receiving the document knows which font is needed to view the text and has that font loaded on their computer. Anyone without that font would see only "garbage" on their screen when they viewed the document.

This last technique was used by an illegal drug supplier. He took a photograph of a handwritten sign that contained the instructions and location of how and where a drug transaction was to take place. The drug dealer hoped that anyone monitoring or "sniffing" his network traffic would be unable to "read" the message. A forensic examiner using the search functionality in any forensic utility would not see the message. The examiner would have to use the graphics function in the tool to see such a message.

These and many other techniques for finding hidden data are taught in various computer forensic courses. For additional information about this type of training, please visit Neil's Web site at http://www.trcglobal.com.

Trace Evidence

Trace evidence is a term that applies to all physical evidence that may be circumstantial evidence in the trial of a case. Trace evidence, although often insufficient on its own to make a case, can corroborate other evidence or even prompt a confession. Tracing some piece of data present at a crime scene to its origin can assist in arrest and conviction. Similarly, finding some trace of data from a victim or crime scene on a suspect's computer can strongly impact a case.

trace evidence
Traces of data either left behind or found with a criminal that can be used to prove that a crime was committed.

slack space

The space on a hard disk between where a file ends and where the disk storage cluster ends.

Computer evidence is often found in file slack and in unallocated file space called *slack space*. Sometimes a good portion of a computer's hard disk may contain data fragments from word processing documents, or almost anything that has occurred in the past. This space can be a valuable source for computer evidence because of the large volume of data involved and because most everyday computer users are oblivious to it. In Figure 6.13, a utility called Karen's Disk Slack Checker was used to check slack space on a hard disk. As you can see, there is quite a bit of stuff here.

Figure 6.13   Karen's Disk Slack Checker

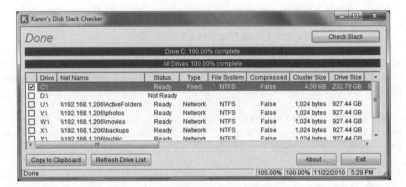

Slack space results from the way data is written to disks. Operating systems normally write in clusters. Clusters are made up of blocks of sectors. Even if the actual data being stored requires less storage than the cluster size, an entire cluster is reserved for each file. For example, if the cluster size is 32KB and you create a file that is 2KB in size, that file is allocated 32KB of space. This means that 30KB is unused. That's a lot of slack space! Let's go a bit further and say that you create a 31KB file. You decide that you no longer need the file and delete it. At some point in the future, you create another file that is 4KB. When the system goes looking for a location to write this new 4KB file, it finds the space where the old 31KB file that you supposedly deleted resides, and places the data there. Now you have 4KB of new data plus the remainder of the old data in the same space. To recover that data, you can extract trace evidence from the first file in the new file. These pieces of files or file fragments can hold a good amount of information.

swap file

Space on the hard disk used as the virtual memory extension of a computer's actual memory.

On computers running a Microsoft Windows operating system, large quantities of evidence can be found in the Windows *swap file*. In Windows XP, Vista, Server 2003, and Server 2008 this file is named PAGEFILE.SYS by the operating system. On Windows 7 and Windows Server 2008 R2 computers the swap file is called READYBOOST.SFCACHE. This is a memory management function within the Windows operating environment. It uses space on the hard drive to swap data in and out of memory to make better use of RAM. Swap space also resides on computers running Linux. When you install the operating system, you specify a Linux swap file partition size.

Trace evidence also appears in backups. Although this option is frequently forgotten, backups can be a great source of information in forensic investigations. Most companies make some type of backup rotation and perform full backups at least once per quarter. Even though files may have been deleted from an individual computer, they may still be available on backups. Third-party service providers frequently back up e-mail and generally keep backups for some period of time. Again, even though files may be gone from a computer, in most cases, e-mail systems are backed up. As a forensic investigator, you can (and should) find out how long messages are kept because you may be able to recover information valuable to your investigation.

Fax buffers, printer buffers, and USB drives also hold trace data and should be examined for evidence as well. USB drives offer another source of trace evidence to forensic investigators. Often people put one or two files on a USB drive and forget about them. USB drives can be imaged and then processed.

Terms to Know

brute force attack	port scanner
cache	protocol
connector	router
Cookie	signature analysis
covert channel	slack space
e-mail header	steganography
IP address	swap file
MAC time	temporary Internet files
metadata	trace evidence
multiboot system	Transmission Control Protocol/Internet Protocol (TCP/IP) network
packet	Trojan horse program
	UPD Datagram

Review Questions

1. What set of rules and conventions governs how computers exchange information over the network medium?

2. Name some factors that motivate criminal activity.

3. As a Word document is written and changed, these changes are tracked and produce a type of evidence that is called what?

4. What types of files should arouse your suspicion when you are examining data?

5. Why should you look at the header of an e-mail?

6. What is steganography?

7. What method can you use to determine if the extension of a file has been changed to avoid suspicion?

8. If you are investigating a case that involves the Internet and pictures, name three areas that could reveal the Internet habits of the suspect?

9. What is a multiboot system?

10. Name three types of trace evidence.

Chapter 7

Passwords and Encryption

Computer forensics is all about perspective and process. A forensic investigator's main perspective must be as a neutral party in all activities. Approach each investigation the same way, ensuring that it is repeatable and sound. After evidence is identified and preserved, analyze it to determine its impact on your case. In many situations, forensic investigators don't have the authority to disclose any evidence except to authorized individuals. It all depends on who owns the computer and who is paying for the investigation. As a forensic investigator, you need to know how to exercise your authority and access protected data properly. The two most common controls that protect data from disclosure are access controls and data encryption. This chapter covers the most common type of access control—the password—and the general topic of encryption.

You will learn basic techniques to obtain passwords to gain access to evidence. You will learn about basic encryption methods and how to recover encrypted evidence.

Passwords

user ID

A string of characters that identifies a user in a computing environment.

Computer users must commonly provide a *user ID* to log on to, or otherwise access, a system. User IDs identify a specific user and tell the security subsystem what permissions to grant to that user. Unfortunately, some computer users attempt to impersonate other users by fraudulently providing another person's user ID. By doing so, the impersonator can perform actions that will point back to the stolen user ID owner's account when audited. As a forensic investigator, you'll need to determine the difference between actions taken using a valid user ID and actions conducted by an impersonator using a stolen or otherwise compromised user ID.

 Real World Scenario

Who Are You, Really?

Fred is an enterprising university student who enjoys testing the limits of his school's computer use policy. The policy clearly states that users may only use their own user IDs to access the computer system. If Fred wants to create some mischief on the university's computer system, he could ignore the policy and use Mary's user ID to access the system. In effect, he could pretend to be Mary. With no controls in place to stop him, Fred could cause many problems and to the untrained eye, it would appear that Mary was the guilty party. A control is anything that stands between Fred and his unauthorized actions. In this case, there actually is at least one control to deter him—the university's computer use and access policy. The university's computer use policy is an administrative control. While administrative controls dictate proper behavior and the penalty of noncompliance, they don't stop unauthorized actions by those who are determined to ignore such policies (as in Fred's case).

---

password

A string of characters that security systems use to authenticate, or verify, a user's identity. Security systems compare passwords a user provides during login to stored values for the user account. If the value provided (password) matches the stored value, the security subsystem authenticates the user. Most operating systems store passwords when users create login accounts.

There is a simple solution. User IDs provide identification for users. Another piece of information that only the real user should know provides authentication that the user is who he or she claims to be. The most common method of authentication is a *password*. To authenticate using a password, users provide not only a user ID, but the proper password as well during login. The security system then validates that the password provided matches by comparing it to the stored value for that user ID. If the two match, the security system authenticates and trusts the user and allows access to the computer system.

There are two main reasons for investigators to crack passwords. First, you may need a password to log in to a computer or access a resource. Second, you may need a password or key to access encrypted data that may be vital to the success of the investigation.

During an investigation, forensic investigators commonly need access to one or more computer accounts. When a suspect or other knowledgeable user cooperates with an investigation, obtaining a user ID and password can be as easy as asking for it. Never forget to try the simple approach: When users cooperate, it can save valuable time. Always ask for any needed user IDs and passwords. When passwords aren't readily available, here are three alternative methods to acquire them:

1. Find passwords
2. Deduce passwords
3. Crack passwords

Forensic investigators not only understand what each of these three techniques is, but know when and how to use each one as well.

Although passwords are the most common user authentication technique, they aren't always secure. In the next sections, we'll examine each password recovery technique and show you how quickly and easily some passwords can become available.

Finding Passwords

By far, the easiest way to obtain a password is simply to ask someone who knows the password to provide it to you. If asking nicely doesn't work, try social engineering. Build trust with a person who knows information you need to further the investigation. This person could be anyone who knows the password. The password or other information sought could be as simple as a phone call away.

For example, you could call and pretend to be a member of the network administrator team. A simple statement like, "Hi, this is Tom from network support. Your computer looks like it is sending out a virus to other computers. I need to log on to stop it. What is the user ID and password you used to log on this morning?" Fortunately for the forensic investigator, far too many people are only too willing (and in fact, often eager) to help and quickly provide the requested information. Mission accomplished! When using social engineering techniques to gather information, experienced forensic investigators will ensure they have permission to conduct these types of activities before proceeding. As long as you abide by any applicable security policies, encouraging a suspect to give you the information you need is perfectly fine. Law enforcement officials are good at doing this. Ask them for help, especially if this is a criminal investigation.

If social engineering isn't an option, or the person who knows the password won't cooperate, then there are other simple approaches you can try. There are two basic types of passwords: those that are easy to remember and those that are hard to remember. With more people becoming aware of security issues, passwords now tend to be more secure than in the past. Most people equate password complexity with security. That is, long, hard-to-remember passwords appear to be more secure than simple ones.

Longer passwords can be less secure than shorter ones. Passwords that expire frequently can be less secure as well. The reason is that when a user must use a password that is too hard to remember, he will often write it down. The hassle of retrieving a lost password often encourages users to keep sticky notes with passwords written on them. When encouraging the use of strong passwords, allow users to create ones they can remember.

Because a password is a string of characters that authenticates a user's identity, it is important that the user always have access to the password. The more complex a password is, the more likely it is that the user has it written down or otherwise recorded somewhere. Look around the computer for written notes. It's not uncommon for forensic investigators to find sticky notes with passwords written on them in plain sight, or in some cases, even taped to the computer system itself. You'll find that this phenomenon occurs in a surprisingly large percentage of the sites you investigate. As a forensic investigator, you'll become an expert at recognizing common "hiding places" for password notes, such as:

◆ On the monitor (front, sides, top, etc.)

◆ Under the keyboard

◆ In drawers (look under pencil holders and organizers)

◆ Attached to the underside of drawers

◆ Anywhere that is easily accessible from the seat in front of the computer but not readily visible

◆ Personal digital assistants (PDAs) and smartphones

◆ Obvious files on the hard disk (such as `passwords.txt`)

While this approach may seem too simple and obvious, never dismiss this important method for finding passwords. Few people trust their memories for important passwords. There is a good chance some users you'll be investigating wrote down their passwords and put them somewhere handy.

Deducing Passwords

So, you've looked all around the physical hardware and desk but you still can't find the password you are looking for. What next? Don't worry—there are still other options available to obtain passwords. In spite of all the common rules for creating "strong" passwords, many users routinely break the rules. If you are trying to guess a password, try the obvious ones. The more the forensic investigator knows about the user, the better the chances of guessing the password. Try some of these ideas:

◆ User ID

◆ Birth date

◆ Social security number

◆ Home address

◆ Telephone number

◆ Spouse/children/friend name

◆ Pet name

◆ Favorite team name or mascot

◆ Common word or name from a hobby

Use this section as a lesson for creating your own passwords. Because so many people ignore password best practices, take it upon yourself to be unique. Take the time to create strong passwords and keep them secure. Passwords can also easily be secured through the use of password vault programs such as RoboForm Pro (www.roboform.com).

NOTE

Although guessing a password is possible, it isn't very productive in most cases. Don't spend a lot of time trying to guess a password. This method is most effective if you have a strong hunch that you will be successful. It may be possible for forensic investigators to solve password puzzles by piecing several pieces of information together. People often hide the real password but leave clues that can help you to guess the password contents. For example, during an investigation, a note was found that read "me 4 her -7." After trying several combinations, we hit on a password that consisted of the subject's initials, "ajd," and his wife's initials, "rgd." The password was "ajd4rgd7. (Just in case you're wondering, this wasn't the actual password—the initials were changed to protect the innocent!)

Even though you might get lucky occasionally, really "guessing" a password isn't very common. It looks good in the movies, but it doesn't happen that often in the real world. Deduced passwords normally come from piecing several pieces of information together. For instance, when analyzing a subject's activity, keep track of visited Web sites and locally protected applications. Cookies for recently visited Web sites may be left behind that store an unprotected password. People are creatures of habit and many tend to use the same passwords repeatedly, so if you find an unprotected password for one resource, try it in other areas.

As much as it violates good security practices and common sense, the same password is often used to protect both secured servers and to subscribe to a Web site's news services. If you find a password, see if the user also uses it elsewhere.

—————— *NOTE* ——————

When poking around and guessing passwords, forensic investigators might end up locking the resource they are attempting to access owing to excessive failed logon attempts. Always make sure you have at least two copies of media. If one copy is corrupted, you can always make a new working copy from your second image. You never want to explain to the judge that you had to check out the original media from the evidence locker twice because you messed up the first copy.

Up to now, our password discussion has focused on nonspecific strategies. Finding, guessing, or deducing a password is more of an art than a science. It involves knowing your subject and knowing how people think. It might take a lot of homework, but it is fun and can yield that gold nugget that opens up the evidence you need.

Cracking Passwords

password cracking
Attempting to discover a password by trying multiple options and continuing until you find a successful match.

The last method of obtaining a password is the most technical and complete. When a password can't be obtained by any other means, forensic investigators try a process known as *password cracking*. Cracking a password involves trying every possible combination, or every combination in a defined subset, until the right one is found.

Different utilities allow forensic investigators to crack passwords online or offline. These utilities employ several different methods. Because older UNIX systems stored encoded passwords in a single file, the /etc/passwd file, several utilities emerged that tried different combinations of password strings until they found a match for each line in the file. All forensic investigators had to do was copy the /etc/passwd file to their own computer, launch the password cracker, and let it run.

This approach became so popular and dangerous that newer flavors of UNIX, and now Linux, go to great lengths to hide encoded passwords in another file. Most UNIX and Linux systems store passwords in the /etc/shadow file. This file has highly restricted access permissions and requires super user permission to access. If you are investigating a computer system running UNIX or Linux, look at the /etc/passwd file. An x character between two colons indicates that the actual password is stored in the shadow file. For example, here is what a line from the /etc/passwd file looks like if password shadowing is in use (notice the "x" after the user name, msolomon):

```
msolomon:x:517:644::/home/msolomon:/bin/bash
```

Real World Scenario

Tales from the Trenches: The Contract Ends Now!

Several contractors were working at a manufacturing plant in southern California. These contractors filled various functions, including project management and application development. The project goal was to modify a manufacturing software package to meet the client's specific needs. One morning, the company's system administrator noticed that his assigned IP address was in use when he booted his computer. After a couple comments under his breath, he rebooted again and found that the IP address was available. He took note of the people who were in the office that morning and started doing a little investigative work on his own to find out if anyone was using his IP address. He found that a particular contractor had installed a common password cracker in his home directory. A further look at the contractor's history file showed that he had been engaging in attempts to crack the system's password file.

The system administrator immediately removed the contractor's access and had him terminated. The company's policy regarding appropriate use of computing systems forbade any use of password-cracking software and provided grounds for immediate termination.

There are many password-cracking utilities available to forensic investigators. Some commons ones include:

- Cain and Abel (http://www.oxid.it/cain.html)
    - Cain and Abel is a free (donation requested) password recovery utility for Microsoft Windows operating systems that uses several techniques to find passwords.
- John the Ripper (http://www.openwall.com/john/)
    - John the Ripper is an open source password cracker that reveals weak passwords in most operating systems.
- Hydra (http://freeworld.thc.org/thc-hydra/)
    - Hydra is a free, fast network authentication cracker. Hydra can attack the most common network protocols.
- ElcomSoft (http://www.elcomsoft.com/)
    - ElcomSoft produces a variety of commercial software that recovers passwords from operating systems and application software.

- LastBit (http://lastbit.com/)
  - LastBit produces a variety of commercial software that recovers passwords from operating systems and application software.
- L0phtCrack (http://www.l0phtcrack.com/)
  - L0phtCrack is a commercial tool that recovers passwords and more from computers running multiple operating systems.
- RainbowCrack (http://project-rainbowcrack.com/)
  - RainbowCrack is a free tool for cracking Linux and Windows passwords using precomputed hash tables, called rainbow tables.

Anytime passwords are found stored in a file or database, forensic investigators can use offline password-cracking techniques. Online password cracking methods are used if the password repository can't be found or you don't have access to it (it might reside on another system). Online password cracking is much slower and may fail more frequently (and for more reasons) than offline cracking. Online password-cracking utilities attempt to pass logon credentials to target systems until it finds a successful user ID/password pair. The number of attempts that are necessary to find a password is the same as an offline cracking utility, but the act of passing the logon credentials to another process requires substantially more time. If the target computer is remote to the client password-cracking utility, network propagation further slows the process and adds to the possibility of failure.

Unauthorized Password Cracking is Illegal

Never attempt to crack passwords unless you have specific, and written, authority to do so. The person or organization who owns the computer system can provide the necessary permission. Without written permission, you may be at risk of substantial civil and criminal penalties. Ensure that the permission you receive comes from someone with the authority to give it to you, is in writing, and is specific about what you can (and can't) do.

The main reason to crack a password is to obtain password-protected evidence. Permission to crack a password is obtained from the computer owner or a court. In cases where the computer's owner is unwilling to provide permission to crack a password, a court order will suffice.

Regardless of the type of utility used, there are three basic approaches, or "attack types," that password-cracking utilities commonly employ.

Dictionary Attack

A *dictionary attack* is the simplest and fastest attack. The cracking utility uses potential passwords from a predefined list of commonly used passwords. The password dictionary stores the list of passwords. The larger the dictionary, the higher the probability the utility will succeed (but the longer it will take to attempt the entire dictionary file). A little research on the Internet will yield several dictionaries of common passwords.

An offline dictionary attack calculates hashed values of passwords from a password dictionary. The utility compares the hashed value with stored passwords to find a match. Since the cracking utility spends most of its time calculating hash values, there is an opportunity to speed up the process. If you plan to use a password dictionary for several attempts at password cracking, you can precompute the password hashes from the password dictionary. These precalculated password hashes, or rainbow tables, make offline dictionary attack processes much faster. As a forensic investigator you'll find that passwords are statistically located halfway through any given process. For example, if given the choice to choose a password between 1 and 100, 50 percent of people will choose a password below the number 50 while the other half will choose a password above 50.

The reason this type of attack works so well lies in human nature. People tend to use common, easy-to-remember passwords. Most would be surprised to find their favorite password in a password dictionary. Any passwords found in a password dictionary are too weak and should be changed.

AccessData's Password Recovery Toolkit offers a great benefit when used with their FTK software. The investigator exports a "dictionary" file from FTK and then uses it as the dictionary file to crack encrypted files found on the suspect hard drives. The dictionary file is made up of every word found on the suspect hard drive. This enables you to crack a password by using a list of every word on the suspect computer, potentially including when the user entered the password (as is the case with a password that was cached from memory).

Brute Force Attack

On the other end of the spectrum is the brute force attack. A brute force attack simply attempts every possible password combination until it finds a match. If the utility attempts to use every possible combination, it will eventually succeed. However, the amount of time required depends on the complexity of the password. The longer the password, the more time it will take to crack.

Brute force attacks should never be your primary method for cracking passwords for two reasons. First, brute force attacks are slow. They can take a substantial amount of investigative time. Also, the length of the password may not be known.

dictionary attack
An attack that tries different passwords defined in a list, or database, of password candidates.

In this case, the utility will have to try many, many combinations that won't succeed before finding the right one.

Second, the client, resource server, or authentication credentials (passwords) may be located on different computers. If so, the brute force attack will generate a huge volume of network traffic. Excessive network traffic and multiple failed logon attempts may make a tangible impact on the network. Unless you can set up a copy of the suspect network in your lab, you may not be able to secure permission to launch a brute force attack.

Hybrid Attack

hybrid attack
A modification of the dictionary attack that tries different permutations of each dictionary entry.

The final type of attack, the *hybrid attack*, combines the dictionary and brute force attack methods. In a hybrid attack, the utility starts with a dictionary entry and tries various alternative combinations. For example, if the dictionary entry were "lord," the hybrid attack utility would look for these possible alternatives:

◆ Lord

◆ l0rd

◆ 1ord

◆ 10rd

And many, many others. As you can see from this list, it is common to obscure passwords derived from dictionary words by replacing the letter "l" with the digit "1," or replacing the letter "o" with the digit "0." Don't do this with your own passwords. Even simple cracking utilities know this trick.

Regardless of the type of utility used, there are tools that can help you get the passwords you need to access evidence.

The next section addresses one of the methods of protecting data from disclosure—encryption.

Encryption Basics

After they gain access to the file that contain needed evidence, forensic investigators may well find that the file itself is unreadable. As computer investigators begin to use more sophisticated tools, both regular and malicious users are taking more sophisticated steps to hide information. One method used to hide information is to modify a message or file in such a way that only the intended recipient can reconstruct the original.

NOTE   This chapter does not cover the mathematics behind encryption in any detail (such a discussion is beyond the scope of this book).

Cryptography scrambles the contents of a file or message and makes it unreadable to all but its intended recipient. In the context of a computer investigation, a forensic investigator is an unintended recipient. The word cryptography comes from Greek words *krypto*, which means "hidden," and *graphein*, which means "to write."

Although cryptography's importance has become more widely acknowledged in recent years, its roots are traced back 5,000 years to ancient Egypt. The Egyptians used hieroglyphics to document many rituals and procedures. Only specially trained agents could interpret these early hieroglyphics.

Around 400 B.C., the Spartans used an innovative method to *encrypt*, or hide, the meaning of military communication from unauthorized eyes. They would wrap a strip of parchment around a stick in a spiral, similar to a barber's pole. The scribe would write the message on the parchment and then unwind it from the stick. With the parchment stretched out, the message was unintelligible. In fact, the only way to read the message, or *decrypt* it, was to wrap the parchment around another stick of the same diameter and equal, or greater, length. The "secrets" to reading the message were the dimensions of the stick and the knowledge of how to wrap the parchment. Anyone who possessed these two components could read the secret message.

Roman Emperor Julius Caesar was the first to use a cryptography method, or *cipher*, similar to the decoder rings popular as children's trinkets. He used a method called a *substitution cipher*, to send secret messages to his military leaders. This cipher encrypts a message by substituting each letter of the original message with another letter. A substitution table provides the static mapping for each letter. For example, here is a simple Caesar cipher mapping table:

Original: ABCDEFGHIJKLMNOPQRSTUVWXYZ

Mapped: DEFGHIJKLMNOPQRSTUVWXYZABC

For each character in the original message, read the character directly below it in the mapped character string. The string "HELLO" would become "KHOOR."

The recipient decrypts the message by reversing the process. The recipient translates each letter from the encrypted message to the original letter by reading the mapping table backward. The resulting message is identical to the original. One must possess the translation table to encrypt and decrypt messages using a simple substitution cipher. The main weakness of the cipher is the table itself. Anyone who discovers or acquires the translation table can decrypt messages.

Although the algorithms used in current encryption implementations are far more complex than the Caesar cipher, the basic approach and goals are the same. Next, we'll examine some common encryption practices.

cryptography
The science of hiding the true contents of a message from unintended recipients.

encrypt
To obscure the meaning of a message to make it unreadable.

decrypt
To translate an encrypted message back into the original unencrypted message.

cipher
An algorithm for encrypting and decrypting.

substitution cipher
A cipher that substitutes each character in the original message with an alternate character to create the encrypted message.

Common Encryption Practices

In general, encryption provides:

Confidentiality   Assurance that only authorized users can view messages

Integrity   Assurance that only authorized users can change messages

Authentication   Assurance that users are who they claim to be

Nonrepudiation   Assurance that a message originated from the stated source

To a forensic investigator, the most common exposure to encryption occurs when confronted with encrypted files. Encryption is becoming more common for hiding file contents. Though there are other valuable uses for cryptography, such as securing communication transmissions and authenticating the originator of a message, they are beyond the scope of this discussion.

As a forensic investigator, you must understand cryptography basics and how you should react when you encounter encrypted files.

Usually you'll recognize encrypted files when an attempt to open a file with a known extension fails. For example, you might attempt to open an encrypted Microsoft Word document in Microsoft Word, but you receive an error message instead. The text of the error message tells you that you need a converter to read the file. In other words, Microsoft Word doesn't recognize the contents of the encrypted file.

Another sign of encrypted files is a collection of meaningless filenames. Many encryption utilities change filenames to hide the meaning and type of the file.

There are two main types of encryption algorithms. (An algorithm is the detailed sequence of steps necessary to accomplish a task.) Each type has strengths and weaknesses, but they both serve the same function.

Private key algorithms use the same value to encrypt and decrypt the original text. Private key algorithms are sometimes referred to as symmetric key algorithms because the same key is used to encrypt and decrypt files.

Public key algorithms (also known as asymmetric key algorithms) use one value to encrypt the text and another value to decrypt it. One implementation is to use public and private key pairs.

Transposition cipher
An encryption method in which the positions of plaintext characters are shifted by a defined number of places to produce ciphertext. Ciphertext created with a transposition cipher is a permutation of the plaintext.

Encryption algorithms transform an original message, called plaintext, into an encrypted message, called ciphertext. The algorithm also generally provides a method for reversing the process by translating the ciphertext back into the original plaintext message. We looked at the Caesar cipher, which is a substitution cipher, in the previous "Encryption Basics" section. Another type of cipher is a transposition cipher. For example, suppose you want to send a message to a particular recipient that no one else can read. You choose a block transposition cipher to change the order of the letters in the original message. First, write the original message in a block with a specific number of columns. Next, you create the ciphertext by reading down each column.

Our plaintext message is:

`I would like to meet with you in private at pier 42 tonight at midnight.`

Using a block width of 10, you rewrite the message:

```
iwouldlike
tomeetwith
youinpriva
teatpier42
tonightatm
idnightxxx
```

You can add specific characters to make the message fill up the last row. Next, construct the ciphertext by reading down the columns.

Our encrypted message is:

`ityttiwooeodomuannueitiilenpggdtpihhlwrettiiiraxktv4txeha2mx`

All you have to do to decrypt the message is to rewrite it in a block and read the message across the rows. The key to the process is knowing that the original block used 10 columns. Once you know the number of columns in the original block, simply divide the length of the ciphertext, 60, by the number of columns, 10. This tells you there are six rows in the original plaintext block. Write the ciphertext in columns using six rows and you can read the original message.

All algorithms use some type of value to translate the plaintext to ciphertext. Each algorithm performs steps using the supplied value to encrypt the data. The special value that the algorithm uses is the *encryption key*. Some encryption algorithms use a single key, while others use more than one. The Caesar cipher uses a single key value. The key value tells how many positions to add to the plaintext character to encrypt and the number to subtract from the ciphertext character to decrypt. As long as the sender and receiver both use the same algorithm and key, the process works.

encryption key
A code that enables the user to encrypt or decrypt information when combined with a cipher or algorithm.

Private, or Symmetric, Key Algorithms

The easiest type of encryption to understand and use is the *private key algorithm*, also referred to as a symmetric key algorithm. It is symmetric because the decrypt function is a simple reversal of the encrypt function. In other words, it looks the same on both sides. (See Figure 7.1.)

This type of algorithm is simple, fast, and a frequent choice for encrypting data. The key and the algorithm are all that is required to decrypt the file. (Sounds simple doesn't it? And it is, *if* you have the key and algorithm.) Although this type of algorithm is common for encrypting files, it can be more difficult to use for message encryption. The problem is managing the encryption key. The key is required to decrypt a file or message. Plus, you have to find a way to get the key to the recipient in a secure manner.

private key algorithm
An encryption algorithm that uses the same key to encrypt and decrypt. Also known as symmetric key algorithm.

Figure 7.1   Symmetric key algorithm

Symmetric Algorithm

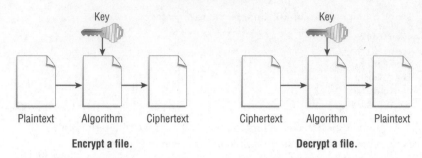

Encrypt a file.   Decrypt a file.

If someone is eavesdropping on all communication between you and your intended recipient, then he or she will likely intercept the encryption key as well as any encrypted data. With the key, they will be able to decrypt files at will. For the purposes of computer forensics, you will more likely find symmetric algorithm–encrypted files on media. The simple reason for this is that symmetric algorithms are fast and easy to use. Because you have only a single key, you don't need to specifically generate keys and then keep up with multiple values. That means you need the single key.

Don't assume that computer investigators only deal with file encryption using symmetric keys. You will encounter various types of encryption and algorithms. Encryption is a discipline in itself. This section just highlights those issues you are most likely to encounter.

Key discovery is similar to password discovery. Forensic investigators need to find, deduce, or crack the encryption to get to the key. The biggest difference between cracking passwords and cracking encryption keys is that cracking encryption keys is usually much harder and takes far longer. The simple explanation is that the plaintext for a password is generally limited to a couple dozen characters. The plaintext for a file could be gigabytes. Cracking the encryption key takes substantially longer than cracking a password.

Many well-known symmetric encryption algorithms exist. Here are a few of the more common ones forensic investigators are likely to encounter:

◆ Data Encryption Standard (DES)

     ◆ First published in 1977

     ◆ Adopted by the U.S. government standard for all data communications

     ◆ Uses 56-bit key (plus eight parity bits)

     ◆ Old and weak by today's standards

- Triple DES (3DES)
  - More secure than DES
  - Uses three separate DES encryption cycles
- Blowfish
  - Stronger alternative to DES
  - Key size can vary from 32 bits to 448 bits
- Advanced Encryption Standard (AES)
  - The latest, strongest standard adopted by the U.S. government after an exhaustive competition among algorithms designs developed by leading world experts in cryptography
  - Based on the Rijndael cipher
  - Key sizes are 128, 192, or 256 bits
- Serpent
  - Came in second place in the AES competition
  - Similar block sizes and key sizes to AES
- Twofish
  - Related to the Blowfish algorithm
  - One of the five finalists in the AES competition

Each algorithm in the previous list can effectively encrypt files. For more security, use a newer algorithm and a secure key. Research some of the common encrypt/decrypt utilities and compare the algorithms they support.

Advanced Encryption Standard (AES) competition
Sponsored by the National Institute for Standards and Technology (NIST), the AES competition was for an encryption standard to replace DES. The competition began in 1997 and culminated with the announcement in 2000 that the winner of the Advanced Encryption Standard was the Rijndael cipher.

Public, or Asymmetric, Key Algorithms

The other type of encryption algorithm is the *public key algorithm*. This type of algorithm is also called asymmetric because the decrypt process differs from the encrypt process. An asymmetric encryption algorithm addresses the issue of key distribution by requiring two keys to complete the encrypt-decrypt process.

The process starts with key generation. The software that encrypts plaintext will also have a utility to generate keys. When asked, the user supplies a *passcode* and the utility uses the passcode to generate a private key and a public key. This is called a key pair. Private keys are meant to be secret and should not be disclosed to anyone. On the other hand, public keys can be distributed to anyone. The encryption algorithm uses the private key to encrypt plaintext and the public key to decrypt resulting ciphertext. (See Figure 7.2.)

The resulting process allows you to encrypt data with your private key. Anyone who has the public key can decrypt the file or message. This process lets anyone verify that a file or message originated from a specific person. If you can decrypt a file with Fred's public key, Fred had to encrypt it with his private key. Although

public key algorithm
An encryption algorithm that uses one key to encrypt plaintext and another key to decrypt ciphertext. Also called asymmetric algorithm.

passcode
A character string used to authenticate a user ID to perform some function, such as encryption key management.

this is great for sending messages and verifying the sender's identity, it doesn't add much value if all you want to do is encrypt some files.

Figure 7.2   Asymmetric algorithm

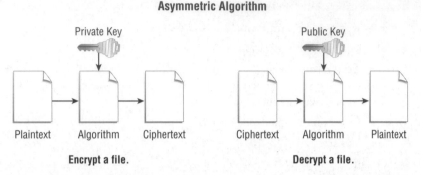

The most common type of encryption you will run into during evidence analysis is file encryption. For that reason, we focus on symmetric key algorithms.

Steganography

Both symmetric and asymmetric encryption algorithms share one common trait: Encrypted files can be recognized by examining their contents. The fact that a file has encrypted content draws attention to its value. A forensic investigator may want to decrypt a file just because it contains encrypted content and, therefore, probably contains some data of value or other evidence.

Encrypt It All!

If you are going to use encryption, then it's generally a good practice to encrypt everything to avoid drawing attention to particular encrypted files. As an analogy, if every letter mailed was written on a post card, and you suddenly found a post card placed inside of an envelope, you'd want to know why. Placing the post card in an envelope would draw attention to the fact that something might be hidden in that message. The same is true for encrypting files. If forensic investigators find encrypted files when all other files are unencrypted, they'll want to know what the user is hiding in the encrypted file.

There is another approach. Steganography is the practice of hiding one message in another, larger message. The original message, or file, becomes the carrier and the hidden message is the payload. Large pictures and sound files make good carriers because the payload can be inserted without changing the original file in an obvious way. Steganographic utilities insert payload bytes into the carrier by slightly changing bytes in the carrier file. If the original data in the carrier separates the changed bytes by wide enough margin, changes are unnoticeable. If you change every 100th pixel in a picture by a single shade of color, the resulting picture appears almost identical to the original.

Steganography allows users to embed desired data into seemingly innocent files and messages. A secret message embedded in a picture file can be sent via e-mail as an attachment and raise no suspicion. Or better yet, the user can simply post the picture on a Web site and there won't be a direct connection between the user and the person they are communicating with. The ease with which anyone can obtain steganographic utilities makes covert data communication and storage easy.

Real World Scenario

Keeping Secrets

Intelligence experts suspect that the terrorists who planned and carried out the attacks on New York and Washington, D.C. on September 11, 2001, may have used steganography to communicate with one another. Investigators suspected the terrorists of embedding messages in digital pictures and then e-mailing the pictures (and embedded messages) as attachments to normal e-mail messages. The messages looked like common e-mails with attached pictures. The pictures could have been anything. Nothing was there to provide a clue that the pictures held secret messages. That is the power of steganography.

Detecting steganography is difficult. It can be detected only by noticing the changes to the carrier file or using statistical analysis to detect an anomaly. Detecting changes to the carrier file requires a noticeable difference that you can see or hear. Statistical analysis depends less on human perception because it compares the frequency distribution of colors of a picture with the expected frequency distribution of colors for the file. For audio carrier files, a statistical analysis utility would use sound patterns instead of colors.

Another method for detecting steganography is finding steganographic utilities on a suspect machine. Although the mere presence of such software doesn't prove steganography is in use, it certainly provides motivation to look harder for carrier files with embedded messages. Few people go to the trouble of acquiring and installing steganographic utilities without using them.

Here are a few steganographic utilities that you might encounter in your career as a forensic investigator. Look at several of these for more information about and examples of how steganography works:

◆ Puff (`http://members.fortunecity.it/blackvisionit/PUFFV200.HTM`)

The freeware Puff steganography tool runs in Microsoft Windows and handles many carrier file types.

◆ Invisible Secrets (`www.invisiblesecrets.com`)

Invisible Secrets is a full-featured commercial Microsoft Windows application that makes it easy to hide data in several different types of carrier files.

◆ PhilTools Image Steganography (`http://philtools.com/image_steganography/`)

PhilTools is a Web site that allows users to submit an image file and a message. The web site hides the message in the image and returns the new image to the user. Hidden messages can also be extracted from a carrier image at this site.

Remember that the appeal of steganography is that its very nature masks the existence of the message. Forensic investigators can look at a suspect drive and easily overlook embedded data if they aren't careful. Look for utilities that create steganographic files. Also, look for files that would make good carriers. If the circumstantial evidence points to hidden data, chances are steganography is in use.

Next, let's examine the quality of encryption by considering key length and key management.

Strengths and Weaknesses of Encryption

Encryption is not a perfect safeguard. With some effort, forensic investigators can access encrypted data. Encryption is far from worthless, though. As a forensic investigator, you'll likely need to access information that is encrypted and break the encryption algorithms.

Before you're ready to defeat file encryption, you need a better understanding of the strengths and weaknesses of encryption. This knowledge will provide a better awareness of where to start and what steps to take for each unique situation.

Key Length

The length of the encryption key directly relates to the encryption algorithm's strength. Although there are differences in the relative strength of each algorithm, the key length choice has the greatest impact on how secure an encrypted object will be. Simply put, longer keys provide a larger number of possible combinations used to encrypt an object.

A key that is 4 bits in length can represent 16 different key values, because $2^4 = 16$. A key length of 5 bits allows 32 key values, and so forth. It may be easy to decrypt a file or message with only 32 different key values. However, larger keys mean more potential key values.

Some older algorithms approved for export by the U.S. government used 40-bit keys. These algorithms aren't secure by today's standards because of their small key length. A 40-bit key can hold one of 2^{40} values, or 1,099,511,627,776 (1 trillion). Assuming that you have a computer that can make 1.8 million comparisons per second, it would take about a week to evaluate all possible key values.

The Data Encryption Standard (DES) algorithm uses 56-bit keys. Although DES is too weak for most security uses, it is far stronger than a 40-bit key algorithm. A DES key can store one of 2^{56}, or 72,057,594,037,927,936 (that is 72 quadrillion) values. Using the same computer as before, it would take about 1,260 years to evaluate all possible key values.

As key values increase in size, the computing power required to crack encryption algorithms grows exponentially. At first glance, it looks like an algorithm with a key length that requires over 1,000 years to crack is sufficient. Unfortunately, that isn't the case. Today's supercomputers can evaluate far more than 1.8 million comparisons per second. With parallel-processing capability, you could realistically create a unit that can crack DES in a matter of minutes (or even seconds). That is the reason key lengths are commonly over 100 bits. Longer keys provide more security by reducing the possibility of using a brute force attack to discover the encryption key.

Using Amazon to crack passwords

In November 2010, an article reported that a security researcher was able to crack SHA-1 passwords by renting processing power on Amazon's EC2 cloud computing service:

http://threatpost.com/en_us/blogs/cloud-makes-short-work-strong
-encryption-111910

Key Management

Because the encryption key is crucial to the encryption process, it must be protected at all costs. If the key is disclosed, the encrypted data is no longer secure. Symmetric algorithms use a single key. The sender and receiver must both posses the key to encrypt and decrypt the data. For local file encryption, the same person is likely to encrypt and decrypt the data. The purpose of encryption in such a case is to protect file contents from any unauthorized access.

As a forensic investigator, you may find encrypted files on both hard disks and removable media. In fact, suspects with a basic knowledge of security will often encrypt files before archiving them to removable media. In many such cases, an encryption utility is found on the main computer. Look for a stored copy of the key. Many people keep copies of important information in ordinary text files. Look for a file with an obvious name (such as key.txt or enc.txt) or one that contains a single large number and little else. Personal notes or other personal information manager files with an unusually large number that seems to have no other meaning are also great places to look. A forensic investigator's task in such a situation is similar to finding passwords.

The next section addresses proper handling of encrypted data by first identifying encrypted files and then decrypting them to extract the data.

Handling Encrypted Data

At some point in the investigation, you'll likely encounter encrypted data. The course of action depends on the particular type of encryption and the value of the expected evidence once the data is decrypted. If you suspect the encrypted data holds a high value for your case, it will warrant more time and effort to get at that data. Decrypting data can require a substantial effort. Only pursue that course of action when necessary.

Identifying Encrypted Files

Identifying encrypted files is easy. You try to access a file with the appropriate application and you end up getting garbage. The first step you should take in this instance is to find out the type of file you're dealing with. Most operating systems make assumptions about file types by looking at the file's extension. For example, a file with the .doc extension is normally a word processing document, and a file with the .zip extension is normally a compressed archive file. Never trust extensions. One way to "hide" files from casual observers is simply to change their extensions to another file type.

For example, an easy way to hide pictures from standard viewer applications would be to change the extension from .jpg to .txt. Any extension would work, but the .txt extension would represent all such files as text files in most file browser windows. If an unscrupulous user wants to represent hidden pictures as another file type, it's simple to use another defined file extension. Alternatively, an undefined file extension, such as 'xxx', could be used, but these files would likely attract more attention.

As a forensic investigator, you need to ensure that you aren't simply looking at altered file extensions. Always use a file viewer that looks at both the file extension and the file contents. Such a utility will notify you if it finds files that use a non-standard extension. When you find such files, you may be dealing with files that someone deliberately hid.

Another telltale sign that you are dealing with encrypted data is a generated filename. Many encryption utilities have the option to obscure the filename as they encrypt the plaintext file. It is harder for a forensic investigator to identify a file named 100455433798.094 than one named My Illegal Activities.doc. Although many applications generate filenames, any time a collection of files with obviously generated filenames is found, the experienced forensic investigator finds out why. They might be encrypted files.

In summary, if during the course of an investigation, forensic investigators find files that don't fit their extensions or have unknown extensions, the investigators should consider them potentially encrypted. Look at their location in the file system, and check any path history of file accesses and encryption utility activity. The file encryption utility might keep track of recent write locations. Take hints wherever you find them.

Decrypting Files

Assume that you have identified one or more encrypted files. What does the forensic investigator do next? The simple answer is to crack the encryption. The complete answer is a little more complex.

Before exhausting an investigative budget on the latest encryption busting utilities, take the simple approach first. Ask the suspect. If you haven't found encryption keys written down or otherwise recorded in obvious places, just ask. If you're lucky (and you might be), your suspect might provide the keys voluntarily. If asking doesn't work or you know the suspect is unlikely to cooperate, use social engineering next. If a suspect can be convinced to divulge secrets like encryption keys, lots of time and work can be saved. Only resort to technical means when you have exhausted all conventional methods of collecting information.

The suggestion to use social engineering doesn't mean that forensic investigators should engage in questionable activities. Make sure all activities are documented and approved before you engage in social engineering activities. Evidence that the court deems as inadmissible is worthless to any case.

NOTE

First, evaluate the type of encryption you see. A common type of encryption is provided by popular applications. Microsoft Office and WinZip both provide options to encrypt the contents of its data files. Although convenient, application-supported encryption tends to be very weak. There is a wide variety of utilities that specialize in cracking application encryption available for use by forensic investigators. Here is a short list of utilities that help recover file contents of specific file formats:

◆ **Zip Password by LastBit** (http://lastbit.com/zippsw/)—Password recovery utility. Decrypts ZIP/WinZip/pkzip files

◆ **Passware Password Recovery Software** (http://www.lostpassword.com)—Recovers passwords from MS-Office application files

◆ **ElcomSoft password recovery software** (http://www.crackpassword.com)—These products recover passwords from various application files

NOTE   **Many other utilities are available to help forensic investigators defeat application-specific file encryption. Their wide availability should emphasize that such encryption has far less value than generic file encryption algorithms. In short, don't rely on any application vendor to provide strong embedded encryption for your own privacy needs.**

After ruling out embedded encryption, forensic investigators need to move to more sophisticated methods. Always begin by looking for low-hanging fruit. Let's assume you are looking at an encrypted document. Find out as much as possible about the file's context. Here are a few questions to consider:

◆ Does the file have a defined extension?

  ◆ Unless you have information to the contrary, assume the file's extension is valid.

  ◆ Encrypting a file and then changing the extension to throw off an investigator is too much work for most people.

◆ Where is the file located?

  ◆ File location, especially unusual locations, may give clues to the originating application.

  ◆ If you find files stored in unusual locations, check the default document directories for installed applications. That information might tell you what application created the file.

◆ What application(s) likely created the file?

  ◆ If you know, or suspect, what application created the file, see if the application uses a cache or temporary files.

  ◆ Look at deleted files in the application's temporary directory. Any files here are likely to include pre-encryption data.

◆ What is the last access time for the file?

  ◆ Look for any deleted files with access times just prior to the last access time of the encrypted file. Although good encryption utilities won't leave such obvious traces behind, the application that generated the file might not be so careful.

- ◆ Do installed applications create temporary files during creation/editing?
  - ◆ Attempt to recover all the files you can. Even the most innocent ones may be valuable.
- ◆ Are there any files in the Recycle Bin?
  - ◆ Don't laugh; it happens!

These questions will get you started. The best outcome from searching for deleted and unencrypted copies of files is to find a pristine, unencrypted copy of the one file you need. Although it's possible to find just what you're looking for, it is more likely that you will simply find another piece of the puzzle. Any unencrypted file or file fragment that relates to an encrypted file will increase chances of successfully decrypting files. Let's look at a few attack methods to decrypt suspect files.

Real World Scenario

Tales from the Trenches: Opening Encrypted Files

Customers retain computer forensic experts to open encrypted files from time to time.

One day, Bill, a previous client, contacted me and insisted I meet with him right away. Naturally, I told him I would be right over. He said we needed to meet "away from the office" and suggested a local restaurant where we could talk in private.

As soon as I arrived, Bill told me he was having major troubles at work with a small group of employees whom he thought were planning to leave the company, form their own firm, and compete against him. Bill knew there was nothing he could do to keep the employees from leaving, but he wanted to ensure that they didn't take any proprietary information belonging to his company with them when they left.

He was specifically concerned because the company's "network guy" came to him and reported that he had recently observed an unusually large amount of network activity for a few employees, including accessing the customer database and billing system. While this type of access wasn't against company policy and was within the employee's job description, it was unusual enough for the network guy to report it. Bill asked him to "keep an eye open" for any more unusual activity.

A few days later, the network guy informed Bill he observed an increase in the amount and size of e-mail these same employees were sending through the company e-mail server. When he explored further, he noted these employees sent a large number of encrypted e-mails to a former employee. He was, of course, unable to read the e-mails. Encryption wasn't normally used by the company, but it wasn't against the company policy to use encryption, either.

Continues

Bill needed proof that these employees were sending proprietary information out of the company to this former employee so that he could terminate their employment and so that he could obtain a "cease and desist" order against his former employee to prevent him from using the proprietary information.

As expected, while examining the employees' computers, I located a large number of encrypted files and attempted to crack the password protection so I could see the content of the files. The employee protected the majority of files with PGP, a very strong encryption utility. I knew that the possibility of cracking a PGP-protected file was very slim, but I also knew that I had human nature working in my favor.

On one of the computers, I located a small collection of Microsoft Word documents that were password protected using the built-in Microsoft password-protection security. This protection scheme can be very simple to crack using a variety of available commercial cracking utilities. I was able to open each of these files within a few minutes and review their contents. The fact that none of these files had anything to do with the case didn't deter me. I learned a long time ago that people are generally very lazy when it comes to choosing passwords and typically will use the same password in several places.

I attempted to use the recovered password to open the PGP files and was able to access all of the information that was stored on this employee's computer. I located enough evidence to assist Bill in obtaining the "cease and desist" order and to terminate the employees without fear of being sued for wrongful termination.

Although this is one example of overcoming an encryption technology by using a weakness in the implementation of the technology (the human weakness of reusing passwords) and not a weakness in the technology itself, you will find many situations where a weak encryption technology works in the investigator's favor.

Known Plaintext Attack

known plaintext attack
An attack to decrypt a file characterized by comparing known plaintext to the resulting ciphertext.

The *known plaintext attack* is a method of cracking encryption that uses the plaintext and the associated ciphertext. If a forensic investigator is lucky enough to have both the unencrypted and encrypted versions of a file, the relationship between the two can be analyzed and the encryption key deduced. Some archive file password crackers utilize this type of attack. Simply provide an unencrypted file and an encrypted ZIP archive, and the utility will compare the two and attempt to find the key used in the encryption.

As a part of an investigation, forensic investigators often have access to files that may appear to be unrelated to the evidence that is needed. Savvy forensic investigators won't be deterred by this because they know these files could help provide the key the suspect used to encrypt the files. Keeping track of multiple encryption keys is difficult, so forensic investigators are often able to use that discovered key to decrypt other encrypted files.

Chosen Plaintext Attack

Forensic investigators may have access to the encryption engine, but not the key. It is possible the encryption utility allows users to encrypt files using stored credentials without disclosing those credentials. In such cases, forensic investigators may be able to discover the encryption key using a *chosen plaintext attack*. In a chosen plaintext attack, files are encrypted and then compared to the resulting encrypted file. After you create the plaintext and ciphertext, the attack progresses just like the known plaintext attack.

chosen plaintext attack
An attack to decrypt a file characterized by comparing ciphertext to a plaintext message you chose and encrypted.

Brute Force Attack

The brute force attack method for decrypting files is the worst choice and should be used only after exhausting other methods first. It uses the same approach as brute force password cracking. The utility tries every possible key value to see if the decryption results in an intelligible object. Use this option as your last resort.

Which Way to Go?

Each type of attack requires different input, output, and access to the encryption utility. Always try the easiest methods first. If these don't work, move on to more complex approaches. There are no guarantees that discovering a method to decrypt files will be successful within a reasonable timeframe. A brute force attack will always work eventually. However, remember that "eventually" can mean several thousand years.

Use what you can and take the time to think about the evidence. Evidence collection and analysis is very much like assembling a puzzle. Forget about the picture; look at how the pieces fit together.

Terms to Know

chosen plaintext attack	known plaintext attack
cipher	passcode
cryptography	password
decrypt	password cracking
dictionary attack	private key algorithm
encrypt	public key algorithm
encryption key	substitution cipher
hybrid attack	user ID

Review Questions

1. What is a password?

2. What is the process of getting someone to carry out a task for you?

3. Are more complex passwords stronger or weaker than simpler passwords?

4. What method should you first use to get a password?

5. What type of password attack tries passwords from a predefined list?

6. Which type of password attack uses passwords from a list and then tries variations on each element from the list?

7. What is an algorithm for encrypting and decrypting data?

8. What term describes an encrypted message?

9. The Rijndael cipher is the basis for which symmetric encryption algorithm?

10. Which symmetric encryption algorithm uses 56-bit keys?

Chapter 8

Common Forensic Tools

In this chapter, you'll learn more about:
- Explore disk imaging tools, forensic software tool sets, and miscellaneous software tools
- Understand computer forensic hardware
- Assemble your forensic tool kit

The first steps in any investigation nearly always involve old-fashioned detective work. As a forensic investigator, you need to observe and record your observations first. Once you start examining media contents, you'll need some tools to help you find and make sense of stored data.

Forensic investigators and computer examiners need several different types of tools to identify and acquire computer evidence. Some evidence is hidden from the casual observer and requires specialized tools to find and access. In this chapter, we'll examine a sampling of some common and popular tools available to carry out computer forensic tasks.

Disk Imaging and Validation Tools

After identifying the physical media that they suspect contains evidence, forensic investigators must make sure media is preserved before any further steps are taken. Preserving the media is necessary to provide assurance the evidence acquired is valid.

Chapter 3, "Computer Evidence," and Chapter 4, "Common Tasks," both emphasize the importance of copying all media first and then analyzing the copy. It's usually best to create an exact image of the media and verify that it matches the original before continuing the investigation. It's rare to examine the original evidence for any investigation that might end up in court. For other types of investigations, however, forensic investigators might perform a targeted examination on the original evidence. For example, assume the job is to examine a user's home folder on a server for suspected inappropriate material. It might be impossible or extremely difficult to create a mirror image of the disk drive, but the disk can be scanned for existing or deleted files while it is in use. Although examining media while in use might not always be the best practice, informal investigations use this technique frequently.

To Copy or Not to Copy?

Whenever possible, create a duplicate of the original evidence, verify the copy, and then examine the copy. Always invest the time and effort to copy original media for any investigation that might end up in a court of law. If you are sure your investigation will not end up in court, you might decide to analyze the original evidence directly. This is possible and desirable in cases where copying media would cause service interruptions.

Your choice of tools to use depends on several factors, including:

- Operating system(s) supported
    - Operating system(s) in which the tool runs
    - File systems the tool supports
- Price
- Functionality
- Personal preference

The following sections list some tools used to create and verify media copies. Some products appear in two places in the chapter. That's because several products play multiple roles. This section lists several products that are part of larger forensic software suites. While most suites of forensic software handle image acquisition, this section highlights those tools investigators tend to use most frequently.

The list in this chapter is not exhaustive. There are many useful tools not listed here; thus, the exclusion of any tool need not diminish its merit. Where possible, web addresses and URLs have been included for tools examined.

NOTE

dd

The dd utility tool is a mainstay in UNIX/Linux environments. This handy tool is installed with most UNIX/Linux distributions and is used to copy and convert files. As briefly discussed in Chapter 5, "Capturing the Data Image," dd is commonly used in forensics to copy an entire UNIX/Linux environment. Using dd you can specify the input and output file, as well as conversion options. This utility uses two basic arguments:

> if specifies the input file
>
> of specifies the output file

The dd utility abides by operating system file size limits (normally 2 GB) and truncates individual files larger than the limit. (The 2 GB limit does not apply when using the dd utility with device files.) Use caution when copying large files with dd.

If you want only to copy files smaller than the maximum file size, dd is a handy tool to keep in your forensic toolbox.

For example, to copy a simple file from a source (such as /home/user/sn.txt) to a destination (such as /tmp/newfile), you would issue the following command:

```
dd if=/home/user/sn.txt of=/tmp/newfile
```

Figure 8.1 shows the results of the above command.

Figure 8.1   Using the dd utility to copy a text file

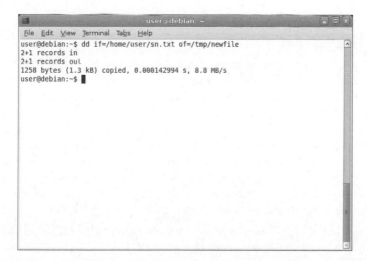

Using similar syntax, an entire hard disk drive can easily be copied. To copy a drive located at /dev/sdb to an image file named /home/user/case1234img, use this command:

```
dd if=/dev/sdb of=/home/user/case1234img
```

Figure 8.2 shows the results of the above command.

Figure 8.2   Using the dd utility to copy an entire hard disk drive

The dd utility is already on any computer running UNIX or Linux, and an Internet search produces a list of places to obtain dd for Windows. Chrysocome provides a version of dd for Windows at http://chrysocome.net/dd. Type **man dd** in UNIX or Linux for a man (manual) page that documents the command syntax.

DriveSpy

DriveSpy is a DOS-based disk imaging tool, developed by Digital Intelligence, Inc. An extended DOS forensic shell, DriveSpy provides an interface similar to the MS-DOS command line, along with additional and extended commands. The entire program is only 125 KB and easily fits on a DOS boot floppy disk. Unfortunately, DOS boot floppy disks aren't as common as they once were. Also, it takes some work to prepare media to use DriveSpy. The payoff is usually worth the effort. DriveSpy does a great job of capturing and searching disk content. All you have to do is create a DOS bootable device with the DriveSpy executable on it. The most common portable boot devices are CD/DVDs and USB devices.

To create a DOS bootable device:

1. Start DriveSpy and use the DRIVES or V command to list the drives and partitions attached to a computer. (See Figure 8.3.)

Figure 8.3   Listing the drives on a system

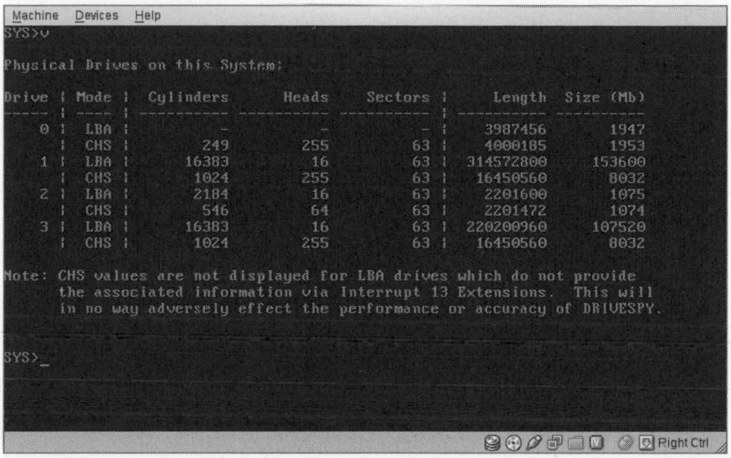

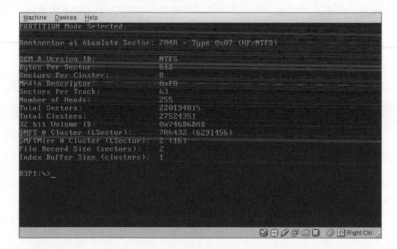

2. Choose a drive and partition for the investigation target from the SYS> prompt.

3. Select Drive 3 from the D3 command.

4. Select partition 1 at the P1 command. The partition information is displayed. (See Figure 8.4.)

Figure 8.4   Partition information

DriveSpy provides many functions necessary to copy and examine drive contents. The program logs all activities, optionally down to each keystroke. Logging can be disabled at will. Forensic investigators can examine DOS and non-DOS partitions and retrieve extensive architectural information for hard drives or partitions.

DriveSpy does not use operating system calls to access files, and it does not change file access dates.

DriveSpy also lets you perform the following tasks:

- ◆ Create a disk-to-disk copy (supports large disk drives).
- ◆ Create a MD5 hash for a drive, partition, or selected files.
- ◆ Copy a range of sectors from a source to a target, where source and target can span drives or reside on the same drive.
- ◆ Select files based on name, extension, or attributes.
- ◆ Unerase files.
- ◆ Search a drive, partition, or selected files for text strings.
- ◆ Collect slack and unallocated space.
- ◆ Wipe a disk, partition, unallocated, or slack space.

DriveSpy provides basic command-line functionality and is portable enough to carry on a simple boot device or media to use at the scene. For pricing and more information, visit the Digital Intelligence, Inc. Web site at `http://www.digital intelligence.com/software/disoftware/drivespy/`.

EnCase

forensic suite
Set of tools and/or software programs used to analyze a computer for collection of evidence.

The EnCase product family from Guidance Software is one of the most complete *forensic suites* available. More of EnCase's functionality and its different products are covered in the "Forensic Tools" section later in this chapter. EnCase is also included in this section owing to its drive duplication functions.

In addition to providing tools and a framework in which to manage a complete case, EnCase includes a drive duplicator (also known as a drive imager). The drive imager creates an exact copy of a drive and validates the image automatically (See Figure 8.5 and Figure 8.6). It either creates complete images or splits drive images to economize storage. EnCase copies virtually any type of media, creating an identical image for analysis. EnCase calls this static data support.

TIP

EnCase Enterprise Edition also provides support for volatile data. This feature snapshots Random Access Memory (RAM), the Windows Registry, open ports, and running applications. It provides potentially valuable information that disappears when a computer is shut down.

Guidance Software also sells a complete line of hardware disk-write blockers. Their Tableau products provide an extra measure of assurance that no writes occur on a device. You can use the hardware write blocker with EnCase or rely on EnCase's own software write blocking to protect original media. Forensic investigators can also use Tableau hardware write blockers with non-EnCase software.

Figure 8.5   Using EnCase to select a drive for duplication

		Name	Label	Access	Sectors	Size	Process ID	Write Blocked	Read File Syst
☐	1	C	DRIVE_C	Windows	314,363,903	149.9GB	0		•
☐	2	F	Data	Windows	314,566,655	150GB	0		•
☑	3	G	DATA2	Windows	2,195,455	1GB	0		•
☐	4	H	DYNDATA	Windows	220,194,815	105GB	0		•
☐	5	0	VBOX HAR	ASPI	314,572,800	150GB	0		•
☐	6	1	VBOX HAR	ASPI	314,572,800	150GB	0		•
☐	7	2	VBOX HAR	ASPI	2,201,600	1GB	0		•
☐	8	3	VBOX HAR	ASPI	220,200,960	105GB	0		•

Figure 8.6   EnCase acquisition status message with an assigned globally unique identifier *(GUID) and MD5*

Acquire

Status: Completed
Start: 10/16/10 02:22:01PM
Stop: 10/16/10 02:26:02PM
Time: 0:04:01
Name: G
Path: C:\Program Files\EnCase5\G.E01
GUID: 1B8AA05F7AC6434A81D321C00C0CE113
Acquisition MD5: F1B1AC6611E2D44FBB08147B4094C85C

☐ Console   ☐ Note   ☐ Log Record

OK   Cancel

The EnCase products run on Windows workstation and server operating systems. For more information on the EnCase product line and specific system requirements, visit the Guidance Software Web site at www.guidancesoftware.com.

Forensic Replicator

Forensic Replicator, from Paraben Forensic Tools, is another disk imaging tool that accommodates many types of electronic media. Forensic Replicator runs on the Windows operating system. It provides an easy-to-use interface, as shown in Figure 8.7 and Figure 8.8, to select and copy entire drives or portions of drives.

It also handles most removable media, including Universal Serial Bus (USB) micro drives. Forensic Replicator stores media images in a format that the most popular forensic programs can read.

Figure 8.7   Paraben's Forensic Replicator Acquisition Wizard

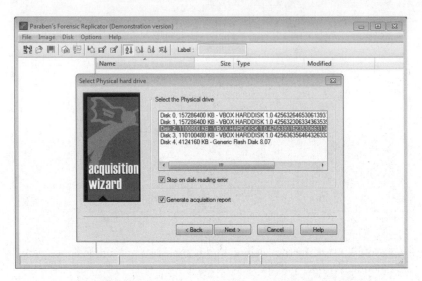

Figure 8.8   Paraben's Forensic Replicator primary user interface

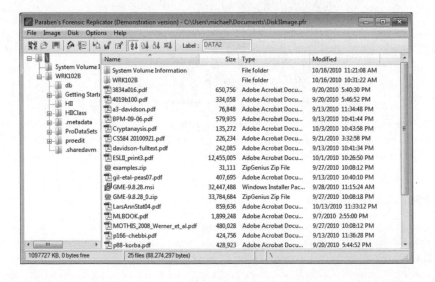

Forensic Replicator also provides the ability to compress and split drive images for efficient storage. The ISO option allows you to create CDs or DVDs from evidence drives that you can browse for analysis. This option makes drive analysis much easier and more accessible for general computers. Copies of the suspect drive don't need to be mounted on a dedicated forensic computer. Standard searching utilities can be used to search the CDs or DVDs. Forensic Replicator also offers the option of encrypting duplicate images for secure storage.

Paraben also sells a FireWire or USB-to-IDE/SATA write blocker, called Paraben's Lockdown V3, as a companion product.

For additional information about the Paraben forensic tools product line, see the "Forensic Tools" section later in this chapter. For more information on the Forensic Replicator product, visit the Paraben Web site at http://www.paraben -forensics.com/replicator.html.

FTK Imager

FTK (Forensic Toolkit) Imager from AccessData Corporation is a Windows-based set of forensic tools that includes powerful media duplication features. (See Figure 8.9.) This free imaging tool allows you to mount a forensic image of the suspect computer so that the suspect's image becomes a letter drive on the investigator's computer.

Figure 8.9   AccessData FTK Imager

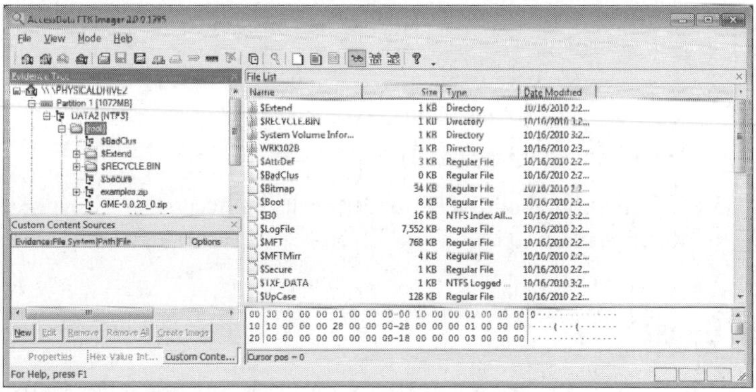

FTK can create media images from many different source formats, including:

◆ NTFS and NTFS compressed

◆ FAT12, FAT16, and FAT32

◆ Linux ext2, ext3, and ext4

◆ HFS, HFS+, CDFS, and VXFS

Figure 8.10 shows the image creation progress message.

Figure 8.10 FTK Imager creating an image

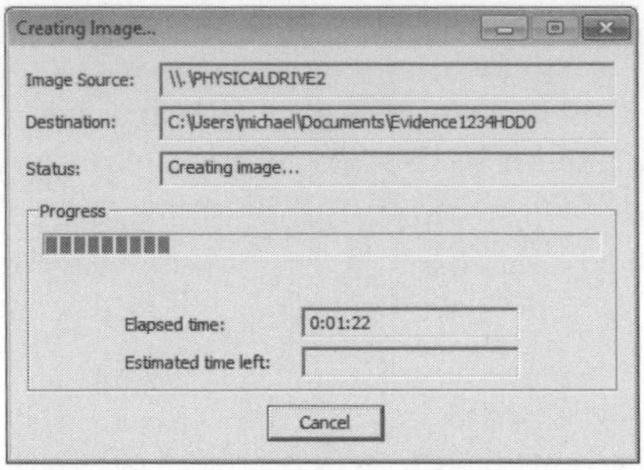

FTK generates CRC or MD5 hash values, as do most products in this category, for disk-copy verification. In addition, FTK provides full searching capability for media and images created from other disk imaging programs. Image formats that FTK reads include:

- EnCase
- SMART
- Expert Witness
- ICS
- Ghost
- dd
- Advanced Forensic Format (AFF)
- AccessData Logical Image (ADI)

For more information about FTK Imager, visit the AccessData Corporation Web site at www.accessdata.com.

Norton Ghost

Norton Ghost, from Symantec, is not strictly a forensic tool, but it does provide the ability to create disk copies that are *almost* exact copies of the original. You can verify the copies you make and ensure each partition is an exact copy, but a complete drive image that Ghost creates commonly returns a different hash value than a hash of the original drive. This means that, although Ghost is a handy tool, it may not provide evidence that is admissible in a court of law. The most common uses for Ghost include backup/restore and creating installation images for multiple computers. Even though Ghost's primary use is not forensics, its utility merits a place in our list of useful tools. (See Figure 8.11.)

Figure 8.11   Norton Ghost

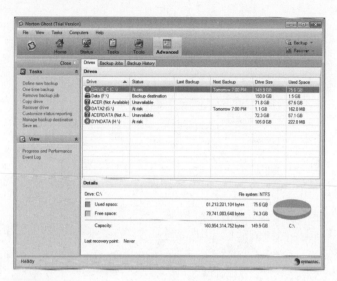

Norton Ghost is a Windows application and requires a Windows operating system. For more information on Norton Ghost, visit the Symantec Web site at http://us.norton.com/ghost.

ProDiscover

ProDiscover, from Technology Pathways, is another suite of forensic tools worth considering for your forensic toolkit. Like other forensic software suites, ProDiscover provides disk imaging and verification features. (See Figure 8.12.)

ProDiscover can create a bit stream copy of an entire suspect disk, including host protected hardware protected area (HPA) sections, to keep original evidence safe. The HPA is an area of a hard disk drive that the disk controller does not report to the BIOS or the operating system. Some disk drive manufacturers use the HPA to hide utilities from the operating system. (For more information, see Chapter 5.)

Another interesting feature of ProDiscover is that it allows you to capture a disk image over a network without being physically connected to a suspect computer.

ProDiscover also automatically creates and records MD5 or SHA-1 hashes for evidence files to prove data integrity. Figure 8.13 shows the main project window.

Technology Pathways provides several different versions of ProDiscover, to meet specific forensic needs. As with other forensic suites, we cover additional features in a later section of this chapter.

All Technology Pathways products include disk imaging and verification and require a Windows operating system. For more information on ProDiscover, visit the Technology Pathways Web site at www.techpathways.com.

Figure 8.12   Capturing a disk image with ProDiscover

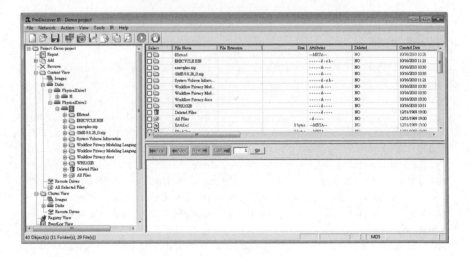

Figure 8.13   ProDiscover project

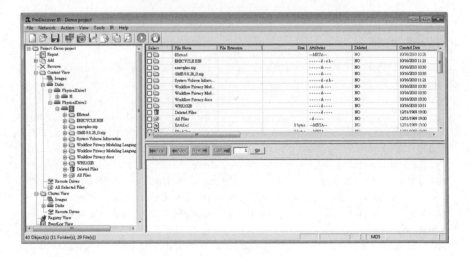

SMART Acquisition Workshop (SAW)

The SMART Acquisition Workshop (SAW) product from ASR Data Acquisition & Analysis, LLC, is a stand-alone utility that creates forensic-quality images from storage devices. SAW runs on Windows, Linux, and Mac computers. Regardless of the operating system, SAW uses a GUI that makes creating images of evidence data easy. (See Figure 8.14.)

Figure 8.14   SAW interface

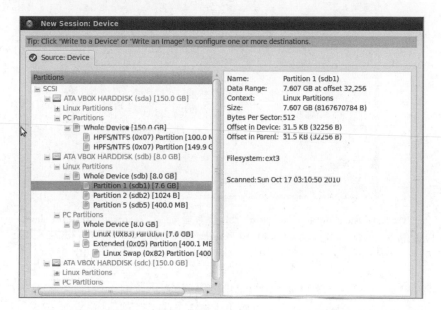

Although SAW works as a stand-alone utility, it also works with another ASR Data utility, SmartMount. SmartMount uses image files from SAW and several other imaging tools, to ensure fast performance for many common forensic activities. ASR Data states that SmartMount exceeds competitors' performance by running up to twenty times faster for searches, indexing, and analysis operations.

Even without SmartMount, SAW provides a solid method to create images of many different types of storage media using a straightforward GUI. For more information on SAW, visit the ASR Data Acquisitions & Analysis Web site at http://www.asrdata.com/forensic-software/saw/.

SMART

SMART comes from the same organization that produces the SAW utility, ASR Data Acquisition & Analysis, LLC. The suite comprises several tools integrated into a full-featured forensic software package. Two tools in the package are SMART Acquisition, which provides disk imaging, and SMART Authentication, which provides verification functionality.

SMART runs in Linux and provides a graphical view of devices in a system (Figure 8.15). The first step in creating a disk image is to calculate a hash value for the source device.

Figure 8.15   SMART displays devices in a system.

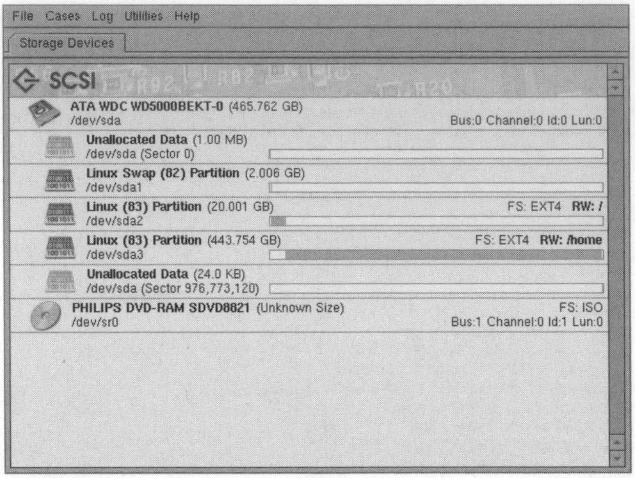

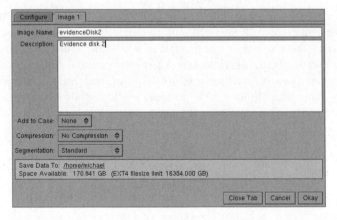

After SMART generates and stores the hash value, it creates one or more device images. SMART can create multiple image files, use compression, split images to fit on smaller devices, and associate images with existing case files (Figure 8.16).

Figure 8.16   Creating an image file with SMART

For more information on SMART, visit the ASR Web site at http://www.asr data.com/forensic-software/smart-for-linux/.

WinHex

WinHex, from X-Ways Software Technology AG, is a Windows-based universal hexadecimal editor and disk management utility. It supports recovery from lost or damaged files and general editing of disk contents. Its disk cloning feature is most relevant to this section.

WinHex clones any connected disk (see Figure 8.17 and Figure 8.18) and verifies the process using checksums or hash calculations.

Figure 8.17   Starting the clone process in WinHex

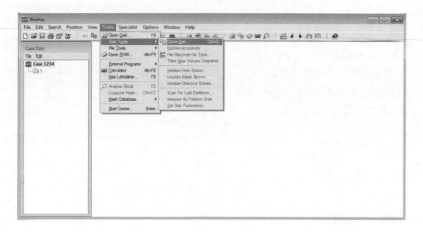

Figure 8.18   The Clone Disk dialog box in WinHex

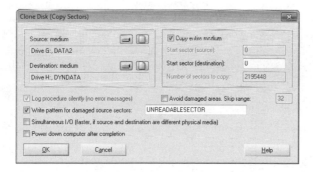

WinHex provides many features beyond disk imaging and verification. You can use WinHex to examine, and optionally edit, disk contents. You can also search disks for text strings using WinHex's search engine. Its support for various data types and its ability to view data in different formats make WinHex a valuable forensic tool.

For more information on WinHex and its additional capabilities, visit the X-Ways Software Technology Web site at http://www.x-ways.net/winhex/.

Forensic Tools

After you make a verified copy of original media, you're ready to begin analysis. The tools discussed in the following sections can perform many forensic functions. Your choice of tools depends on specific investigative needs. The following sections include common software and hardware tools and cover their capabilities.

As with disk imaging tools, your choice of tools to use depends on the following:

- Operating system(s) supported
- User interface preferences
- Budget
- Functionality/capabilities
- Vendor loyalty

Software Suites

Several companies specialize in developing and providing forensic tools. These companies produce software and/or hardware with diverse functionality. Some suites of forensic software are tightly integrated and have mature user interfaces. Other forensic suites are little more than collections of useful utilities. Consider the following tools and try out the ones you like. Your final choice of forensic tools should enable you to perform the examinations you will encounter. Although bells and whistles are nice, it's more important to get the tools you really need.

EnCase

Guidance Software produces the EnCase product line. EnCase was originally developed for law enforcement personnel to carry out investigations. This product line has grown to support commercial incident response teams as well.

The general concept of a case is central to the EnCase product. The first action you take is to create a case file. All subsequent activities (see Figure 8.19, Figure 8.20, and Figure 8.21) relate to a case.

Figure 8.19   EnCase interface

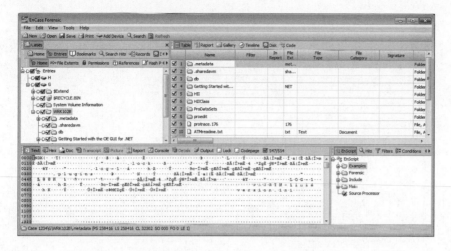

Figure 8.20   Using EnCase to search for keywords

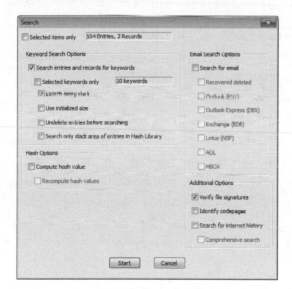

Figure 8.21   Viewing IP addresses with EnCase

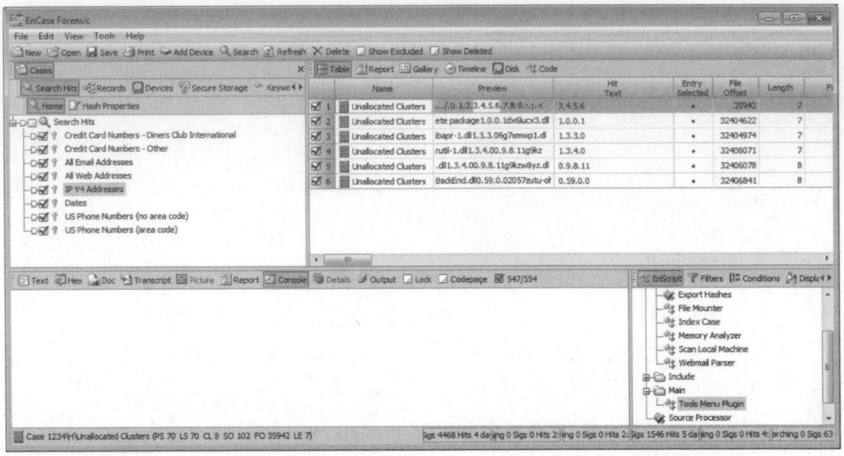

EnCase is an integrated Windows-based GUI tool suite. Even though the EnCase functionality is impressive, you are likely to need other utilities at some point. Fully integrated solutions can increase productivity, but don't hesitate to use another tool when you need it.

Here are just a few features of EnCase:

- Snapshot enables investigators to capture volatile information including:
  - RAM contents
  - Running programs
  - Open files and ports
- Organizes results into case files and manages case documents
- Helps maintain the chain of custody
- Provides tools for incident response teams to respond to emerging threats
- Supports real-time and postmortem examinations

EnCase provides the functionality to acquire and examine many types of evidence. The organization around a case provides the structure to keep information in order. Overall, EnCase is one of the premium suites of software you definitely should evaluate when selecting forensic tools. For more information on EnCase, visit the Web site at www.guidancesoftware.com.

Forensic Toolkit (FTK)

Another forensic suite that provides an integrated user interface is AccessData's Forensic Toolkit (FTK) (Figure 8.22). FTK runs in Windows operating systems and provides a powerful tool set to acquire and examine electronic media.

Figure 8.22   FTK Evidence Processing options

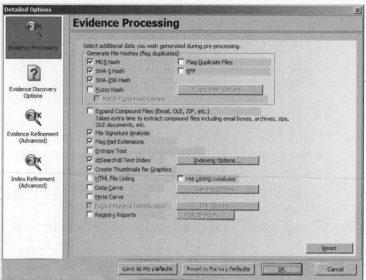

As discussed in "Disk Imaging and Validation," earlier in this chapter, FTK contains a disk imaging tool. This imaging tool provides one or more copies of primary evidence for analysis.

FTK provides an easy-to-use file viewer that recognizes nearly 300 types of files. It also provides full text indexing powered by dtSearch (we cover dtSearch features later in this chapter in the "Miscellaneous Software Tools" section). FTK's integrated file viewer and search capabilities enable it to find evidence on most devices.

FTK works with media images created by several imaging utilities, including:

- FTK
- EnCase
- SMART
- dd

Search capabilities include e-mail and archive file analysis. FTK also enables users to quickly examine files in many different formats. Results are organized by case and presented in a case content summary. For more information on FTK, visit the AccessData Web site at www.accessdata.com.

The Sleuth Kit (TSK)

The Sleuth Kit (TSK) is a popular, free, open source forensic software suite. TSK is a collection of command-line tools that provides media management and forensic analysis functionality.

TSK has a few features that deserve separate mention. TSK supports Mac partitions and analyzes files from Mac file systems. It also runs on Mac OS X. TSK can analyze volatile data on running systems.

The core TSK toolkit contains five different types of tools.

◆ File System Tools

File System Layer   The fsstat tool reports file system details, including inode Numbers (file system data structures that contain file information), block or cluster ranges, and super block details for UNIX-based systems. For FAT file systems, fsstat provides an abbreviated FAT table listing.

File Name Layer   The ffind and fls tools report allocated, unallocated, and deleted filenames.

Meta Data Layer   The icat, ifind, ils, and istat tools report on file metadata (file details) stored in file systems.

Data Unit Layer   The blkcat, blkls, blkstat, and blkcalc tools report file content information and statistics.

File System Journal   The jcat and jls tools report journal information and statistics.

◆ Volume System Tools

The mmls, mmstat, and mmcat tools provide information on the layout of disks or other media.

◆ Image File Tools

The img_stat, and img_cat tools provide details and content information for image files.

◆ Disk Tools

The disk_sreset, and disk_stat tools detect and remove an HPA on an ATA disk.

◆ Other Tools

hfind   The hfind tool looks up hash values.

mactime   This tool uses fls and ils output to create timelines of file activity, such as create, access and write activity.

sorter   This tool sorts files based on file type.

sigfind   This tool searches for a binary value in a file, starting at a specific offset location.

For more information on TSK, visit the TSK Web site at www.sleuthkit.org.

ProDiscover

Technology Pathways provides two different versions of the ProDiscover tool suite: Forensics and Incident Response (IR), depending on your particular forensic needs. (ProDiscover IR is shown in Figure 8.23 and Figure 8.24.) Both ProDiscover products run in Windows with an integrated GUI.

Figure 8.23   Using ProDiscover IR to add comments to a file

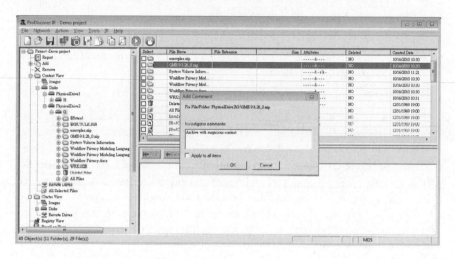

Figure 8.24   Search results in ProDiscover IR

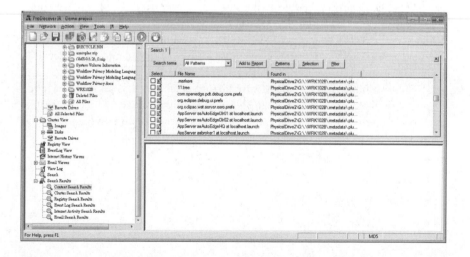

Here are some notable ProDiscover features:

◆ Allows live system examination

◆ Identifies Trojan horse programs and other software intended to compromise system security

◆ Utilizes a remote agent that allows centralized examination and monitoring, along with encrypted network communication to secure analysis data

◆ Creates a bit stream copy of an entire suspect disk, including hidden HPA sections, to keep original evidence safe

◆ Ensures integrity of acquired images using MD5 or SHA-1 hashes

◆ Supports FAT12, FAT16, FAT32, all NTFS versions, Linux ext2/ext3, and Sun Solaris UFS file systems

◆ Generates reports in eXtensible Markup Language (XML)

ProDiscover provides functionality similar to other full-featured forensic software suites listed in this section.

Technology Pathways also offers a free version of ProDiscover Basic. ProDiscover Basic is a complete GUI-based computer forensic software package. It include the ability to image, preserve, analyze, and report on evidence found on a computer disk drive. This version is freeware and may be used and shared free of charge.

Take a look at the full product line for more details on specific features. To learn more about ProDiscover, visit the Technology Pathways Web site at www.techpathways.com.

SIFT

The SANS Investigative Forensic Toolkit (SIFT) is a collection of open source (and freely available) forensic utilities. SANS originally developed SIFT as a toolkit for students in the SANS Computer Forensic Investigations and Incident Response course. The students liked the toolkit so much that word spread and SANS decided to repackage and release it to the public.

SIFT is available either as a VMware virtual machine or as an ISO image to create a bootable CD. It provides the ability to examine disks and images created using other forensic software. This toolkit allows users to examine the following file systems:

◆ Windows (FAT, VFAT, NTFS)

◆ Mac (HFS)

◆ Solaris (UFS)

◆ Linux (ext2/ext3)

SIFT tools support the following evidence image formats:

◆ Raw (dd)

◆ Expert Witness (E01)

◆ Advanced Forensic Format (AFF)

SIFT includes these individual tools:

◆ The Sleuth Kit (TSK file system analysis)

◆ Log2timeline (generates timelines)

◆ Ssdeep and md5deep (generates hashes)

◆ Foremost/Scalpel (file carving)

◆ Wireshark (network analysis) (http://www.wireshark.org/) (See Figure 8.25.)

Figure 8.25   Wireshark Network Analyzer

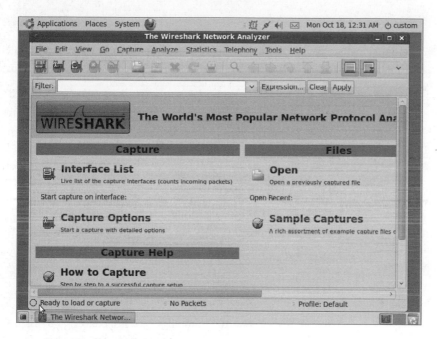

◆ Vinetto (thumbs.db analysis)

◆ Pasco (Internet Explorer history analysis)

◆ Rifiuti (examines Recycle Bin)

◆ Volatility Framework (memory forensics)

- ◆ DFLabs (GUI front end for TSK)
- ◆ Autopsy (GUI front end for TSK)
- ◆ PyFLAG (log and disk analysis)
- ◆ Guymager (GUI imager for evidence acquisition)

Figure 8.26   Guymager open source forensic manager

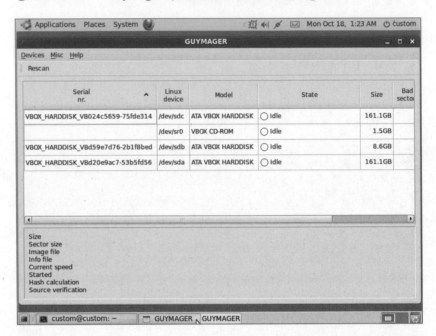

SANS also provides users with documentation (including a series of "how-to" tutorials) on using SIFT in a forensic investigation. For more information on SIFT, visit the SANS Web site at https://computer-forensics2.sans.org/community/downloads/.

X-Ways Forensics

X-Ways Forensics, from X-Ways Software Technology AG, is a collection of forensic tools that assist in examining media images. Compared to other forensic suites in this section, it's a little more lightweight. However, it does provide several forensic tools that include some large package features at a very reasonable price.

Some of the main X-Ways features include:

- ◆ Case management
- ◆ Automatic activity logging
- ◆ Automated reports in HyperText Markup Language (HTML)

◆ A display of existing and deleted files, sorted by file type category

◆ Gallery view for graphics

◆ Skin color detection helps in isolating pictures that may contain pornography

◆ File extension/file type mismatches detection

◆ EnCase media image support (read)

This list only covers a few of the many features of X-Ways. For more information on this product, visit the X-Ways Software Technology Web site at http://www.x-ways.net/forensics/.

Miscellaneous Software Tools

In addition to drive imaging software and complete forensic software suites, there are many targeted tools and utilities that are of value to computer forensic investigators. No matter how many features your forensic suite of choice may have, your investigation might have specific needs that require other special tools.

The following sections cover a few special-purpose tools. As with previous sections, consider each of these tools and choose the best ones for your forensic needs.

DriveSpy

DriveSpy was introduced earlier in the "Disk Imaging and Validation Tools" section. It's included here as well to remind you that DriveSpy does a lot more than just duplicate drives. For instance, you can:

◆ Select files based on name, extension, or attributes

◆ View the sectors and clusters in built-in hex viewers.

◆ Search a partition or drive for specific text strings

DriveSpy provides basic command-line functionality that is portable enough to carry on a single floppy disk and use at the scene of a forensic investigation. After an image of a drive is created, DriveSpy also assists you in examining image content.

For pricing and more information, visit the Digital Intelligence, Inc. Web site at http://www.digitalintelligence.com/software/disoftware/drivespy/.

dtSearch

After you create an image of suspect media, you'll need to search it for possible evidence. The dtSearch product line, from dtSearch Corporation, provides solutions that enable you to search terabytes of text in a short time. Although not strictly a forensic tool, dtSearch (Figure 8.27) supports a highly necessary forensic function.

Figure 8.27   dtSearch

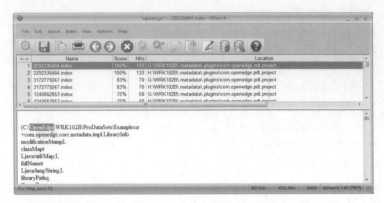

The dtSearch products offer the following features:

◆ Over 25 search options, including indexed, unindexed, field content searching for supported file types, and full-text search options

◆ Convert results to HTML, XML, or PDF, with search results highlighted (exposes the search results context)

◆ Support for distributed searching for high performance

The dtSearch product line includes several different products for different forensic investigative needs, including:

dtSearch Desktop   Searches stand-alone machines

dtSearch Network   Searches across networks

dtSearch Spider   Extends a local search to a remote Web site

dtSearch Web   Supports instant text searching for online documents

dtSearch Publish   Publishes an instant searchable database on CD/DVD

dtSearch Engine   Empowers developers to add dtSearch's functionality to applications

For a forensic examiner, the Desktop and Network products provide the capability to find possible evidence on multiple machines. For more detailed product information, visit the dtSearch Corporation Web site at www.dtsearch.com.

NetAnalysis

NetAnalysis, from Digital Detective, is a software utility that recovers and then analyzes Internet browser artifacts. NetAnalysis (Figure 8.28) empowers investigators to search and analyze browser history from suspect computers. Even if a user deletes all browser history, NetAnalysis can still recover much of that deleted content and reconstruct past actions.

Figure 8.28   NetAnalysis

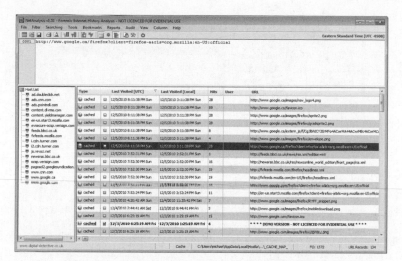

NetAnalysis enables investigators to reconstruct visited Web sites from locally cached data. It can read several standard forensic image formats, including images generated by EnCase. The Auto Investigate function helps investigators save time by automatically identifying suspicious Web sites that may contain specific content, such as child pornography. It also analyzes search terms, user IDs, and passwords it finds on the suspect computer.

NetAnalysis helps investigators recover and identify the most valuable information to an investigation. Using NetAnalysis to find questionable browsing activity is much easier than performing a manual analysis. NetAnalysis also allows users to develop standard key terms and queries to share and use with other investigations.

For more detailed product information, visit the Digital Detective Web site at http://www.digital-detective.co.uk/netanalysis.asp.

Quick View Plus File Viewer

Quick View Plus, from Avantstar, is a general-purpose file viewer. Quick View Plus (Figure 8.29) allows you to view files in over 300 formats. Quick View Plus also allows you to view parts of files and print them or cut and paste into your own applications.

From a forensic perspective, Quick View Plus provides examiners the ability to search many types of files for text strings and view the results in the context of the original file.

Find more details on Quick View Plus by visiting the Avantstar Web site at www.avantstar.com.

Figure 8.29 Quick View Plus file viewer

ThumbsPlus File Viewer

ThumbsPlus File Viewer, from Cerious Software Inc., is a general-purpose file viewer and editor. It allows you to view files in many formats. A good file-viewing tool makes browsing through several graphics files far easier. ThumbsPlus (Figure 8.30) makes it easy to collect and browse most common graphic formats.

Figure 8.30 ThumbsPlus Pro

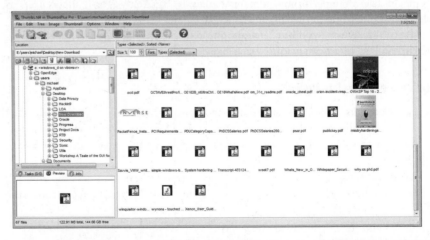

You can find many more details on ThumbsPlus by visiting the Cerious Web site at http://www.cerious.com/featuresv7.shtml.

Paraben Tools

Paraben Corporation provides a wide array of forensic tools. The Forensic Replicator was introduced earlier. In this section, you'll learn about three additional Paraben tools. At the end of the Paraben Tools section, be certain to follow the link to learn about other forensic tools offered by Paraben.

Device Seizure

Paraben's Device Seizure (Figure 8.31 and Figure 8.32) is a software tool that enables investigators to acquire and analyze data from over 2,400 different mobile devices. This includes mobile phones, PDAs, and GPS devices. Paraben also sells hardware accessories that work with Device Seizure to allow you to physically connect to all supported mobile devices.

Figure 8.31   Paraben's Device Seizure Welcome Wizard

Device Seizure acquires and organizes a large amount of mobile data, including:

- Active and deleted text messages
- Phonebook entries from memory and the SIM card
- Call history with call details
- PDA common information (calendar, to-do list, etc.)
- File system contents
- GPS information
- E-mail information

Figure 8.32   Paraben's Device Seizure main screen

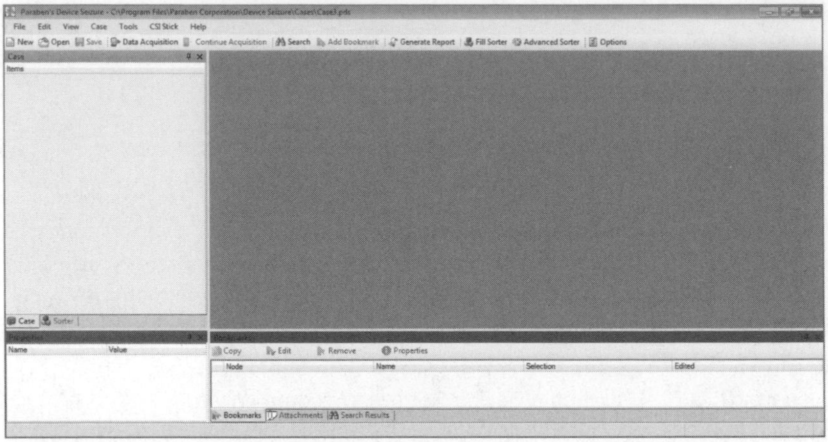

Device Seizure can also translate GPS coordinates into Google Earth data. This makes it easy to present evidence in a form that anyone can easily see and understand. Paraben designed Device Seizure to be a solid forensic tool for mobile device investigations.

Chat Stick

Paraben provides several consumer products for home and corporate use, such as the Chat Stick. The Chat Stick is a USB thumb drive that comes preloaded with software.

Using the Chat Stick is easy. Simply insert the Chat Stick in a USB port on a target computer. The Chat Stick software automatically launches and lets you search for chat logs from most popular instant message (IM) software, including:

◆ Yahoo
◆ MSN
◆ ICQ
◆ Trillian
◆ Skype
◆ Hello
◆ Miranda

Chat Stick identifies chat logs and copies these logs to the USB thumb drive. From there, Chat Stick software (Figure 8.33) allows users to view and create reports on all IM conversations.

Chat stick makes it easy for parents to check up on IM activities on home computers. Businesses also use Chat Stick to ensure their employees uphold their acceptable use policies for computer equipment at work.

Figure 8.33   Paraben's Chat Stick software

Paraben Porn Stick

Paraben's Porn Stick is another consumer product distributed on a USB thumb drive. The Porn Stick contains preloaded software that searches a target computer for suspicious images—specifically pornography.

As with the Chat Stick, the Porn Stick software automatically launches when the thumb drive is plugged into a USB port. Users can search one or more drives on the target computer for suspicious images.

The Porn Stick stores thumbnails of suspicious images on the USB thumb drive. Images can be previewed once the scan is finished. To make the process more palatable, the Porn Stick blurs image thumbnails. You can select any image and use the mouse pointer to see a small portion of the unblurred image (see Figure 8.34). This feature makes it difficult to "accidentally" view objectionable material.

The Porn Stick is a consumer product that home and business users typically purchase. As with the Chat Stick, parents can use it at home and businesses can use it in the office to check for acceptable use policy violations.

For more information on any Paraben products, visit their Web site at www.paraben.com.

Snagit

Snagit, from TechSmith Corporation, is a full-featured tool designed to capture and manage screenshots. Sometimes, the best way to document the state of evidence is to save an image from the screen. Snagit (Figure 8.35) makes it easy to take screenshots using over 40 different methods. You can record any aspect of what's on a computer monitor.

Figure 8.34   Detection results from Paraben's Porn Stick software

Figure 8.35   Snagit

Once you take a screenshot, Snagit allows you to edit it (see Figure 8.36) and add features to highlight specific areas on that image. Snagit also helps in sharing, cataloging, and storing screenshot images. Snagit can help to simplify any investigation.

Figure 8.36   Snagit Editor

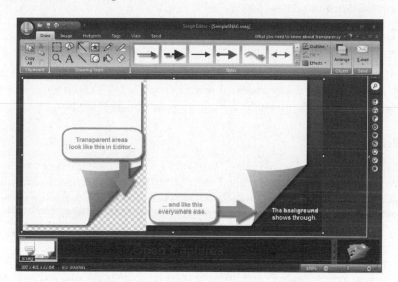

For more information on Snagit, visit the TechSmith Web site at http://www .techsmith.com/snagit/.

Hardware

Up to this point, we've ignored the requirement that all software tools must run on hardware of some type. Although forensic tools run on general-purpose machines, using dedicated computers for forensic investigations is often advisable. Using dedicated hardware decreases the possibility of accidental contamination by nonforensic applications.

Although actual evidence contamination cannot occur on the original evidence when analyzing an image of the original, other applications might affect the evidence image copy you are examining. Your forensic machine probably has special-purpose hardware elements such as a disk-write blocker, keystroke logger, or multiple format disk controllers.

Because forensic examination computers tend to support special-purpose hardware and software, several companies offer hardware devices and complete computer systems built from the ground up to serve as forensic hardware devices. Some of these systems can be expensive, but if you need a prebuilt forensic hardware platform, the cost is probably justified. Carefully consider your needs based on:

- Where will you analyze media?
  - At the scene
  - In the lab
- How often do you use forensic software?
- What type of operating system and hardware must you analyze?
- Will the evidence you collect be presented in a court of law?

Answers to these questions will help you to decide whether you need special-purpose forensic hardware and what features you need. The following sections describe the products offered by some forensic hardware providers.

Cellebrite

Cellebrite produces a line of forensic hardware for use in mobile device forensics. Their Universal Forensic Extraction Device (UFED) enables forensic investigators to extract information from more than 3,600 mobile devices, including phones and GPS units. UFED is used by militaries, law enforcement agencies, governments, and intelligence agencies around the world to extract information from mobile devices during investigations.

UFED comes in multiple versions to support user-specific requirements. The UFED system includes over 100 different connectors that allow investigators to attach any type of mobile device. UFED software supports many features investigators need, including:

- Extract existing and deleted phone data
  - Call history
  - Text messages
  - Contacts
  - Images
  - Geotags
- Search, reconstruct, and analyze phone data
- Integrate GPS information with Google Maps and Google Earth

For more information on Cellebrite UFED products, visit the Web site at http://www.cellebrite.com/forensic-products.html.

ICS Solo 4

Intelligent Computer Solutions (ICS) specializes in data duplication hardware. They produce a line of forensic acquisition products for both field and lab use. Their forensic products use high-speed hardware and hardware write blockers to duplicate evidence media. Instead of using software tools to create images of evidence media, ICS provides hardware to accomplish the same task. The tool also has the ability to capture video played on Web sites.

The main advantage to using hardware data acquisition is increased speed. ICS products transfer data at rates up to 18 GB/min. That is far faster than any software image acquisition. ICS products, such as the ICS Solo-4 (Figure 8.37), provide a convenient method to extract images from a suspect computer, even without removing its hard drive(s).

Figure 8.37   Image MASSter Solo-4 from ICS

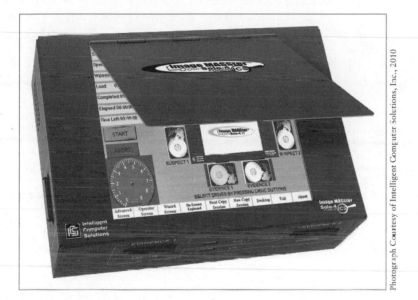

Photograph Courtesy of Intelligent Computer Solutions, Inc., 2010

For more information on the ICS line of forensic acquisition products, visit the ICS Web site at www.ics-iq.com.

Your Forensic Toolkit

Now that you've reviewed a selection of tools available to forensic investigators, you must decide which tools work best for you. Every forensic investigator has slightly different needs. The particular tools you acquire depend on many factors, including:

- ◆ Expected types of investigations
    - ◆ Evidence to be presented in a court of law
    - ◆ Evidence for internal reporting/auditing

◆ Operating system needs and preference

◆ Background and training

◆ Budget

◆ Status

    ◆ Law enforcement

    ◆ Private organization

Consider your specific forensic needs, then carefully consider the products available. In general, you should acquire only the functionality you need and nothing more. The problem is that it can be difficult to know exactly what functionality you will need under any and all circumstances. Each investigation is different and may call for different approaches. In such cases, tool needs change. To the best of your ability, develop a list of anticipated forensic tool needs.

 Real World Scenario

Tales from the Trenches: Forensic Tools

The care and maintenance of your computer forensic tools begins well before you are asked to perform any forensic evaluation.

Each time you purchase a new hard drive, you must complete a procedure to sanitize that drive to ensure that there is no data present prior to using it in an imaging process. This is a process that can require many hours to complete.

The CEO of a company once asked me to perform a forensic evaluation of a very senior employee's computer to look for evidence that this employee was planning to leave the company. The CEO was very concerned because this employee had access to sensitive trade secrets that could put the company at a great disadvantage if they were revealed to a competitor.

The CEO wanted me to go into the employee's office in the middle of the night and image the hard drive without his knowledge and leave everything as I had found it so the employee would not know I had been there. I had only one problem. The CEO wanted the imaging done that night and I didn't have a hard drive with me that had been sanitized to comply with the U.S. Department of Defense specification DoD 5220.22-M standard.

I was out of town teaching a forensic class when the request was made. If I had been at home, I simply would have opened the safe at my lab and taken out one of the many sanitized hard drives (of varying sizes) that I keep prepped and ready to go. As a matter of procedure, each time I purchase a new hard drive, I use the ICS Image MASSter Solo 4 Forensic unit to sanitize the drive and then I store the drive in my safe and complete an entry in a log to begin its chain of custody.

Continues

Because I did not have a prepped drive, I drove to one of the local computer super centers and purchased a drive. I had previously asked the CEO what size hard drive he thought the employee had in his computer and he told me the company standard was an 80 GB hard drive. Of course, I purchased a 120 GB hard drive to make sure I was buying a large enough drive.

I went back to my hotel and began sanitizing the drive, which takes many hours to complete on a 120 GB hard drive. The CEO told me he would meet me at the office whenever I was ready. The process completed at 4 a.m. and I called the CEO. We went to the office, and I was able to image the employee's computer and leave the building before any of the other employees arrived for work. After inspecting the hard drive, we discovered evidence that the executive was planning to leave and was collecting data to take with him. We were able to prevent him from taking the data. Very soon after, he did leave the company and, because of his actions, did not receive a severance package.

From this experience, I learned to bring a sanitized 250 GB hard drive with me when I travel out of town— just in case. From this story, you should learn that you would be wise to purchase a variety of hard drives and sanitize them before you ever talk to your first customer about performing a forensic examination.

Although it's important to be adequately prepared, one common pitfall is to overbuy. The impulse in all things is to pack any acquisition with the maximum number of options available. Think about it. Have you ever used all the options in your video camera? Look at the owner's manual and see all the cool things it can do. You probably heard about those features when you purchased the camera and promptly forgot about most of them once you started using it. Forensic tools may include options you simply don't need. Avoid paying for options you'll never use: It will save you money.

Each Organization Is Different

In choosing a forensic tool set, consider how your organization approaches investigations. Do you need the ability to examine machines remotely? If so, you can narrow your search to a few options. Are you a UNIX shop with a small budget? Open source tools might fit the bill in this situation.

There is no "one size fits all" forensic toolkit. Ask questions. Take the time to attend training and view tutorials. Test as much software as possible. Investing a substantial amount of time in this process will help you make decisions that are more informed. Thoroughly consider how your organization conducts investigations, what kind of investigations you'll need to participate in, and what features you'll need to get the job done.

Most Examiners Use Overlapping Tools

Unless a single set of forensic tools satisfies all of your needs, consider selecting multiple tools while weighing the costs involved. When you do select multiple tools, they will most likely overlap. That's okay. Get what you need. There's nothing wrong with having three disk imaging tools. Use the one that makes the most sense.

Most forensic examiners use tools from several vendors. Some may use commercial and open source tools. The source is not important. The important points are that you have the tools to get the job done, you know how to use them, and you verify that the tools do what they are supposed to do before you use them on a real case.

One last point: Get the necessary training to use the tools you acquire most effectively. Great tools can hamper or ruin an investigation if you don't know how to use them. Forensic tools can be highly effective or highly destructive, depending on the knowledge of their user. Get the tools, and then get the training to use them properly.

After you have built your toolbox, and know how to use the tools in it, you are ready to tackle the next investigation.

Terms to Know

forensic suite

Review Questions

1. Which utility, originally created for the UNIX platform, copies and converts files using two basic arguments (if and of)?

2. Which software suite provides an enterprise edition that specifically supports volatile data analysis on a live Windows system?

3. Which disk imaging software operates as an extended DOS command shell?

4. What are MD5 and SHA-1?

5. Which forensic software suite integrates the dtSearch Engine in its searching function?

6. What two software suites are free?

7. Name two vendors of forensic hardware.

8. After creating an image of a drive, what must you do to ensure that the copy matches the original?

9. You have many factors to consider when choosing appropriate forensic software. Name two.

10. Which two forensic products can extract both active and deleted text messages from a mobile phone?

Chapter 9

Pulling It All Together

In this chapter, you'll learn more about:
- Creating proper and thorough documentation
- Formulating a concise analysis report summary
- Exploring model analysis reports and sample reports
- Using software to create reports

Throughout the forensic process, an investigator extracts and examines mounds of information. In the end, all this information must be processed into a succinct report that is understandable to a judge and a jury.

Your top priority is to properly document all steps taken during the evidence-gathering process. Good documentation, along with sound forensic procedures, is essential for successful prosecution of criminal cases. Crucial evidence is subject to question, and qualifications of any expert witness can become an issue if computer evidence is not documented systematically. (Before you're allowed to provide expert opinions, you must first be qualified as an expert in computer forensics. Qualifications of an expert witness can be challenged at any time, even when evidence has been gathered and documented properly.) This is what makes the ability to accurately reconstruct and recite the details of an investigation such a critical skill.

In this chapter we'll look at the information you might need and how to put all the pieces together in an analysis report that is concise yet detailed enough to explain your findings. This chapter examines the process of documenting evidence gathering and works through several sample reports to "show and tell" the type and quality of documentation you will need for a case.

Creating Easy-to-Use Reports

Every report should begin with a clear and concise summary of the facts of the case and evidence gathered. The purpose of the summary is to provide the client (or court) with a high-level overview of the evidence gathered and the conclusions drawn based on the evidence. The summary is meant to provide the client or court with a snapshot of the facts and evidence. Remember, the client or court will be able to read the full details in the body of the report—the summary is merely an overview.

During an investigation, it's easy to gather large amounts of evidence. While such evidence can be stored on an 8 GB USB flash drive (also known as UFD), if its contents were printed, it could generate a stack of paper approximately 1,000 feet tall. Even though you can't have too much documentation, when it comes to presenting any case, you need balance. You won't want to weed through tons of evidence again later, but you don't want to appear incompetent. For example, if you are asked about log events or a specific activity, you don't want to respond, "I know that I saw that somewhere." If the activity is captured in a Tcpdump log file, you'll need not only to be able to locate it again, but also to locate it quickly.

You need to organize relevant evidence in a report. When formulating a concise report, it is important to:

- ◆ Understand the importance of the report
- ◆ Limit the report to specifics
- ◆ Use a layout and presentation that is easy to understand
- ◆ Understand the difference between litigation-support reports and technical reports
- ◆ Write clearly
- ◆ Provide supporting material
- ◆ Explain methods used in data collection
- ◆ Explain results

The basic guidelines for your reports should be to document your steps clearly, use a template to organize the report, and be consistent. Documenting clearly and concisely helps ensure that the details can be recalled or conveyed when the need arises. To do this thoroughly, the scope of your original documentation must be broad and you should document every step of the process. Many of the tools we discuss in Chapter 8, "Common Forensic Tools" include report generation facilities that you'll use to build your report, and to help you produce a summary to guide the judge, jury, and officers of the court through your painstakingly compiled evidence and information.

Often lawyers want to have electronic evidence produced for them in paper format. But evidence is much simpler to handle in electronic form, where it can be filed, cross-referenced, and indexed. Most law firms now have the technology to do this. A complete forensic analysis will usually fit on a single CD-ROM. Various software programs, such as AD Summation, permit evidence to be processed more efficiently than piles (and files) of paper. Find more information on AD Summation at http://accessdata.com. In particular, investigate CaseVantage at the following URL:

```
http://accessdata.com/products/ediscovery-litigation-support/ad-summation
-casevantage
```

Kroll Ontrack is another software program that attorneys use. It provides software tools that let you view, search, sort, bookmark, and generate reports on data after the evidence is extracted. For more information go to www.krollontrack.com.

X-Ways Investigator offers a broad range of capabilities, including serving as an automated forensic examiner. It can come in handy during civil litigation when one party wants to examine the other party's computers. Investigator is a product of X-Ways Software Technology AG. You can find information at http://www.x-ways.net/investigator/.

Document Everything, Assume Nothing

As an investigator, the better you understand a case, the better you'll be able to sense each logical step in the investigation process. An experienced investigator knows that the success of a forensic investigation relies not only on the ability to uncover evidence but also on following sound methodology while collecting and handling evidence, so it can be used in court. Under *Federal Rule of Civil Procedure 26*, section (a)(2)(B), parties involved in legal cases are required to disclose the identities of their forensic experts or risk not being able to call those experts to testify at trial. This rule states that testimony must be accompanied by a written, signed report. The report must contain:

Federal Rule of Civil Procedure 26
Federal Rule 26 states the General Provisions Governing Discovery and Duty of Disclosure. Section (a) states Required Disclosures and Methods to Discover Additional Matter.

◆ A complete statement of all opinions and the basis and reasons for such

◆ Any data or other information relied upon in forming the opinions

◆ Any exhibits to be used in support of or summary for the opinions

◆ The qualifications of the witness, including a list of all publications authored by the witness within the last ten years

◆ Amount of compensation to be paid for the study and testimony

◆ A list of any other cases in which the witness has testified as an expert at trial or by deposition within the last four years.

Attorneys may ask the forensic investigator write and sign an affidavit attesting to these items instead of preparing a full report. On December 1, 2010, Rule 26 was amended and a new section, Rule 26(a)(2)(C), added. Under this rule, witnesses who do not normally testify, or who were not hired for the purpose of providing expert testimony, are only required to provide a summary of the subject matter, facts, and opinions about which they'll testify.

Under Rule 30(b)(6), an organization's designated agent needs to testify to matters known by or reasonably available to the organization. This could include providing additional items of more specific information, such as:

◆ Quantity and locations of computers in use

◆ Operating systems and application software installed and dates of use

◆ File-naming conventions and which directories data is saved to

◆ Backup disk or tape inventories and schedules

◆ Computer use policies

◆ Identities of current and former employees responsible for systems operations

◆ E-mail with dates, times, and attachments

◆ Word documents, tables, graphs, and database files

◆ Internet bookmarks, cookies, and history logs

You begin the documentation process long before you start dealing with any data used as evidence in a case. Prior to seizing equipment or data, make sure you have the necessary paperwork filed and have proper permission to seize the computer or equipment in question. Remember that the Fourth Amendment limits the ability of government agents to search for evidence without a warrant, but consent remains the most relevant exception to this Amendment. When a proper computer use policy is in place, it can cover an employee's consent to search their system. If you don't know whether a warrant is needed, the manual *Searching and Seizing Computers and Obtaining Electronic Evidence in Criminal Investigations* on the Computer Crime and Intellectual Property Section of the United States Department of Justice Web site at http://www.cybercrime.gov/ssmanual/ can provide guidance. Of course, don't overlook the obvious—always consult an attorney when in doubt about whether a warrant is required.

NOTE

Although the excitement of working in the computer forensic field comes while performing the investigation and "catching the bad guy," the "real work" is achieved when the investigator "kills a few trees" and completes the paperwork. As a computer forensic investigator, you must remember that your job is not complete until your report is filed.

Document everything carefully, consistently, and neatly. As discussed in Chapter 3, "Computer Evidence," you need to record the who, what, when, where, why, and how of the case. You'll also want to pay special attention to procedural details. You may want to start with a bound paper notebook, making notes in pen with dates and initials. This type of documentation can provide a good point of reference for jogging the memories of the forensic investigators when the case is lengthy. Chapter 3 provides a brief explanation of documentation and a sample log sheet. The National Institute of Justice offers a document titled *Forensic Examination of Digital Evidence: A Guide for Law Enforcement*. Appendix C in that document has a wide variety of sample forms that you can tailor for your needs. The document, with sample forms, is located online at http://www.ojp.usdoj.gov/nij/pubs-sum/199408.htm.

A large percentage of your time will be spent writing reports and completing logs. All the documentation you create might be used at a later time by the courts. When you write the report, remember that it may take years for the case to reach the courts. The more details you include in the report you write now, the easier it will be for you to recall facts about the case when you have to testify in the future.

Interviews and Diagrams

If you interview anyone, create a list of who you interviewed, including their names, e-mail addresses, what they saw, and when, where, and how they saw it. In cases such as the release of malware or denial of service (DoS) attacks, you can sometimes obtain more information than you expect just by asking. You might even end up with a confession.

Using diagrams is another method to document a case. Remember that jurors might not know about the workings of computers and networks, so you may want to use pictures or drawings to get your point across. For example, if you are asked to prove that the data presented has not been altered, you must present documentation proving that you made the image of the original evidence correctly. Let's say that you used MD5 verification to ensure that the procedure did not corrupt the data. In your report, you would explain that when using MD5, even a change to one bit of information on a large drive packed with data results in a new message digest. By comparing the original disks and the copy, you can ensure that an image is an exact replica of the original. By using a drawing like the following one, you can help the jury better understand how this procedure works.

Figure 9.1   How MD5 verification works

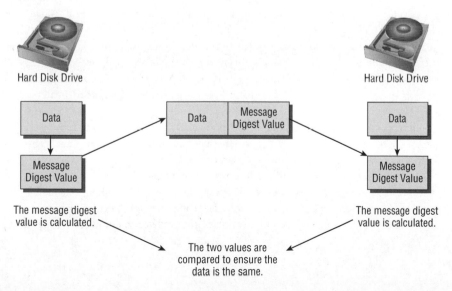

Real World Scenario

Tales from the Trenches: Reports

The ability to write clear and concise reports will greatly benefit the computer forensic investigator.

When I was testifying in a deposition a few years ago, an extremely well-prepared attorney for the opposing side questioned me for hours about the minutest details of the case. I had been called to analyze a hard drive belonging to a publishing company. The drive in question had been used by an editor and was suspected to contain highly inappropriate material prohibited by the company's acceptable use policy. I located many evidence items on the drive and documented each and every one, as well as the procedures I used to process the case.

When it was time to testify, the opposing attorney was very well briefed on the details of the case and on forensic procedures. If I had not properly prepared my report during that investigation, I would have performed poorly while I was being "grilled." I was properly prepared to testify because I reviewed my report before the deposition and because I wrote an extremely detailed report at the time of the investigation. This particular investigation occurred three years and many investigations before I testified, but I was able to easily recall the necessary facts just by reviewing the report.

Keep in mind that the work you do today to prepare a report may very well more than pay for itself many years down the road.

Videotapes and Photographs

If at all possible, videotape the entry of all persons into the crime scene. By taping the actual entrance of a forensic team into the area, you can help refute claims that evidence was planted at the scene. You might also want to take photographs of the actual evidence and take notes at the scene. For example, in the case of an intrusion, you may want to take a photograph of the monitor. However, time is usually of the essence. Consideration should be given to the possibility of destructive processes running in the background or a time-delayed password-protected screen saver.

Pictures of the computer should be taken from all angles to document the system hardware components and how they are connected. Be careful to label each wire so that the original computer configuration can be restored. Remove the case cover of the PC or server, and carefully photograph the interior. Note the serial number, internal drives, and peripheral components. Documentation should include a physical description and detailed notation of any identifying markings or numbers. Make sure you document the configuration of the cables and connection types as well. Next, label the evidence and then once again photograph the evidence after the labels have been attached.

Most forensic investigators use digital cameras instead of 35mm film cameras to take their photographs. However, using digital images is not without risk because they're easy to manipulate and tamper with. Be prepared to defend the authenticity of any digital images gathered as a part of an investigation. Documentation should include the following information:

- The type of digital camera used
- Who took the digital photographs
- Any special training or expertise of the investigator taking the digital photographs
- Documentation showing all procedures used when inputting or outputting the digital images
- Information regarding any software used in retrieving or reproducing the digital image.

Ideally, one person documents while another person handles the evidence. Document everything that goes on. The designated custodian for the chain of custody should initial each item after double-checking the list you have created. It is important to do this at the scene to eliminate the possibility of evidence tainting at a later date. You want to be able to prove that you did not alter any of the evidence after the computer came into your possession. Such proof will refute allegations that you changed or altered the original evidence.

Transporting the Evidence

The computer most likely will be moved to a secure location where a proper chain of custody can be maintained and the processing of evidence can begin. Therefore, the next step in the documentation process is to document the transporting of the evidence to the lab. Photograph or videotape and document the handling of evidence leaving the scene to the transport vehicle. Be careful to guard against *electrostatic discharge (ESD)*. Although ESD won't hurt you, it can certainly kill your computer components. Integrated circuits (such as processors, memory, and expansion cards) are especially sensitive to ESD. During transportation, *electromagnetic fields* created by magnets and radio transmitters can alter or destroy data as well. To ensure the integrity of the data stored on the media, avoid exposing the computer or media to conditions such as moisture, high humidity, and extreme heat or cold. At the examination facility, videotape or photograph and document the handling of evidence from the transportation vehicle to the lab.

Leave original evidence untouched unless extenuating circumstances occur. Do not leave a computer unattended unless it is locked in a secure location. You don't want to risk the destruction of any crucial evidence.

electrostatic discharge (ESD)
Buildup of electrical charge on a surface that is suddenly transferred to another surface when it is touched.

electromagnetic fields
Produced by the local buildup of electric charges in the atmosphere. They can damage computer components. They are present everywhere in our environment but are invisible to the human eye.

Documenting Gathered Evidence

When gathering and preparing evidence, keep in mind that normal computer operations can destroy evidence in memory, in the file slack, or in the swap file. When documenting physical evidence such as hard disks or portable media, put the original evidence in a bag and seal it with tape that can't be unsealed without leaving a mark. Clearly mark the sealed evidence bags with the case information. Tamper-proof evidence bags can be purchased from companies such as SecurityBag.com (the e-commerce division of Packaging Horizons Corporation) at http://evidence bags.info/. Be sure to keep extra plastic bags with ties for storing evidence along with numerous blanks for all incident-handling forms.

The U.S. Department of Justice, Office of Justice Programs at the National Institute of Justice has established a guide for forensic computer and digital evidence examinations. This guide includes lists of the types of items to be documented. It is published as *Forensic Examination of Digital Evidence: A Guide for Law Enforcement* and you can find it at http://www.ncjrs.gov/pdffiles1/nij/199408.pdf. Document all standard procedures and processes used in the examination of the evidence and note in detail any deviations from standard procedures. All recovered data should be properly marked.

Complementary Metal Oxide Semiconductor (CMOS) chip
On-board semiconductor chip used to store system information and configuration settings when the computer is either off or on.

Timelines for computer usage and file accesses offer valuable sources of computer evidence. Computer investigators rely on evidence stored as data and the timeline of dates and times that files were created, modified, or last accessed by a computer user. If the system clock is one hour different from the actual time because of Daylight Saving Time, then file time stamps will also reflect the wrong time. To adjust for such inaccuracies, documenting the system date and time settings at the time the computer is taken into evidence is crucial. The accuracy of the time and date stamps on files depends on the accuracy of the time and date stored in the *CMOS chip* of the computer. It is important to document the accuracy of these settings on the seized computer in order to validate the accuracy of the times and dates associated with any relevant computer files. Compare the current time and date with the date and time stored in the computer. The current time can be obtained from official time sites such as www.greenwichmeantime.com or www.worldtimeserver.com. Normally, the date and time are checked by simply booting into the BIOS and then checking the time and date in the BIOS settings.

File dates and times are important when documenting backdating of computer files. Sometimes criminals purposely change the date and time on their computers. They do this for several reasons; one of the most common is to defeat valid software licensing. Another reason the computer date and time may not be current is because the CMOS battery is dead. When a CMOS battery dies, the computer no longer keeps correct time, causing the computer date and time to be inaccurate. When settings on the computer are inaccurate, times and dates associated with relevant files can sometimes be established by a computer forensic specialist through the painstaking collection of information about time discrepancies on the system, date of occurrence, and so forth. Be prepared to review and confirm date and time information on any files where reported time and actual, correct time differ. Be prepared to respond to challenges to your findings from the opposing side. AFind is one program that is available from Foundstone's Web site (www.foundstone.com, search for AFind). AFind lists the last access time for files without tampering with their data.

Always remember to make a bit stream backup of the hard drive before running the computer or checking the time and date. It's important!

Activity timelines can be especially helpful when multiple computers and individuals are involved in the commission of a crime. A computer forensic investigator should consider timelines of computer usage in all computer-related investigations. The same is true in computer security reviews concerning potential access to sensitive and/or trade secret information stored in the form of computer files. The time and date that files were created can be important in cases involving computer evidence. Forensic software, such as Guidance Software's EnCase, allows you to build a timeline in your casework (Figure 9.2).

Figure 9.2   EnCase timeline options

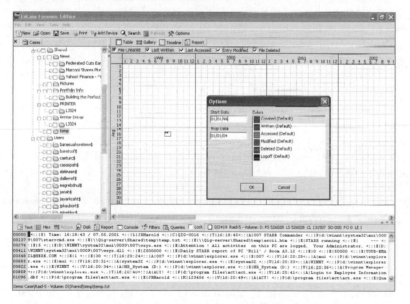

Using forensic software, you can create a case and then enter details such as case description, examiner name, organization, and comments. The next section discusses these in finer detail. When working in a case file, you have the option of logging all your actions, including exact dates and times and screenshots of dialog boxes.

Documenting the process from entering the scene to gathering the evidence is important. You aren't done yet, though. Forensic investigators may need to gather a couple of additional pieces of documentation before the report is actually written.

Additional Documentation

If someone intends to prosecute for damages caused to an organization, all losses the organization suffered as a result of the incident should be documented. Ask the organization for such data as:

◆ Estimated number of hours spent in response and recovery

◆ Cost of damaged equipment

◆ Value of data lost

◆ Amount of credit given to customers because of the inconvenience

◆ Loss of revenue

◆ Value of any trade secret information lost or stolen

Document and Validate Evidence

A basic rule of evidence is that it must be the best available, which means evidence that is primary or first-hand. Computer forensic involves the use of tools and procedures to guarantee accurate preservation of evidence. Most computer forensic specialists use multiple software tools, created by separate and independent developers, to help them preserve evidence accurately. By using different, independently developed tools to validate results, you can avoid inaccuracies owing to software design flaws or bugs. By validating evidence with software tools and procedures, you help eliminate the likelihood of a successful challenge to the integrity of results based on the accuracy of software tools used. By documenting everything, you should be able to refute claims that evidence was mishandled or that the tools used in your investigation were unacceptable.

Hacker Acquitted

Aaron Caffrey, 19, was acquitted after a jury unanimously decided he was not guilty of unauthorized computer access related to an attack on the Port of Houston's web-based systems in September 2001. Caffrey claimed that the evidence against him was planted on his computer by attackers who used an unspecified Trojan horse program to gain control of his PC and launch the assault. A forensic examination of Caffrey's PC found attack tools but no trace of a Trojan infection. The case depended on whether the jury accepted the argument that a Trojan could remove itself or accepted expert testimony from the prosecution that no such technology existed.

Continues

> As a forensic investigator, it's important to document your findings, validate the evidence gathered, and be prepared to present that evidence to a court so that the jury understands the facts and your conclusions regarding those facts. The final outcome of the case may depend on how well you document, gather, and present the evidence. That's why it's so important to be competent, convincing, and—above all else—clear.

Now that you are familiar with all the information you should document, it's time to decide how to put all this information into a report format that a judge and jury can understand easily.

Formulating the Report

Before preparing a report, make sure that your client wants a report prepared. Not every client wants written documentation of an investigation. Federal Rules of Civil Procedures used to require disclosure of all draft reports prepared by expert witnesses along with all communications between attorneys and their expert witnesses. In some jurisdictions, attorneys may still be required to produce copies of draft reports, along with e-mails between the attorney and forensic expert, as a part of the court record. Such documentation could include information that the client does not wish to make public or be generally known. For this reason, some clients avoid reports.

The Federal Rules of Civil Procedure were amended on December 1, 2010. (See the discussion of Rule 26(b)(4)(B) and Rule 26(b)(4)(C) in "Document Everything, Assume Nothing," earlier in this chapter.) Under the new rules, greater protection from disclosure is now provided to draft reports prepared by expert witnesses as well as attorney-expert witness communications. As of the writing of this book, it's too early to fully understand how these new rules will work in the real world for expert forensic witnesses.

As noted in "Tales from the Trenches: Reports," earlier in this chapter, if you do prepare a report, you might have to use it to recall events years after the fact. Therefore, reports should contain focused and specific information. Each forensic investigator has his or her own way to formulate reports, but establishing a standardized template is important. This way, your work will be consistent. The more you use a template, the more proficient you will become. You also want the items you refer to in your report to be consistent so you don't confuse your audience. For example, if you discuss a "hard drive" in your report, be sure that all instances refer to it as just that. Using the terms "hard disk," "hard drive," and "fixed disk" interchangeably in the same report can cause confusion for its readers. It's a good idea to define terms in the report to avoid future confusion. For example, you might define "hard drive" in reports by saying: "We located a 120 GB, Western Digital Hard Drive, s/n 123456–789012 (hereafter referred to as

'Hard Drive')." In fact, including a glossary can help define items listed in your report. Here are some items the report should contain:

- Name of the reporting agency and case investigator
- Case number
- Date of the report
- Numbered pages (e.g., Page 3 of 12)
- List of the items examined
- Description of the examination process
- Results and/or conclusion

A typical report format consists of several independent sections, which include the preceding information. These sections are presented in the following order:

Executive Summary or Summary of Findings   The summary is a brief explanation of the circumstances that required the investigation and a short detail of the significant findings. Include the names of all persons involved in the case and the date.

Objectives   This section states the specific purpose for the investigation—for example, to determine if a subject used a laptop computer as an instrument in the crime of identity theft and/or as a repository of data related to that crime. Include the name of the reporting agency and investigator.

Analysis   This section provides a description of the evidence and the steps taken to process that evidence.

Findings   The findings include specific information listed in order of importance or relevance. This can include data and graphic image analysis, Internet-related evidence, and techniques used to hide data.

Supporting Documentation   This section includes how you arrived at the findings in the previous section. The supporting documentation is usually the longest section of the report. It can also contain the printouts of items of evidence and chain of custody documentation. To authenticate printout pages as a part of the report information, the forensic investigator preparing the report should initial and date each page in the bottom corner.

Glossary   This section can be included to help the reader understand technical terms contained in the report.

Now that you have some idea of the format the report should have, let's look at a few sample reports.

Sample Analysis Reports

In this section, you'll look at some sample analysis reports. Most of them are taken from the various software programs described in Chapter 8. The samples show different sections of the reports. In addition to these reports, you can find two sample reports and case summaries in Appendix A of the *Forensic Examination of Digital Evidence: A Guide for Law Enforcement* document by the National Institute of Justice at www.ncjrs.org/pdffiles1/nij/199408.pdf.

The following sample report starts with a case brief explaining the particulars of the incident.

Sample Report for Copyright Piracy Case

On June 1, 2009, a concerned citizen contacted the police department regarding possible copyright piracy. He explained that he searched the Internet seeking to purchase Acme Accounting accounting and finance software. He purchased that software from a Web site called Knockoff.com that advertised it as "authentic," but he was unable to register the software he purchased.

When the police department contacted Acme Accounting, they were informed that several other buyers also complained they were also unable to register Acme Accounting software purchased from the same Web site. The case arose from a 14-month investigation led by U.S. Immigration and Customs Enforcement working with the Department of Justice Computer Crimes and Intellectual Property Section.

The investigation was conducted by the Bureau of Immigration and Customs Enforcement. After making an undercover purchase of software from the Web site through the Customs Cyber Center, the agents obtained a warrant to search the suspect's residence for computers and materials used in making counterfeit software and other evidence related to the theft charges. The agents submitted a desktop computer to the computer forensic laboratory for analysis.

Now let's move on to the objective of the case. As you follow along, note some of the particulars of the case, such as:

- Computer type
- Operating system
- Offenses committed with the computer
- Case agent
- Where the exam took place
- Tools used

Objective

Determine if the suspect used the desktop computer as an instrument in the crime of copyright infringement and/or as a repository of data related to those crimes.

- ◆ **Computer type**: Compaq Deskpro desktop computer
- ◆ **Operating system**: Microsoft Windows XP
- ◆ **Offenses**: Criminal copyright infringement
- ◆ **Case agent**: Customs Cyber Center investigator, D. Brown
- ◆ **Where examination took place**: Computer Forensic Laboratory
- ◆ **Tools/Software used**: AccessData's Forensic Toolkit (FTK) and Password Recovery Toolkit

Initial Assessment

This section of the report gives an initial assessment of the case. It establishes proper documents were provided, the goals of the examination were set, and that the case was assigned.

1. The initial documentation provided by the investigator was reviewed. This review determined that:

    a. Legal authority was established by a search warrant obtained specifically for the examination of the computer in a laboratory setting.

    b. Chain of custody was properly documented on the appropriate departmental forms.

    c. The request for service and a detailed summary explained the investigation, provided keyword lists, and provided information about the suspect, the counterfeit software, and the Internet web address.

2. The computer forensic investigator met with the case agent and discussed the investigative avenues and potential evidence being sought in the forensic examination.

3. Evidence intake was documented:

    a. The computer was marked and photographed.

    b. A file was created and the case information was entered into the laboratory database.

    c. The computer was properly stored in the laboratory's property room.

4. The case was assigned to a computer forensic investigator.

Disk Imaging

The next section of the report documents the analysis. It explains how the evidence was assessed, how the drive was imaged, and how the data was analyzed.

1. The desktop computer was examined and photographed.

   a. The computer cover was removed and the hardware was examined and documented.

   b. The computer was booted to the BIOS setup screen. The BIOS information was documented, and the system time was compared to a trusted time source and documented. The boot sequence was checked and documented. (Figure 9.3 shows an example of the BIOS setup screen.)

Figure 9.3   BIOS setup screen showing system time

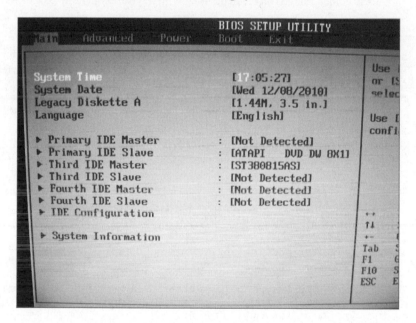

   c. The desktop computer was powered off without making any changes to the BIOS.

2. Access Data's FTK Imager was used to create an evidence file containing the image of the desktop computer's hard drive.

   a. The hard drive was removed from the suspect computer.

   b. A hardware write blocker, Intelligent Computer Solutions' Super DriveLock (http://www.ics-iq.com/), was connected to the forensic computer.

    c. The hard drive which was removed from the suspect computer was then plugged into Super DriveLock.

    d. Access Data's FTK Imager was used to make a forensic dd image of the suspect hard drive.

    e. A MD5 hash was created of both the suspect hard drive and the dd image and the results compared to validate that the dd image was an exact duplicate of the original hard drive. (The validated dd image is sometimes referred to as the "golden" image.)

3. After the dd or "golden" image was validated, steps were taken to preserve and safeguard this image and return the original suspect computer.

    a. The hard drive was returned to the suspect computer, and then returned to the proper legal authorities. (As a forensic investigator, you'll keep the golden image you created, along with any subsequent images to conduct your investigation. You'll return the original suspect computer to legal authorities.)

    b. The golden image was replicated, and the new image was validated by doing an MD5 hash and comparing the results to ensure it was an exact duplicate.

    c. The golden image was then returned to the forensic laboratory safe and locked up.

4. Now there were two copies of the original suspect hard drive—the golden image, which was locked up in the safe, and the second authenticated image, which became the working copy. Now, the investigators were ready to begin the analysis of the image.

Analysis

This section of the report describes the evidence and the steps taken to process the evidence.

1. A laboratory computer was prepared by the investigator using licensed copies of Windows XP, AccessData's FTK version 1.43, and WinHex version 10.45 SR-2.

2. The FTK evidence files from the desktop computer were copied to the laboratory computer's hard drive.

3. A new FTK case file was opened, and the suspect computer's evidence files were examined using FTK.

    a. Deleted files were recovered by FTK.

    b. File data, including filenames, dates and times, physical and logical size, and complete path, were recorded.

    c. Keyword text searches were conducted based on information provided by the investigator. All hits were reviewed.

    d. Graphics files were opened and viewed.

    e. HTML files were opened and viewed.

    f. Data files were opened and viewed; four password-protected and encrypted files were located.

    g. Unallocated space and slack space were searched.

    h. Files of interest were copied from the FTK evidence file to a compact disk.

4. Unallocated clusters were copied from the FTK evidence file to a clean hard drive, which had been wiped to U.S. National Institutes of Science and Technology (NIST) Special Publication 800-88: Guidelines for Media Sanitization, which can be found at http://csrc.nist.gov/publications/nistpubs/800-88/NISTSP800-88_rev1.pdf.

5. FTK was then used to carve images from unallocated space.

6. The carved images were extracted from FTK, opened, and viewed.

7. WinHex was used to verify the results obtained. A total of 3,592 images were extracted.

8. AccessData's Password Recovery Toolkit works directly with FTK. (The FTK notifies you that files are encrypted.) The encrypted files were imported into the Password Recovery Toolkit from the FTK, and passwords were recovered for the password-protected files.

9. Once the passwords were cracked, the files were imported back into the FTK and reprocessed.

10. The files were opened using the passwords and viewed.

Findings

This section summarizes the findings that are valuable to the investigation.

The analysis of the desktop computer recovered 265 files of evidentiary value or investigative interest. The recovered files included:

1. Ninety document files including documents containing the suspect's name and personal information. Text in the files included names of customers who had purchased the software, their methods of payment, and shipping information. In addition, text that described the counterfeit software and pricing structure was found.

2. Fifty-seven graphics files, including high-resolution image files of software labels and packaging materials, certificates of authenticity, registration cards, and copies of checks made out to Knockoff. Most graphics were scanned.

3. Eighty-three HTML files, including Hotmail and Yahoo e-mail inquiries about the software and e-mails between the suspect and customers (including the concerned citizen who reported his inability to register the software he had purchased).

4. Thirty-one graphics files carved from unallocated space depicting copies of checks.

5. Four password-protected and encrypted files.

    a. Microsoft Word 2000 document containing a list of personal information about several individuals including names, addresses, dates of birth, credit card numbers and expiration dates, and other information. Password: [gotya].

    b. Microsoft Word 2000 document containing information on how to crack the license for the Acme software products. Password: [crack].

    c. Microsoft Excel spreadsheet containing the dates and dollar amounts of payments made through PayPal and eBay. Password: [money].

    d. Microsoft Excel spreadsheet containing a list of various software products and their licensing key numbers. Password: [moremoney].

Supporting Documentation

This section contains the most detailed information. It describes how investigators arrived at the conclusions in the findings sections. It includes documents and tables that outline all the steps taken to meet the investigation's objective. The section begins with details about the media analyzed and then moves on to subsections showing string searches and log file analysis.

Figure 9.4 is the file overview. It summarizes the number of items included in the case.

Figure 9.5 is a sampling of the evidence list. These are some of the items that should be included in the supporting documentation part of the report.

As you can see from this sample report, the sections outlined are the starting point for your reports. From here the forensic investigator must formulate a report that is understandable to a judge and jury.

Additional Report Subsections

Often, forensic reports include additional subsections, especially if a case is extensive or contains data from many devices and computers. If a report becomes too long, include a table of contents so that everything stays organized in logical fashion. The audience can scan it and get a better idea of the purpose of the report.

Some additional subsections might include:

◆ If you are investigating an intrusion, include a methodology section on attacks to help the audience understand how attacks are conducted or how the particular attack in the case took place.

Figure 9.4   File overview showing number of items in case

Aug 6, 2004
Evidence Items
Evidence Items: 4

File Items
Total File Items: 5002
Flagged Thumbnails: 0
Other Thumbnails: 2025/

File Status
KFF Alert Files: 0
Bookmarked Items: 1645
Bad Extension: 394
Encrypted Files: 0
From E-mail: 13
Deleted Files: 0
From Recycle Bin: 0
Duplicate Items: 880
OLE Subitems: 277
Flagged Ignore: 0
KFF Ignorable: 180

File Category
Documents: 679
Spreadsheets: 0
Databases: 0
Graphics: 2025
E-mail Messages: 13
Executables: 198
Archives: 26
Folders: 0
Slack/Free Space: 0
Other Known Type: 150
Unknown Type: 1924

◆ If the case involves an employee illegally accessing confidential information on a vendor Web site, a section on Internet activity could be added to show the browsing history and Internet activity of the employee. This section could also be used to show the download of malicious tools or evidence erase programs.

◆ When an employee illegally accesses confidential information on a vendor Web site, a user applications section is usually included. The applications section should include a list of all installed applications such as "hacker tools" or malicious software and a description of what they do.

◆ Sometimes a final summary and/or conclusion may be included with a report.

Figure 9.5　Sampling evidence list

Aug 6, 2006
Display Name: Cookies
Evidence File Name: Cookies
Evidence Path: C:\Documents and Settings\Diane Barrett
Identification Name/Number:
Evidence Type: Contents of a folder
Added: 8/6/2004 12:53:47 PM
Children: 17
Descendants: 17
Investigator's Name: D. Barrett
Comment:

Display Name: Documents and Settings
Evidence File Name: Documents and Settings
Evidence path: C:
Identification Name/Number:
Evidence Type: Contents of a folder
Added: 8/6/2004 1:01:46 PM
Children:
Descendants: 4659
Investigator's Name: D. Barrett
Comment:

Display Name: Favorites
Evidence File Name: Favorites
Evidence path: C:\Documents and Settings\Diane Barrett
Identification Name/Number:
Evidence Type: Contents of a folder
Added: 8/6/2004 12:53:52 PM
Children: 3
Descendants: 7
Investigator's Name: D. Barrett
Comment:

Display Name: Temp
Evidence File Name: Temp
Evidence path: C:\Windows
Identification Name/Number:
Evidence Type: Contents of a folder
Added: 8/6/2004 12:53:50 PM
Children: 2
Descendants: 17
Investigator's Name: D. Barrett
Comment:

In the copyright piracy case described in the previous section, "Sample Report for Copyright Piracy Case," the final summary and conclusion might look like the following.

Summary

Based on the information revealed by the computer analysis, several new avenues of investigation were opened. By contacting the victims listed in the password-protected Microsoft Word document, investigators learned that the victims all purchased software from the suspect through either his Web site or his direct mail. The Hotmail and Yahoo e-mail messages found on the suspect's computer provided information on additional victims. The password-protected Microsoft Excel spreadsheet containing the dates and dollar amounts of payments made through PayPal and eBay documented that the suspect had sold 2,578 illegal copies of Acme software with a retail value of $750,250.00.

NOTE

In the case we just examined, the suspect eventually pled guilty and was sentenced to 5 years in prison. Since the report is prepared before the case goes to trial, obviously information on the final disposition of the case would not be included in the report.

Follow-Up Reports

Information regarding the disposition of the case can be included in follow-up reports. Forensic investigators usually issue an Initial Report documenting findings. Supplemental Reports may also be issued as new evidence is discovered and documented.

Recommendations

Instead of a summary or conclusion, you might add a Recommendations section to your report. This can be especially helpful if the case probably won't end up in court—for example, when the company doesn't want to prosecute and just wants to know how to reduce its risk in the future.

Glossaries and Appendixes

Use a glossary to define technical terms that the average person might not understand. You might also want to include an appendix for detailed information that would interrupt the flow if it were included in the report proper. When investigating accounting fraud, you will frequently come across large spreadsheets. These sheets are hard to print in a format that is easily viewable. In instances such as this, you will want to attach an electronic appendix.

Using Software to Generate Reports

Nearly all commercial forensic software produces a report for the beginning of your documentation. Let's look at a sample report from Paraben's Case Agent Companion. To save space, most of the bookmarks have been deleted, but this will give you a general idea of what a generated report looks like.

Case #234—Acme Accounting Copyright Piracy Summary

Header

    Agent: Customs Cyber Center

    Examiner: D. Brown

Notes

    Subject: Software Evidence

    Body: The bookmarked files are part of a program that is used to generate software labels.

    Author: D. Brown

    Created: Fri Sep 10 13:42:28 GMT-07:00 2004

    Modified: Sat Sep 11 06:16:35 GMT-07:00 2004

Analysis Logs

1. A laboratory computer was prepared by the investigator using licensed copies of Windows 2000 Professional, AccessData's FTK version 1.43, and WinHex version 10.45 SR-2.

2. The FTK evidence files from the desktop computer were copied to the laboratory computer's hard drive.

3. A new FTK case file was opened, and the suspect computer's evidence files were examined using FTK.

    a. Deleted files were recovered by FTK.

    b. File data, including filenames, dates and times, physical and logical size, and complete path, were recorded.

    c. Keyword text searches were conducted based on information provided by the investigator. All hits were reviewed.

    d. Graphics files were opened and viewed.

    e. HTML files were opened and viewed.

    f. Data files were opened and viewed; four password-protected and encrypted files were located.

Continues

    g. Unallocated space and slack space were searched.

    h. Files of interest were copied from the FTK evidence file to a compact disk.

4. Unallocated clusters were copied from the FTK evidence file to a clean hard drive, which had been wiped to U.S. Department of Defense recommendations (DoD 5200.28-STD). FTK was then used to carve images from unallocated space. The carved images were extracted from FTK, opened, and viewed, and subsequently verified using WinHex. A total of 3,592 images were extracted.

5. AccessData's Password Recovery Toolkit was run on the files, and passwords were recovered for the password-protected files. The files were opened using the passwords and then viewed.

Bookmarks

Images Excluded

Contraband Images Included

Full Text Excluded

nero.exe

Description:

Name = nero.exe

Path = C:\Program Files\Ahead\Nero

Created = Sun Dec 16 13:40:06 GMT-07:00 2001

Modified = Wed Feb 20 10:53:58 GMT-07:00 2002

Last Accessed = Sun Apr. 11 13:40:06 GMT-07:00 2004

Size Actual = 18421

Size Allocated = 18421

PFS Type = 10000709

MD5 Hash = fc3031a83d9d82add6b9ab5df15a0d338

Cluster Map = []

Incident Counter = 0

Deleted = false

Encrypted = false

FOCH Hit = false

Volume = Volume0

System = Windows 2000

Continues

Author: D. Brown

Created: Fri Sep 10 13:49:23 GMT-07:00 2004

Modified: Fri Sep 10 13:49:23 GMT-07:00 2004

NeroCmd.exe

Description:

Name = NeroCmd.exe

Path = C:\Program Files\Ahead\Nero

Created = Sun Dec 16 13:40:06 GMT-07:00 2001

Modified = Wed Feb 20 10:53:58 GMT-07:00 2002

Last Accessed = Sun Apr. 11 13:40:06 GMT-07:00 2004

Size Actual = 71266

Size Allocated = 71266

PFS Type = 10000708

MD5 Hash = fe45230445a0b16fb0c3b483b21aa0c5

Cluster Map = []

Incident Counter = 0

Deleted = false

Encrypted = false

FOCH Hit = false

Volume = Volume0

System = Windows 2000

Author: D. Brown

Created: Fri Sep 10 13:49:23 GMT-07:00 2004

Summary

The analysis of the desktop computer recovered 265 files of evidentiary value or investigative interest. The recovered files included: 90 document files including documents containing the suspect's name and personal information; text in the files included names of customer who had purchased the software, their methods of payment, and shipping information. Text describing the counterfeit software and pricing structure was also found. Fifty-seven graphics files, including high-resolution image files of software labels and packaging materials, certificates of authenticity, registration cards, and copies of checks made out to Knockoff.

Continues

Most graphic files were scanned, including:

◆ Eighty-three HTML files including Hotmail and Yahoo e-mail inquiries about the software including e-mails between the suspect and customers (including the concerned citizen who reported his inability to register the software he had purchased).

◆ Thirty-one graphics files carved from unallocated space depicting copies of checks.

◆ Four password-protected and encrypted files.

The software allows you to add or remove sections and sort them to suit your needs, as shown in Figure 9.6.

Figure 9.6   Customizing a report in Paraben's Case Agent Companion

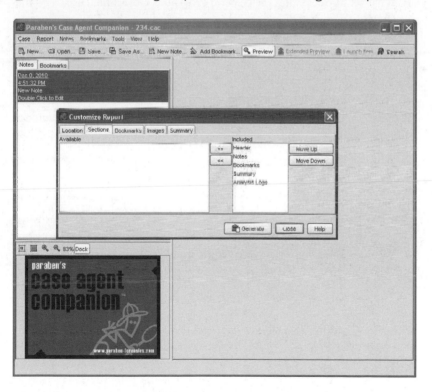

Whether you choose to use a reporting method similar to one demonstrated here, or create your own, your report should document facts so that they may be easily understood. The goals of the report are to accurately recount the details of the case in an understandable format while including all required information to explain your findings and withstand legal examination.

Terms to Know

Complementary Metal Oxide Semiconductor (CMOS) chip

electromagnetic fields

electrostatic discharge (ESD)

Federal Rule of Civil Procedure 26

Review Questions

1. What set of rules states the General Provisions Governing Discovery and Duty of Disclosure?

2. What are some of the items of information that a forensic examiner might be asked to provide under Federal Rule of Civil Procedure 30(b)(6)?

3. Why is a template recommended for reports?

4. Where can you find out how to properly document and sample log sheets?

5. When should you consider using diagrams as a method of documentation?

6. Why should you videotape the entry of all persons into the crime scene?

7. Why is it important to be cautious when you are transporting evidence from the crime scene to the lab for analysis?

8. When formulating a concise report, what are some items you should consider?

9. Why are timelines of computer usage and file accesses important when processing computer evidence?

10. What are some items that your report should contain?

Chapter 10

How to Testify in Court

As a computer forensic professional, you collect evidence for the sole purpose of discovering the truth. Once you do collect evidence, you must be prepared to present it to someone to convince them of its truth and veracity. Some evidence you collect may be destined only to grace the pages of a summary report to your boss. At other times, you may be asked to testify in court. This chapter covers the basics of how to present yourself and your evidence in a court of law.

All the material covered in this chapter also applies to more informal proceedings, but your ability to present basic evidence matters most in court. Our goal is not to provide legal advice. You can research the specific laws that govern your actions as a witness. This chapter covers only the most important things you need to know to be an effective witness in a courtroom.

Preparation Is Everything

The best way to be a successful witness is to be well-prepared. You probably won't be successful if you arrive at the last minute and attempt to answer questions off the top of your head. This would likely make you appear both unprepared and unprofessional. Never allow yourself to be unprepared when presenting your evidence.

In all things, act in an impeccably ethical manner. Never sacrifice your personal or professional ethics by participating in questionable actions. Remember that all actions and statements must adhere to strict ethical standards.

expert witness
A person called to testify in a court of law who possesses special knowledge or skill in some specific area that applies to a case.

In many cases, your role in a trial will be as an *expert witness*. To be considered an expert witness, you need to acquire or demonstrate special knowledge of computers and computer evidence and skill at retrieving evidence from computers. Achieving the status of expert comes through education and experience. You become an expert witness when you appear in court for the purpose of presenting evidence or opinion. Most witnesses are allowed to testify only to facts they have perceived first-hand. That is, a regular witness can tell only what she has seen, heard, touched, felt, and smelled. After you are accepted as an expert in your field, however, your status as an expert witness allows you to provide an opinion about the evidence as well.

Take note: You will be required to justify your status as an expert in your field. You will have to produce documented qualifications, including education and practical experience from valid sources. This information will be provided to both parties. In other words, opposing counsel will receive a copy of your credentials and justification as an expert witness. Generally speaking, a résumé is not enough. You also need to provide additional information, such as:

- Education received and degrees earned
- Professional training received
- Certifications held
- Experience details
- Other times you testified as an expert

summons
A court order that compels a witness to appear in court and answer questions.

You are generally requested to appear in court either by receiving a *summons* or by a client request. In either case, your testimony should be completely unbiased and independent. The weight of your testimony depends on your credibility. When you receive a summons, make sure you are prepared before you appear in court.

Most attorneys recognize that an expert in a particular field is not necessarily expert in presentation skills as well. For those who appear in court, however, an ability to convey and explain information is nearly as important as possessing such information. If you are uncomfortable speaking in front of audiences, spend some time with a member of your legal team working on your delivery skills. Take the time necessary to ensure you are effective at getting your message across.

Expert Witness Training and Practice

Numerous trial support companies do business all over the United States (and elsewhere, to be sure). If you have never testified in court, or haven't seen the inside of a courtroom lately, you can—and probably should—request your legal team to send you to an expert witness school or to a jury and courtroom consultant. These firms or individuals provide one-on-one training and coaching, along with practice at giving testimony and being cross-examined in a mock trial situation. One of your authors attended such a school at Bloom Strategic Consulting in Dallas, TX, and found the experience not just educational and helpful, but invaluable in preparing him to testify effectively in court.

The legal team and all expert witnesses must spend time preparing for a case. Attorneys usually want to meet with witnesses early in the process. Expert witnesses are sought only when they are needed to explain evidence or strengthen its impact. As an expert, you will be asked to provide information on your experience in one or more areas of expertise. You will need to recite information about other times you have testified. Be prepared to field the following questions:

- What is your educational background, including degrees earned?
- What experience do you have in the area in which you are an expert?
- How are you qualified as an expert in this area?
- Are you aware of any conflicts of interest you might have with respect to this case?
- Have you ever testified in court?
- If so, were you called as an expert witness?

In most cases, initial contact and an interview take place before a formal agreement to testify is put in place. The initial conversation becomes billable time only if you are ultimately hired. If you want to work as an expert witness, collect as much background information as possible before the initial interview so you won't waste uncompensated time during initial conversations.

After you are hired as an expert witness, the legal team should question you thoroughly to uncover any issues that could hurt their case. Such issues could include past complaints or claims filed against you, conflict of interest issues, or involvement in activities that reduce your objectivity. During the initial conversations and interview, you'll be asked to state that you are not aware of any conflicts of interest, or perceived conflicts of interest, that could arise during the trial that warrant the attention of opposing counsel.

Conflict of Interest

We've all heard the rules of radio giveaways: "Employees of Mega Radio Corporation and their families are not eligible to win this contest." Avoiding a conflict of interest is the reason for this restriction. If Mega Radio Corporation gave prizes to its employees and their families, eyebrows would be raised. It might look as if the advertisers' money were being spent on employee bonuses. As a result, listeners might lose interest and start tuning into other radio stations that give them a better chance to win prizes. Fewer listeners mean advertisers get less return on their advertising investments. Such situations result from allowing the interests of one party (the employees' desire for bonuses) to conflict with the interests of another party (the advertisers' desire to entice more listeners by using contests). When you find yourself in a situation in which you have incentive to make a decision in a particular direction, a conflict of interest probably exists. Such situations are best avoided whenever possible.

deposition
Testimony that is reduced to written form. (Video recorded depositions are also transcribed and reduced to written form, and both the written transcription as well as the video recording of the testimony may be admitted in court.)

Your first opportunity to share your knowledge may occur before the trial. A common pretrial activity involves taking *depositions* from witnesses. Depositions are conducted under oath and the testimony you give is admissible in court. A court reporter will take down and transcribe every word you say while you are "on the record." In addition, your deposition may also be videotaped.

During a deposition, you are asked questions that pertain to your area of expertise and aspects of the case by counsel for both sides. You can exert a material impact on the case at this point. If you provide strong testimony and speak with authority, you may influence opposing counsel to explore a settlement without going to trial. On the other hand, weak and unsure testimony might encourage the other side to pursue a trial.

If your deposition is videotaped, it's important to recognize that the camera is your audience. The temptation is to ignore the camera and concentrate on your questioner. If you do this, and your video testimony is shown in the courtroom, you will appear to be looking away from the audience. This is commonly perceived as insincere, arrogant, or untruthful to audiences who are used to seeing people on-camera looking straight ahead at the camera lens at all times.

It's important to remember that you're also talking to people who will be watching the video, possibly in a court room, not to the attorneys and the court reporter in the deposition room with you as you testify. Even if you look at the attorney who's questioning you while he or she is talking, remember to look straight at the camera as you give your answers.

NOTE — The section titled "What Matters Is What They Hear," later in this chapter, discusses techniques to get your point across.

When a case goes to court, you will participate in two basic phases of the trial—direct examination and cross examination. *Direct examination* is where attorneys ask questions that allow a witness to provide testimony. Your legal team should provide you with a list of the direct examination questions they plan to use. Opposing counsel then has an opportunity to question you. Their line of questioning is called *cross examination*. The purpose of cross examination is generally to weaken your testimony. The best approach to handling cross examination is to be fully prepared with answers to likely questions.

direct examination
Initial questions asked to a witness to extract testimony.

cross examination
Questions asked by opposing counsel to cast doubt on testimony provided during direct examination.

Understand the Case

As early as possible before a court appearance, meet with your legal team to discuss the case. The goal of such a meeting is to understand the basic facts of the case. Although you may have been integral in the evidence collection effort, you may not know about other critical aspects of the case. Becoming an expert in every detail of the case is unnecessary, but understanding the case as a whole will help you testify for your own piece of it. Such knowledge also keeps your testimony from conflicting with other witnesses' testimony. (We'll return to this topic in the section titled "Say Only What You Must" later in this chapter.)

Many attorneys who work with technical cases understand their intricacies and want the whole team to be well informed. If you work with an attorney who seems to guard case information, think long and hard before agreeing to participate. If you do proceed with only limited awareness for a case, you may be surprised—even blindsided—by some of the questions you will be asked when it is your turn in court.

Another reason to understand the case is that you may not be the only expert witness. Other expert witnesses may be called on both sides. You need to understand the likely testimony of each expert before you prepare your own testimony. This knowledge will not change any of the facts in the case, but it will help you determine the scope of your own testimony. For example, if you know your own counsel will use a database expert, you can focus on other areas. Likewise, knowing that the opposing counsel has hired an expert to counter your testimony will direct your preparation. You should talk with your counsel to understand likely questions, or at least a general direction, that you may face during cross examination.

Understand the Strategy

After you have a grasp of the general facts of the case, talk with the legal team about their strategy for arguing the case. They may want to emphasize technical details. Or, they may want to simply touch on the technical evidence and focus more on other aspects. Your involvement depends strongly on the strategy the legal team chooses.

These techniques apply to presentations outside the courtroom as well. If your investigation is part of an incident response effort, the equivalent of a courtroom appearance might be a presentation to clients about the incident. The rules and environment might be different, but the general goals are the same. Your goal is to present evidence and provide an expert opinion as to what it means.

Remember the part you play in the courtroom. You are a witness; the attorneys are the primary players. They direct the action and call you when it's time for you to contribute to the case. You were hired to play a specific role—namely, that of expert witness. Let's talk some more about what that supporting role really involves.

Understand Your Job

The primary purpose of a trial is to provide a forum for an impartial individual or group of individuals to decide which party prevails in a conflict. In some cases, the facts of the case are plain enough for an ordinary individual to understand them. For example, in cases that involve traffic accidents, most people are familiar with traffic laws and the operation of an automobile. Unless unusual circumstances prevail, many attorneys will present the facts directly to a judge or jury.

Cases with important technical aspects tend to be different. They commonly involve details that most people do not understand. A case that involves ballistics and traditional forensic evidence normally requires an expert to present and explain that evidence. We've all seen televised court proceedings with the expert on the stand testifying as to forensic methods employed. Those experts are essential when it comes to explaining the intricacies of such evidence to a judge or jury.

Your job is often harder, though. Few ordinary citizens will profess to understand how ballistics or DNA analysis work. Although they may be familiar with those terms, most will agree that an expert is required to perform the actual analysis. Computers are different. Nearly everyone has a home computer. What's worse, many home computer owners think they are computer security experts. Your first job is often to explain basic security concepts and how popular concepts may differ from reality.

For example, most people know what spam is, in terms of computer activities. Few know how it originates and why it is so difficult to stop. Similarly, most members of the general public do not truly understand malicious code, also known as malware. For example, very few people understand the differences between a virus, a Trojan horse, and a worm.

As an expert in the field of computers and computer forensics, you possess a level of knowledge that goes well beyond the common understanding of such things in our society. Your value to a case is to share your experience and explain how the evidence proves facts in the case. You are a teacher as well as a witness. Simply put, the legal team would not be able to convince the court that the facts presented are true and relevant without your help.

Appearance Matters

Although we often hear that we shouldn't judge a book by its cover, everyone does so anyway, and that includes judges and juries. Your appearance strongly influences your credibility in the courtroom. As unfair as this may seem, you really do need to attend carefully to what you wear and how you carry yourself. Your knowledge and the weight of your testimony will mean little if you do not appear credible and believable. Let's look at a few aspects of your courtroom appearance.

Clothing

First and foremost, dress appropriately. Wear clothes that you would wear to a conservative office. If you are a man, you should wear a suit. Darker colors (such as blue, black, and dark green) tend to exude confidence and authority. Ties should be conservative and shirts tucked in. Do not wear a hat to court. Although you may make a fashion statement with more vibrant colors, conservative colors create an aura of credibility. If you are a woman, a business suit or dress will give the court the impression that you should be taken seriously. Women should wear a brassiere, hose or dress socks, and closed-toed shoes. Avoid wearing high-heeled shoes. Both men and women should remove outerwear or overcoats before testifying.

Even though you may work wearing jeans and a T-shirt, you should never wear them to court. The way you dress gives the judge and jury an impression of how trustworthy you are. When you walk into a courtroom, you will be judged by what clothes you wear. Remember, we're not talking about fairness here—we're talking about making the most of your courtroom appearance. No matter how you dress the rest of the time, always dress to impress the court. It will serve you well.

When choosing clothing for a court appearance, don't overdo it. Women should keep jewelry to a minimum, and wear only tasteful items. Men should avoid jewelry. All in all, dress conservatively and soberly. Many courts, particularly federal courts, have rules regarding acceptable attire within the courtroom. It's always a good idea to ask your legal team if there are any rules regarding appearance that you need to be aware of before you go to court.

Grooming

Grooming is as important as clothing. Your clothes should be pressed and clean. Your physical appearance should match your crisp, clean clothes. Don't show up to court looking disheveled. You are going to testify that you seized evidence, or accepted seized evidence, and handled it in a responsible manner. Responsible people comb their hair. If you are disheveled, you will have a difficult time convincing a jury that you are responsible.

Men, a 5-o'clock shadow gives the impression that you are sloppy. It doesn't matter if you rarely shave before going to the lab; in court, you must impress a judge and jury. Your job is to present yourself as credible and responsible. The way you present yourself says a lot about your ability to be responsible. Women, use neutral colors in your make-up and avoid flamboyant (sorry, no green or pink or purple hair colors) hairstyles. Do not bring a purse or handbag to the witness stand.

Attitude

When you take the stand, remember that the judge and jury are watching and listening to you. Getting them on your side is imperative. A poor attitude can hurt your testimony. It can actually turn a jury against you. When you alienate people, you make it very difficult for them to believe in you and your testimony.

body language
Communication using body movements, gestures, and facial expressions.

While you testify, remain aware of your attitude. A jury will read your emotions and your *body language*. They will watch you to decide if you are sincere. Look at the judge and jury as you speak. Ignoring the jury may appear as if you are being untruthful. Watch your body language as well. When you cross your arms, you become "closed off" and unapproachable. This action gives many people a feeling of inferiority, which is not the best way to convince a jury.

Avoid being sarcastic or overly confident. Such attitudes tend to alienate jurors. You must strive to be sincere, but not overly confident. Avoid swear words, common slang and common and colloquial phrases such as:

◆ Um

◆ You know

◆ Sure

◆ Wow

As you deliver your testimony, be willing to help the judge and jury understand what you are saying. You are as much a teacher as a witness. Avoid being rude or condescending; instead, be as helpful and respectful as possible. Remember that you are an expert who is trying to present evidence in layman's terms to make it understandable. Let's look at how you can get your message across to make the evidence understandable.

What Matters Is What They Hear

You could have the most eloquent delivery ever presented in a courtroom, but if the jury does not hear what you have to say, it's all wasted effort. Although you may present a topic using sophisticated presentation aids, actual success depends on the recipient. Your responsibility is to ensure that the target of your presentation "gets it." Far too many presenters focus on the presentation and not enough on the perception or reception of that presentation.

Take the time to really sell your presentation. Whether you are teaching a jury how a disk drive works, or responding to cross-examination, get your message across.

Communication involves three critical components:

◆ Sender

◆ Message

◆ Receiver

The sender is the party who prepares and sends the message. The sender is responsible for all aspects of the actual message. The sender chooses message content, tone, style, delivery medium, and recipient. It's the responsibility of the sender to ensure that the receiver understands the message.

The message is the actual content that you are sending. The sender creates and sends the message to the receiver via the chosen media. The message itself consists of the body of the message, along with the "tone" of the message. The tone of a message can be influenced by choice of vocabulary, punctuation, and structure. For example, these two text messages are identical except for their tone:

1. Please come to my office.

2. PLEASE COME TO MY OFFICE!!!

Clearly, the second message creates more anticipation (and dread). You can create the same distinction using your vocal tone. You can add emphasis to certain words or phrases to make them stand out. Don't overdo it, though—you must remain believable and credible. If you rely on theatrics to make your points, you will lose credibility in the long run.

Listening

Listening is an important and often overlooked skill. Use your listening ability to take in as much as you can in the courtroom. The judge's statements and actions can tell you a lot about how you should act. It may change daily, too. Judges and juries are regular people who have bad days just like we all do.

Listening allows you to "test the waters" without making a mistake by charging ahead in the wrong direction. Both legal teams can direct you through the questions they ask. As a rule of thumb, go in the direction your own legal counsel leads you. If opposing counsel leads you in some particular direction, pay close attention to what's going on. They could be trying to trip you up.

Listening always helps you to be more prepared when you do take the stand. To communicate well, use your ears more often than your mouth.

Tone

Because you are an expert, you will be perceived to have superior knowledge in one or more specific areas that pertain to the case. Many people are intimidated by people with superior knowledge or experience. Always avoid using tones in your voice that can be interpreted by others as being haughty. You cannot gain respect through intimidation; rather, you risk losing respect if you use a tone that infers superiority, condescension, impatience, or hostility.

Try to switch into "teacher mode." Take the time to explain topics that are not clear to one or more people in the courtroom. A good teacher evaluates where students are and approaches them to move them toward understanding. An expert witness cannot interact directly with jurors in the same manner a teacher does, but you can still be respectful and try to convey the essence of your message. Any time you talk "down" to a judge or jury you risk creating feelings of resentment. Jurors who resent you may not be very favorable to you during deliberations.

It looks like mom and dad were right when they said, "It's not what you say, it's how you say it that counts." Make sure the jury has an opportunity to perceive you as pleasant. It will matter.

Vocabulary

As previously discussed, the job of the expert witness is to explain complex topics or procedures to laypeople. You must use words and phrases that explain and do not confuse judges and juries. Avoid using too many industry-specific terms and acronyms. For instance, talking about the "TCP and UDP packets traveling between the server and the client" will likely confuse most people. To make good use of such language, you will first have to explain:

◆ How information travels across networks

◆ How networks split messages into smaller chunks, called packets

◆ What a server is and what is does

◆ What a client is and what it does

◆ Networking protocols (basic introduction)

◆ TCP and UDP protocols

That might look like a lot of explaining to do just to address a fairly simple concept. But that's your job as an expert witness, so do your best to revel in this work. Make the complex seem simple and be careful which words you choose. The more successfully you use common, everyday language in your explanations, the more effective your presentation will be.

Words Matter

If you tell the truth you don't have to remember anything.

— *Mark Twain*

Although it should go without saying, always tell the truth. Present the facts and offer your professional non-biased opinion. The facts tell a story and your job as an expert witness is to tell that story to the jury in a manner that enables them to easily understand the story the evidence tells. The facts speak to the truth of the evidence, so always speak the truth.

Know Your Forensic Process and Tools

You are a computer forensic examiner. If you are called as an expert witness, you will be asked to explain your process for collecting evidence. Many jurors will find this process interesting, but will perceive it as tedious as well. Most people are unfamiliar with the processes necessary to acquire and store digital evidence in a way that preserves the state of the evidence. You will have to educate them.

You must know your own process and your toolset like the back of your hand. It is imperative that you know, and can clearly explain, the steps you take and the tools you use in an investigation. You will be asked to explain each of your steps as you collected and analyzed evidence. If you need to use notes in your testimony, get permission from the judge first. He or she will usually ensure that your notes have already been admitted into evidence and then allow you to look at them to assist in the accuracy of your testimony. Don't just read your notes to the court — your credibility will suffer if you appear to lean too much on your notes.

The opposing counsel will certainly hammer you if you are unsure about your own practices. Don't provide them that opportunity!

Best Practices

A good place to start in explaining your own forensic process is by referencing industry best practices. A wealth of information that outlines best practices in most security areas is available online. There are several very good Web sites that discuss current computer forensic best practices. Look at several of these Web sites to make sure your processes and tools are consistent with current best practices:

◆ SANS Reading Room http://www.sans.org/reading_room/

◆ United States Secret Service (download) http://www.forwardedge2.com/pdf/bestPractices.pdf

- ◆ **CERT Coordination Center** (mostly related to incident response) http://www.cert.org/tech_tips/win-UNIX-system_compromise.html
- ◆ **Scientific Working Group on Digital Evidence** (downloads; search for "Best Practices") http://www.swgde.org/documents/current-documents/

Many more useful Web sites are available for additional best practices information. Take some time to explore as many of them as you can. They will help your investigation practices, as well as your acceptability as an expert in court.

Your Process and Documentation

The primary source of information for the testimony explaining your forensic process is your evidence documentation. You should have an activity log that shows every action taken with respect to evidence during your investigation. That activity log should commence with evidence acquisition and be current up through the present day.

Complete documentation gives a jury the impression that you have been careful. Although it is possible to win a case without appropriate documentation, it makes your job far more difficult. Make sure you are meticulous in documenting the investigation process. You will need those logs if you are called to appear in court. Organized, written information gives judges and juries the impression that you are responsible and meticulous.

Your Forensic Toolkit

Be prepared to explain the contents of your forensic toolkit. Include all hardware and software you use during an investigation. For each component, explain why you it's in your toolkit, what function it performs, and how you used it for the current investigation. Corroborating third-party information may be helpful.

For instance, your forensic software tools vendor might maintain information on the reliability of its product. Many commercial products provide online resources that make the use of their product more acceptable to a court of law. Showing how your product maintains the chain of evidence gives some jurors the answers they are seeking.

Know exactly what tools you have and which ones you use. Be ready to justify your choice of tools and explain why your choice was sufficient get the job done.

Say Only What You Must

Brevity is the soul of wit.

— *William Shakespeare*

Be careful with the words you choose. They may come back to haunt you. Talking too much is a common witness mistake during testimony. The more you talk, the more you risk becoming a bore and the more information you divulge. Although it may appear that the primary purpose for an expert witness is to divulge information, that's missing the point. Your main job is to provide an expert's view or interpretation, not to dump memory. The most common type of information a person divulges when talking too much is that of weaknesses or revealing information that might be viewed as a conflict with the testimony of other witnesses. When you are on the stand, answer all questions succinctly. Only add enough details to answer the question fully. Resist the urge to say more than is necessary and do not try to answer questions that aren't asked.

Be Complete, But Not Overly Elaborate

Although you want to avoid saying more than is necessary, you can't answer all questions with "Yes" or "No." When you are asked a question, provide a full answer. If more information is needed, the person asking the questions should ask for it. Incomplete answers leave the appearance that there is something to hide.

If you cannot answer a question with a single word, use an answer that is short. For example, look at the following exchange between an attorney and an expert in the area of firewalls:

Attorney: Mr. Jones, do firewalls stop all "bad" messages coming into a system?

Mr. Jones: No.

Attorney: Well then, do firewalls stop any "bad" messages at all?

Mr. Jones: In most cases, they can be set up to stop messages that you define as "bad."

Although your second answer is not exhaustively complete in a technical sense, it does answer the question. The attorney might ask you to explain how firewalls work and how they can block messages. In contrast, here is a poor answer for the second question:

Attorney: Well then, do firewalls stop any "bad" messages at all?

Mr. Elaborate Jones: Firewalls examine all packets that are designated as of interest in the internal configuration. The specific action the firewall takes is contingent upon the rule set and connection status at the time the packet is received. We can block networks, IP addresses, ports, and actual variant packets at will. Most firewalls that are worth using can do all this dynamically. The days of static ACLs are long gone.

How many nontechnical jurors would understand Mr. Elaborate Jones' answer? Here are a few things that are wrong with his answer:

◆ It was too long. He wasn't asked to explain how firewalls work. He was asked for a general positive or negative answer.

◆ He used technical vocabulary. Most people aren't comfortable with terms such as *internal configuration, rule set*, and *variant packets*.

◆ He used technical acronyms. Don't use *IP* or *ACL* unless you explain what they mean.

◆ He expressed an inappropriate opinion. He could have just offended a juror who happens to be a system administrator for a company that uses static tables in a firewall.

In short, get to the point and only use elaboration to explain your answer, not to deliver it. You always must consider the target for your communication. Let's look at the importance of your audience.

Remember Your Audience

Never forget the audience for your testimony. You are speaking to the court. Specifically, you are speaking to the judge and jury. Your attorneys have heard you before. They may be comfortable with some shortcuts. Because you have met with them on several occasions, you may feel comfortable enough to drop some communication formalities. Even so, don't make the mistake of being too informal in court.

 *Real World Scenario*

Tales from the Trenches: Letting the Attorney Tell the Story

The first time I testified in court, I was unaware of the "storytelling" approach that attorneys use. Each time that I was asked a question about the case, I provided an answer to the question asked but would then continue presenting additional information. I wanted to make sure that the jury understood exactly what had happened, and I was anxious to get in all the information. The problem was that instead of helping the attorney to "tell the story," I was distracting the jury with too many details. I was not giving the attorney the opportunity to "set the stage" and prepare the jury to receive the detailed information.

After the case was over, I made an appointment with the attorney to get her opinion of how she thought the testimony had gone. That was when I learned about the storytelling approach to presenting evidence to a jury. Since then, each time I testify, I remember to slow down and let the information flow and let the story be told.

Continues

As a result of what I learned, the best advice I can give to any investigator who is called upon to testify in a legal proceeding is to thoroughly review all documentation associated with the case and then answer each question you are asked directly and politely. Do not offer any additional information during questioning. In other words, answer the question asked and nothing more.

If you feel that additional information needs to be presented because it is relevant to the case, discuss the details with the attorney you are working for before offering information in open court or at a deposition. Once in court, let your attorney lead you into the testimony. Don't rush to present all the details of the case in your first answer. Remember that the attorney you are working with will be trying to tell a story to the jury and your job is to "complete" that story with details of the case as you are asked questions.

To convey your message effectively, always speak to your audience. Remember their level of technical expertise is more limited than your own. If a jury were composed of computer forensic examiners, there would be no reason to call you in as an expert. You are there to make the complex technical details of the case accessible to the judge and jury. Always be aware of how your delivery sounds to your audience. It's a good idea to have someone on your legal team monitor your testimony from the perspective of a nontechnical person. Comments from such a monitor can be invaluable in helping you tailor your testimony style to make the most impact.

Keep It Simple

Always use the KISS method. The old Keep It Simple, Stupid acronym reminds us that simple is better than complex. In fact, almost everyone will reject information that is confusing. If you want to be believed by the judge and jury, make your explanations simple. You'll have to walk a fine line between keeping your explanations accessible and making them too simplistic.

Explaining Technical Concepts

Humans are associative thinkers. We take new information and associate it with information we already know. If we establish a strong enough association, we remember the new information. We can remember information in isolation, but only for a short time. Here's a simple test to make my point:

1. What are Newton's three laws of motion?
2. Write the quadratic formula from memory.
3. What are the Spanish (or French) words for cat, house, and bread?
4. Diagram the first sentence in the preceding paragraph.

At one time, you could probably answer all these questions. If you're like most people, you could do it on the day of the test. But the memory tends to fade after a few days when the stored information is not frequently accessed. If you currently speak Spanish or French, the third question is a snap. The moral is: your audience will retain information longer if you help them associate it with something they already know. They will also understand it far better. Try to explain technical concepts using analogies where appropriate.

Let's assume you are asked to explain how a firewall works. You can start with something like: "A firewall is like a toll plaza. All traffic must pass through a toll booth in the plaza. Traffic is sorted by payment method: fast pass, exact change, and change provided." This starts off with a mental picture your audience can build on. Take time to develop analogies to explain technical concepts. They can go a long way to get a nontechnical audience to understand technical concepts.

Use Presentation Aids When Needed

In addition to helping your audience use mental pictures, bring some pictures of your own. The old adage "A picture is worth a thousand words" is absolutely true. When appropriate, use various presentation aids to clarify your point. However, don't use presentation aids just to look impressive. Whether you use old-fashioned overhead projectors and cellophane slides, or PowerPoint presentations delivered with computer and projectors, the goal of any presentation is to get your point across to the jury and ensure that they understand the message. The presentation method might vary depending on the evidence—use the method that is most effective for delivering the message you want the jury to understand. Regardless of the delivery media used, ensure that you are completely comfortable with the media and understand how to operate any equipment (such as a computer or projector) so that the delivery is seamless and polished before the court.

If you believe a picture will help your audience understand or remember something, use it. In many cases, projecting a picture onto a screen while you explain a topic helps to cement that topic in the minds of the audience. Pictures are only one of many presentation aids available. When they help your testimony, use any of the following:

◆ Pictures (including crime scene photos)

◆ Illustrations

◆ Animation

◆ Charts or diagrams

The preceding list is not exhaustive. Use the presentation aid you think will make the most impact. That impact is measured in how well your audience understands the points you are making, not in how impressive your presentation looks.

Watch for Feedback

One of the most crucial factors during testimony is audience feedback. Because you make eye contact with the judge and jury, you can see how they react to you. Read their facial expressions and body language. You can tell when you are boring someone. Too few witnesses care, though. When you are presenting any type of information, watch to see what your audience is "saying" to you.

Anytime you lose your audience, do something. If you see that you are losing the jury as you explain how firewalls work, ask for a break. Talk the problem over with your legal team. They may suggest you try a different approach. You may have no other alternative but to push on through. Regardless, try to react to your audience. You might not be able to make the technical exciting, but you can try. Simply responding to the facial expressions and body language of your audience can increase their trust in you.

Be Ready to Justify Every Step

Your own legal team will lead you through justifications and explanations of each step through your investigation. Be prepared to stop at any point and answer "Why" questions. Your team should prepare these questions and answers during trial preparation. Although it can be tedious, you will have to provide detailed explanations that satisfy the most skeptical listeners as to why you performed some action.

The real challenge comes during cross examination. Your own legal team questions you from the perspective that you performed your job appropriately and acquired evidence that proves facts. The opposing counsel will take the opposite approach. To the other side, the evidence does not prove the facts as they are presented or was not acquired properly. You will be asked to defend your actions at each step in the process. Be prepared to justify each action and explain precautions you took to preserve the evidence. Your investigation notebook will be invaluable. Make sure you keep your notebook up-to-date during an investigation and available during a trial.

Summary

As long as you do your homework and document everything in an investigation, your testimony can positively affect the outcome of a case. Of course, if you are poorly prepared, you can have a positive impact for the opposing counsel. There are many resources and books available to help you prepare for the role of expert witness. Neil Broom has an excellent list of recommended reading for those seeking to establish themselves as an expert witness. The list can be reviewed at the following address:

```
http://www.trcglobal.com/Computer_Forensics_Expert_Witness_Books.html
```

Do your homework, know your stuff, be prepared, and above all remember your audience. You'll have a much more pleasant experience, and you may be asked to do it all again.

Terms to Know

body language	direct examination
cross examination	expert witness
deposition	summons

Review Questions

1. How does an expert witness differ from a regular witness?

2. What should you do before you appear in court as an expert witness?

3. Will your résumé validate you as an expert witness?

4. What condition exists when you have personal or business reasons to find in favor of one party over the other?

5. What is the process of taking testimony and reducing it to written form for admission into court?

6. What term describes the process when opposing counsel asks questions to cast doubt on your testimony?

7. Why should you bother dressing up when going to court?

8. What are the three components of communication?

9. Should you be explicit in your testimony?

10. What should you do when you see that you are losing you audience?

Appendix A

Answers to Review Questions

Chapter 1

1. What is electronic discovery?

   Answer: Electronic discovery is the process whereby electronic documents are collected, prepared, reviewed, and distributed in the pursuit of legal or governmental proceedings.

2. Name some examples of electronic discovery items.

   Answer: Examples of electronic discovery items include e-mail, system and devices logs, word-processing documents, plaintext files, database files, spreadsheets, digital art, photos, and presentations.

3. The recovery of data focuses on what four factors?

   Answer: When recovering data, forensic investigators focus on these four factors: identifying meaningful evidence; determining how to preserve that evidence; extracting, processing, and interpreting that evidence; and ensuring that such evidence is acceptable in a court of law.

4. Who works under more restrictive rules, law enforcement officials or corporate employees?

   Answer: Law enforcement officials work under more restrictive rules than corporate employees. Often, law enforcement must obtain a court order to seize evidence.

5. What is incident response?

   Answer: Incident response is an action or series of actions undertaken to respond to a situation to promote speedy and safe recovery of systems, data, and services.

6. Why is social engineering hard to prevent and detect?

   Answer: Social engineering plays on human weaknesses and thus is difficult to prevent. It's also hard to detect because organizations can exercise so little influence over employees' lack of common sense or ignorance, although training can be provided to reduce such ignorance.

7. Why aren't incidents reported in many corporate environments?

   Answer: Corporations are often unsure which law enforcement agency (state or local, FBI, and so forth) to contact regarding incidents. Many organizations also believe that damage to reputation and customer confidence from disclosure of an incident may outweigh the benefits of (or indeed, the legal requirements for) such disclosure.

8. What law was passed to avoid future accounting scandals such as those involving Enron and WorldCom?

   Answer: The Sarbanes-Oxley Act is intended to prevent accounting scandals such as those involving Enron and WorldCom.

9. Name some factors that help to determine which criminal cases get priority.

   Answer: In determining criminal case priority, law enforcement considers such factors as the amount of harm inflicted, crime jurisdiction, success of investigation, availability and training of personnel, and frequency of the crime.

10. Name a good resource for computer forensic training for law enforcement.

    Answer: In addition to training received at the police academy, law enforcement officers interested in a career in computer forensics should consider additional computer forensic training courses such as those offered by Guidance Software, the SANS Institute, AccessData, and the International Association for Computer Investigative Specialists (IACIS).

Chapter 2

1. What is the difference between a server and a PC?

   Answer: Servers are computers with sufficient processing power and storage capacity to provide services to other computers over a network. Personal computers are intended for use by individuals.

2. How many devices can USB support?

   Answer: A standard USB can support up to 127 devices per port.

3. Which has a faster transfer rate, eSATA or FireWire 800?

   Answer: eSATA 2.0 supports data transfer rates of up to 3 Gbps, and eSATA 3.0 up to 6 Gbps, while FireWire-800 supports only 800 Mbps, so eSATA is clearly faster than FireWire.

4. How does Bluetooth communicate?

   Answer: Bluetooth uses a technique called "spread-spectrum frequency hopping" and randomly uses frequencies within a designated range and regularly hops or changes from one range to another. Bluetooth transmitters change frequencies 1,600 times every second.

5. What types of file systems can you find in the Windows environment?

   Answer: Multiple file systems are supported in the Windows environment, including: FAT, Virtual FAT (VFAT), extended FAT (exFAT), New Technology File System (NTFS), and New File System (NFS).

6. What is the difference between NTFS and NFS?

   Answer: The primary function of NFS is to mount directories to other computers. These directories can then be accessed as though they were local. NTFS organizes files into directories, which are then sorted. It also keeps track of transactions against the file system, making it a recoverable file system.

7. What does an incident response team do?

   Answer: Incident response teams create an organizational incident response plan, contain damage, and get systems up and running again. Incident response teams make a determination of the incident, notify appropriate departments, recover essential network resources, prepare an incident report, and potentially communicate with vendors, business partners, and the press.

8. Approximately what percentage of organizations report intrusions?

   Answer: Only 25 percent of organizations report intrusions or incidents.

9. Can an employer search an employee's designated work area or desk?

   Answer: An employer can search an employee's designated work area if (1) the search is a non-investigatory, work-related intrusion or (2) it's an investigatory search for evidence of suspected work-related employee misfeasance.

10. Search and seizure laws are guided by which amendment?

    Answer: Search and seizure are guided by the Fourth Amendment, which limits the ability of government agents to search for evidence without a warrant.

Chapter 3

1. What are two general ways in which computers are involved in security violations?

   Answer: A computer can be used in the commission of crimes or in violation of policy. It can also be the target for an attack.

2. What is computer evidence?

   Answer: Any computer hardware, software, or data that can be used to prove one or more of the five Ws and the H for a security incident—namely, who, what, when, where, why, and how.

3. What is an incident response team?

   Answer: The incident response team (IRT) carries out internal investigations. IRT members are generally specially trained to identify and collect evidence to document and categorize incidents. In addition, team members must also be cognizant when incidents are crimes and require law enforcement involvement.

4. What is real evidence?

   Answer: Real evidence is any physical objects you can actually bring into court and place on a table in front of a jury. Real evidence can be touched, held, or otherwise observed directly.

5. What is documentary evidence?

   Answer: Documentary evidence is written evidence, such as printed reports, log files, database files, computer-based file data, and incident-specific files and reports that supply information about what happened.

6. What is demonstrative evidence?

   Answer: Demonstrative evidence is evidence that is used to explain, illustrate, or recreate other evidence. Usually demonstrative evidence consists of some kind of visual aids and other illustrations.

7. What is a subpoena?

   Answer: A subpoena is a court order that compels an individual or organization to surrender evidence.

8. What is a search warrant?

   Answer: A search warrant is a court order that allows law enforcement to search and/or seize computer equipment without providing advance warning to its owner.

9. What is the chain of custody?

    Answer: *Chain of custody* is a term used to describe careful documentation of all steps that evidence has taken from the time it is located at a crime scene to the time it is introduced in a courtroom. All steps include collection, transportation, analysis, and storage processes. All accesses to the evidence must be documented as well.

10. What is admissible evidence?

    Answer: Admissible evidence is evidence that meets all regulatory and statutory requirements, and has been properly obtained and handled.

Chapter 4

1. What is the first common task when handling evidence?

    Answer: In any investigation, your initial task is to identify the evidence you need for your case. In fact, you'll want to begin your efforts by making a complete photographic survey of the surroundings to document where and when you identified items worthy of investigation.

2. Which type of hardware is seldom of interest to an investigation?

    Answer: Any hardware that does not include built-in storage of some kind – including such things as keyboards, mice, and monitors – cannot provide evidence in an investigation. Thus, it will seldom be of interest to an investigation, either, beyond its role in establishing that a particular person used a computer (such as fingerprints or DNA evidence from a mouse or keyboard, for example).

3. When attempting to prove that an individual used a computer, what clues might computer hardware provide?

    Answer: Computer hardware points you to other sources of evidence. For example, if a scanner is hooked up to a suspect computer, you should expect to find a repository of scanned documents on the computer. Often a computer that an individual uses will store dated files that explicitly illustrate a person's use of that machine (such as e-mail, web cookies, browsing history files, temporary files, and so forth).

4. In addition to hard disk drives, where else might data containing evidence reside?

    Answer: Evidence can be found anywhere and everywhere. Some additional sources may include keyboard, mouse, touchpad, CD-ROM/DVD drive, laptop case, scanner lids, mobile device cradle (especially its buttons and switches), keyboard-video-monitor (KVM) switches, game controller, media storage units (CD/DVDs, tape, floppy cases, and drawers), and much more. Even a keyboard, mouse, or touchpad can provide evidence that a particular user must have touched a specific computer (although such devices, being without RAM or other storage, cannot usually provide more information than that).

5. Should handwritten notes be considered in a computer forensic investigation?

    Answer: Yes. Handwritten notes are a type of documentary evidence. As with other forms of evidence, handwritten notes may also lead to other sources to continue searching for evidence.

6. What is the primary concern in evidence collection and handling?

    Answer: The main concern of evidence collection and preservation is to ensure that absolutely no changes have been made to the evidence since it was collected. Preservation is ensured by logging all access to and use of evidentiary materials, and showing that those materials were properly handled at all times. This is also known as maintaining the *chain of custody*.

7. Can you analyze a system that is intact and running?

    Answer: Live systems can be analyzed with the help of computer forensic software suites that enable you to take a snapshot of the entire system, including memory and disks, while it is still running.

8. What happens when a PDA's battery runs down?

    Answer: When the power runs out on a PDA, the data is lost.

9. What device prohibits any changes to a hard disk drive?

    Answer: You can use a write-blocking device to prevent changes to a hard disk drive. Likewise, software write blockers can also prevent any type of write access to storage devices as well.

10. How can you prove that you made no changes to a disk drive during analysis?

    Answer: By creating a hash upon first inspection of a disk drive as a potential source of evidence, and creating a hash after your inspection of it, you can prove that no changes were made to the evidence during the investigation. If the present hash value and the original hash value match, this is proof positive that no changes were made to the contents of the disk drive.

Chapter 5

1. Why do you need to be careful about the utilities you choose to use for disk imaging?

    Answer: Courts often accept evidence collected by tools that have been used in past trials. You should be prepared to testify to the authenticity and reliability of the tools that you use, otherwise the evidence may not be admissible.

2. What is an HPA?

    Answer: HPA stands for host protected area, an area created on a hard disk specifically to allow manufacturers to hide diagnostic and recovery tools. It is a hidden portion of the disk that can't be used by the operating system. (HPA is sometimes referred to as hidden protected area or hardware protected area.)

3. Name some limitations of virtual environments when used for forensics.

    Answer: Virtual environments are often considerably different from the original computer image, which limits the admissibility in court of evidence gathered (or at the very least makes it subject to challenges by opposing counsel). In addition, some of the installed software products may refuse to start, installed services may not work, and the computer itself might not boot.

4. How can you verify that in imaging the source media, the original media is unchanged?

    Answer: Verification is done by Secure Hash Algorithm (SHA-1) and SHA-2, CRC, or MD5 confirmation. These methods ensure that the copy procedure did not corrupt the original data.

5. Name a tool that can be used to image the data in the memory of a cell phone.

    Answer: Several tools are available to image data in the memory of cell phones, such as Device Seizure from Paraben, Palm dd (pdd) (for Palm OS), BitPim (for use with CDMA phones), Oxygen Forensic Suite 2010 (for use with cell phones, smartphones, and PDAs), Mobilyze (for use with iPhones, iPod Touch, and iPad devices), and Zdziarski's Forensics Guide for the iPhone.

6. What does the Netstat utility do?

   Answer: Netstat displays the active computer connections. This information provides the investigator with a list of what protocols are running and what ports are open.

7. When collecting evidence, which do you want to extract first: the information in memory or on the hard drive?

   Answer: You should collect evidence on a system beginning with the more volatile and proceeding to the less volatile; therefore, memory data should be collected before hard drive data.

8. Why can choosing the method used to shut down a suspect computer be a difficult decision to make?

   Answer: If you disconnect the power cord, you risk losing data, especially on UNIX computers. If you shut down the computer through the normal shutdown method, you risk running destructive programs that will delete data upon shutdown.

9. If you need to boot a suspect computer to make an image copy, how should you do it?

   Answer: You should boot from a controlled boot disk and then create a bit stream of the hard disk using a disk-imaging utility.

10. Name three programs or utilities that can be used to collect forensic images.

    Answer: EnCase, Access Data's Forensic Toolkit (FTK), Technology Pathways' ProDiscover Incident Response (IR), X-Ways Forensics (XWF), the dd utility, WinHex, Grave-Robber, and Incident Response Collection Report (IRCR).

Chapter 6

1. What set of rules and conventions governs how computers exchange information over the network medium?

   Answer: Protocols. A protocol describes the syntax, semantics, and synchronization of communication and may be implemented in hardware, software, or both.

2. Name some factors that motivate criminal activity.

   Answer: Financial gain, anger or revenge, power, addiction, boredom, thrill-seeking, intellectual gain, recognition, sexual impulses, curiosity, and psychiatric illness.

3. As a Word document is written and changed, these changes are tracked and produce a type of evidence that is called what?

   Answer: Metadata. Metadata includes hidden information that Microsoft Office programs add to a file to help people collaborate on writing and editing a document. It can also include information that a person deliberately designates as hidden.

4. What types of files should arouse your suspicion when you are examining data?

   Answer: Files with strange locations, strange names, or dots; files that start with a period (.) and contain spaces; and files that have changed recently.

5. Why should you look at the header of an e-mail?

   Answer: The e-mail header shows the path the message took from the very first communication point until it reached the recipient.

6. What is steganography?

   Answer: Steganography literally means "covered writing." It's a type of cryptology that makes the presence of secret data undetectable.

7. What method can you use to determine if the extension of a file has been changed to avoid suspicion?

   Answer: A technique that you can use to determine if the extension of a file has been changed is signature analysis. Signature analysis is a technique that uses a filter to analyze both the header and the contents of the datagram, usually referred to as the package payload.

8. If you are investigating a case that involves the Internet and pictures, name three areas that could reveal the Internet habits of the suspect?

   Answer: Temporary Internet Files folder, History folder, Cookies folder, and Local Shared Objects (LSOs) or Adobe Flash cookies.

9. What is a multiboot system?

   Answer: It is a system that can boot to more than one operating system. In essence, one operating system is hidden from the other.

10. Name three types of trace evidence.

   Answer: Three main types of trace evidence include slack space (unallocated file space on a hard disk between where a file ends and the disk storage cluster ends), swap file (space on the hard disk used as virtual memory extension of a computer's actual memory), and metadata (data component that describes other data).

Chapter 7

1. What is a password?

   Answer: A password is a type of authentication that enables a user to verify that he or she is who they claim to be. Users supply a password and the authentication system compares the password with the stored password. If the values match, the user authenticates.

2. What is the process of getting someone to carry out a task for you?

   Answer: Social engineering is the process of getting someone else to carry out a task for you.

3. Are more complex passwords stronger or weaker than simpler passwords?

   Answer: Complex passwords are stronger than simple ones if they are kept secret, but in practice they are often weaker than simpler passwords because they are difficult to remember. Users often write down passwords they have difficulty remembering.

4. What method should you first use to get a password?

   Answer: Ask for a password first whenever possible.

5. What type of password attack tries passwords from a predefined list?

   Answer: A dictionary attack attempts to find a password using a predefined list of potential passwords.

6. Which type of password attack uses passwords from a list and then tries variations on each element from the list?

   Answer: A hybrid attack attempts to find a password using a predefined list of potential passwords, and then attempts variations of each element in the list.

7. What is an algorithm for encrypting and decrypting data?

   Answer: A cipher is an algorithm used to encrypt and decrypt data.

8. What term describes an encrypted message?

   Answer: Ciphertext is the term used to describe an encrypted message.

9. The Rijndael cipher is the basis for which symmetric encryption algorithm?

   Answer: The Rijndael cipher is the basis for the AES symmetric encryption standard.

10. Which symmetric encryption algorithm uses 56-bit keys?

   Answer: The DES symmetric encryption algorithm uses 56-bit keys.

Chapter 8

1. Which utility, originally created for the UNIX platform, copies and converts files using two basic arguments (if and of)?

   Answer: The dd utility was originally written as part of UNIX and uses two basic arguments, if and of.

2. Which software suite provides an enterprise edition that specifically supports volatile data analysis on a live Windows system?

   Answer: EnCase Enterprise Edition specifically supports volatile data analysis (live RAM analysis).

3. Which disk imaging software operates as an extended DOS command shell?

   Answer: The DriveSpy utility operates as an extended DOS command shell. Other disk imaging utilities operate as stand-alone programs with their own user interface. While many other utilities have graphical user interfaces (GUI), DriveSpy presents a user interface that operates much like the DOS command shell.

4. What are MD5 and SHA-1?

   Answer: MD5 and SHA-1 are two common algorithms for calculating hash values that are used to verify that the original media is unchanged when imaging source media.

5. Which forensic software suite integrates the dtSearch Engine in its searching function?

   Answer: Forensic Toolkit (FTK) integrates the dtSearch Engine in its searching function.

6. What two software suites are free?

   Answer: SIFT and TSK are open source forensic software suites that are freely available.

7. Name two vendors of forensic hardware.

   Answer: Cellebrite and Intelligent Computer Solutions (ICS) were two hardware vendors discussed in this chapter. Paraben and Guidance Software also sell forensic hardware.

8. After creating an image of a drive, what must you do to ensure that the copy matches the original?

   Answer: After the image is created, compare the copy to the original. This is commonly accomplished by comparing CRC or hash values calculated on the original and the copy.

9. You have many factors to consider when choosing appropriate forensic software. Name two.

   Answer: Factors include:

     ◆ Operating system(s) supported
     ◆ User interface preference
     ◆ Budget
     ◆ Functionality/capabilities
     ◆ Vendor loyalty

10. Which two forensic products can extract both active and deleted text messages from a mobile phone?

    Answer: Both Cellebrite UFED and Paraben Device Seizure support extracting complete data from mobile devices (including phones).

Chapter 9

1. What set of rules states the General Provisions Governing Discovery and Duty of Disclosure?

   Answer: Federal Rule of Civil Procedure 26 contains the General Provisions Governing Discovery and the Duty of Disclosure.

2. What are some of the items of information that a forensic examiner might be asked to provide under Federal Rule of Civil Procedure 30(b)(6)?

   Answer: Under Federal Rule of Civil Procedure 30(b)(6), a forensic investigator may be asked to provide information on such things as: quality and locations of computers in use, operating systems and application software installed and dates of use, file-naming conventions and what directories data is saved to, backup disk or tape inventories and schedules, computer use policies, identities of current and former employees responsible for systems operations, e-mail with dates, times, and attachments, Word documents, tables, graphs, and database files, and Internet bookmarks, cookies, and history logs.

3. Why is a template recommended for reports?

   Answer: Templates help you to organize forensic investigation results in a way that is clear, logical, consistent, and easily understood by others. Templates also aid forensic investigators in recalling facts at the actual time of trial (which may be months or even years after the initial investigation was conducted).

4. Where can you find out how to properly document and sample log sheets?

   Answer: Guidelines for how to document evidence, along with sample log sheets, may be found in Appendix C of *Forensic Examination of Digital Evidence: A Guide for Law Enforcement* produced by The National Institute of Justice.

5. When should you consider using diagrams as a method of documentation?

   Answer: Diagrams are useful to help explain forensic procedures in such a way that jurors better understand them.

6. Why should you videotape the entry of all persons into the crime scene?

   Answer: Videotaping the entrance of a forensic team into the crime scene helps you refute claims that evidence was planted at the scene.

7. Why is it important to be cautious when you are transporting evidence from the crime scene to the lab for analysis?

   Answer: Various conditions (such as moisture, high humidity, or excessive heat and cold) can cause electrostatic discharge (ESD) which can kill your computer components. Exposure to radio transmitters or magnets can create electromagnetic fields which can alter or destroy data as well.

8. When formulating a concise report, what are some items you should consider?

   Answer: When formulating a concise report, it is important to: understand the importance of the reports, limit the report to specifics, use a layout and presentation that is easy to understand, understand the difference between litigation-support reports and technical reports, write clearly, provide supporting material, explain methods used in data collection, and explain results.

9. Why are timelines of computer usage and file accesses important when processing computer evidence?

   Answer: Timelines for computer usage and file access are essential when processing computer evidence because they show the order in which events occurred. Also by cross-correlating the times at which events took place, the duration of a login session, and the identity used to log in, investigators can establish who is responsible for the actions that took place on the timeline. This is important to making the case that a specific individual is involved in certain activities to establish culpability.

10. What are some items that your report should contain?

   Answer: Reports should contain information such as: the name of the reporting agency and case investigator, case number, date of the report, list of the items examined, description of the examination process, and the investigation results and/or conclusion.

Chapter 10

1. How does an expert witness differ from a regular witness?

   Answer: An expert witness possesses special knowledge or a skill in some specific area that a regular witness does not have. Regular witnesses may only testify to matters of fact or personal knowledge, but expert witnesses may also offer opinions to the court.

2. What should you do before you appear in court as an expert witness?

   Answer: Expert witnesses must be completely prepared before appearing in court. Review all aspects of the case with your legal team and completely understand the scope of the case as well as your evidence. You may also want to attend a witness preparation school.

3. Will your résumé validate you as an expert witness?

   Answer: No résumé by itself can validate your status as an expert witness. You'll need to provide additional information regarding your education and degrees, professional training, certifications, related professional experience, and prior experience testifying as an expert witness.

4. What condition exists when you have personal or business reasons to find in favor of one party over the other?

   Answer: When you have a personal or business reason to find in favor of one party over the other, you have a conflict of interest. Conflicts of interest should be avoided at all times, even if that means forgoing expert witness work.

5. What is the process of taking testimony and reducing it to written form for admission into court?

   Answer: Depositions are a form of testimony that is reduced to written form (though usually with video recordings as well as textual transcripts).

6. What term describes the process when opposing counsel asks questions to cast doubt on your testimony?

   Answer: Cross examination is the term used when opposing counsel asks you questions during your testimony.

7. Why should you bother dressing up when going to court?

   Answer: Your courtroom appearance makes a statement to the judge and jury regarding your credibility, professionalism, and trustworthiness.

8. What are the three components of communication?

   Answer: The three components of communication are: sender (person who prepares and sends message), message (the content you're sending), and receiver (the person receiving the message).

9. Should you be explicit in your testimony?

   Answer: All questions should be answered completely with enough detail to ensure that the judge and jury understand the evidence. Avoid lengthy or overly technical explanations.

10. What should you do when you see that you are losing you audience?

    Answer: If you see that you're losing your audience, ask for a break and talk the problem over with the legal team. When appropriate, try a different approach to delivering the information.

Appendix B

Forensic Resources

This appendix lists various sources that should be helpful for your computer forensic research, and possibly even for your investigations. These resources are subdivided into six categories:

◆ Information: Here, you'll find links to resources where you can obtain information about cyber crimes, federal guidelines, national forensic standards, as well as several government agencies such as the Department of Justice and the Department of Defense.

◆ Organizations: In this section, you'll find links to some of the major professional organizations in the field of computer forensics. Such organizations offer invaluable news and resources to help you keep abreast of the latest information and market trends, learn about the newest tools and technologies, and so forth.

◆ Publications: This section contains links to some major publications within the computer forensic field. Publications can also assist you in keeping up with market trends, new laws and cases, technologies, and other related items of interest to computer forensic professionals.

◆ Services: The companies listed in this subcategory provide numerous services in the field of computer forensics, ranging from credit card fraud to child pornography detection and everything in between.

◆ Software: While not exhaustive, you'll find a list of some of the more commonly used forensic software that you're likely to encounter or use during your forensic investigator career, including all the products we mentioned elsewhere in this book.

◆ Hardware: This section provides links to some of the major providers of hardware that are frequently used in forensic investigations, including all the hardware products we mentioned elsewhere in this book.

◆ Training: Formal training is a great way to gain skills and get up to speed in the field of forensic investigation. In this section, you'll find a list of some of the major providers of forensic investigative training, including all the providers mentioned elsewhere in this book.

Information

CERT Coordination Center

http://www.cert.org/tech_tips/win-UNIX-system_compromise.html

Computer Forensics, Cybercrime and Steganography Resources

http://www.forensix.org/links

Department of Defense Cyber Crime Center

http://www.dc3.mil/home.php

Department of Defense, National Industrial Security Program Operating Manual (clearing and sanitizing standard) DoD 5220.22-M

http://www.dtic.mil/whs/directives/corres/pdf/522022m.pdf

Department of Justice Computer Crime and Intellectual Property Section

http://www.cybercrime.gov/

FBI National Computer Crime Squad

http://www.tscm.com/compcrim.html

Federal Guidelines for Searching and Seizing Computers

http://www.knock-knock.com/federal_guidelines.htm

National Institute of Justice Forensic Sciences

http://www.ojp.usdoj.gov/nij/topics/forensics/welcome.htm

National Institute of Standards and Technology (NIST) Computer Security Resource Center (CSRC). (CSRC is maintained by the Computer Security Division of the NIST.)

http://csrc.nist.gov/groups/SMA/ate/

National White Collar Crime Center

http://www.nw3c.org/

National Institute of Standards Technology (NIST) Computer Forensic Tool Testing Program

http://www.cftt.nist.gov/

SANS Information Security Reading Room

http://www.sans.org/reading_room/

Scientific Working Group on Digital Evidence

http://www.swgde.org/documents/current-documents/

United States Secret Service

http://www.forwardedge2.com/pdf/bestPractices.pdf

U.S. Secret Service Electronic Crimes Task Forces and Working Groups

http://www.secretservice.gov/ectf.shtml

Organizations

Digital Forensic Research Workshop (DFRWS 2011)

http://www.dfrws.org/

High Tech Crime Consortium

http://www.hightechcrimecops.org/

High Technology Crime Investigation Association (HTCIA)

http://htcia.org/

International Association for Identification (IAI) Scientific Working Group on Digital Evidence

http://www.theiai.org/disciplines/digital_evidence/index.php

International Association of Computer Investigative Specialists
International Information Systems Forensic Association (IISFA)

http://www.iisfa.info/certification.htm

International Organization on Computer Evidence (IOCE)

http://www.ioce.org/

Publications

Digital Forensics Magazine: Supporting the Professional Computer Security Industry

http://www.digitalforensicsmagazine.com/

Digital Investigation: The International Journal of Digital Forensics and Incident Response (Elsevier)

http://www.elsevier.com/wps/find/journaldescription.cws_home/702130/description

Forensic Examination of Digital Evidence: A Guide for Law Enforcement by the National Institute of Justice

http://www.ojp.usdoj.gov/nij/pubs-sum/199408.htm

International Journal of Digital Evidence (IJDE) (Utica College)

http://www.utica.edu/academic/institutes/ecii/ijde/

iPhone Forensics by Jonathan Zdziarski

http://www.zdziarski.com/blog/?page_id=213

Searching and Seizing Computers and Obtaining Electronic Evidence in Criminal Investigations manual; Computer Crime and Intellectual Property Section Criminal Division of the United States Department of Justice

http://www.cybercrime.gov/ssmanual/index.html

Services

Advanced Data Solutions

http://www.adv-data.com/

Center for Computer Forensics

http://www.computer-forensics.net/

Computer Forensics International

http://www.cf-intl.com/

Computer Forensic Labs

http://www.computerforensiclabsinc.com/

Computer Forensic Services, LLC

http://computerforensicservicesllc.com/index.html

CyberEvidence

http;//www.cyberevidence.com/

Data Recon, LLC

http://www.datareconllc.com/

Digital Mountain, Inc.

http://www.digitalmountain.com/

ESS Data Recovery

http://www.datarecovery.com/

Forensicon, Inc.

http://forensicon.com/

Forentech, LLC

http://www.forentech.com

Kroll Ontrack

http://www.krollontrack.com/

LC Technology International, Inc.

http://www.lc-tech.com/

LuciData, Inc.

http://www.lucidatainc.com/

Midwest Data Group

http://www.forensicdiscovery.com/

Navigant E-Discovery and Forensic Services

http://www.navigantconsulting.com/services/discovery_services/

RenewData

http://www.renewdata.com/

Sassinsky Data Services, LLC

http://www.sassinsky.com/forensics/

Technical Resource Center

http://www.trcglobal.com

Tunstall and Tunstall, Inc.

http://www.datarecoveryservices.com/

Software

AccessData

http://accessdata.com/

Afind (from Foundstone, a division of McAfee)

http://www.foundstone.com

Avantstar Quick View Plus

http://avantstar.com/metro/home/Products/

BitPim

http://www.bitpim.org/

Cain and Abel

http://www.oxid.it/cain.html

Computer Cop

http://computercop.com/

CRCheck

http://www.downloadatoz.com/utility_directory/crcheck/

CryptCat

http://sourceforge.net/projects/cryptcat/

DCode:

http://www.digital-detective.co.uk/downloads.asp

dd utility for Windows by Chrysocome

http://chrysocome.net/dd

Digital Intelligence

http://www.digitalintelligence.com/

DiskJockey File Viewer

http://www.clear-simple.com/

DriveSpy

http://www.digitalintelligence.com/software/disoftware/drivespy/

dtSearch

http://www.dtsearch.com/dtsoftware.html

ElcomSoft Password Recovery

http://www.crackpassword.com

ElcomSoft

http://www.elcomsoft.com/

EnCase

http://www.guidancesoftware.com

Evidor

http://www.x-ways.net/evidor/

Forensic UltraDock from WiebeTech

http://www.wiebetech.com

Forensic Write Blockers from Tableau

http://www.tableau.com

Hashkeeper

http://www.justice.gov/ndic/domex/hashkeeper.htm

Hydra

http://freeworld.thc.org/thc-hydra/

ILook Investigator

http://www.ilook-forensics.org/

Incident Response Collection Report (IRCR)

http://ircr.sourceforge.net/

Intelligent Computer Solutions

http://www.ics-iq.com

Invisible Secrets

http://www.invisiblesecrets.com/

John the Ripper

http://www.openwall.com/john/

Karen's Disk Slack Checker

http://www.karenware.com/powertools/ptslack.asp

Kroll Ontrack

http://www.krollontrack.com

L0phtCrack

http://www.L0phtcrack.com/

LastBit

http://lastbit.com/

Live View

http://liveview.sourceforge.net/

Loki

http://loki.com/

Md5sum Utility for Linux

http://www.gnu.org/software/coreutils

Md5sum Utility for Windows

http://www.etree.org/md5com.html

MS-Office Password Recovery

http://www.interlore.com/office-password-recovery.php

Microsoft Virtual Server

http://www.microsoft.com/windowsserversystem/virtualserver/

Mobilyze from Black Bag Technologies

http://www.blackbagtech.com/

NetAnalysis

http://www.digital-detective.co.uk/netanalysis.asp

Netcat

http://netcat.sourceforge.net/

Norton Ghost

http://www.symantec.com/sabu/ghost/ghost_personal/

Oxygen Forensic Suite 2010

http://www.oxygen-forensic.com/en/

Open Source Digital Forensics

http://www.opensourceforensics.org/tools/windows.html

Paraben Device Seizure, Paraben Corporation

http://www.paraben.com

PDBlock by Digital Intelligence, Inc.

www.digitalintelligence.com

PhilTools Image Steganography

http://philtools.com/image_steganography/

ProDiscover

http://www.techpathways.com/

PsService

http://technet.microsoft.com/en-us/sysinternals/bb897542.aspx

Puff

http://members.fortunecity.it/blackvisionit/PUFFV200.HTM

Quick View Plus

http://www.avantstar.com/metro/visit

RainbowCrack

http://project-rainbowcrack.com/

Remove Hidden Data Tool (RHD)

http://www.microsoft.com/downloads/details.aspx?FamilyID=144e54ed-d43e-42ca-bc7b-5446d34e5360
&displaylang=e

SANS Investigative Forensic Toolkit (SIFT)

http://computer-forensics.sans.org/community/downloads/

SMART

http://www.asrdata.com/

Snagit

http://www.techsmith.com/screen-capture.asp

Super DriveLock, by Intelligent Computer Solutions

http://www.ics iq.com

Symantec Ghost

http://www.symantec.com/themes/theme.jsp?themeid=ghost

Tech Assist, Inc. (ByteBack)

http://www.toolsthatwork.com/computer-forensic.htm

Technology Pathways

http://www.techpathways.com/

The Coroner's Toolkit (TCT)

http://www.porcupine.org/forensics/tct.html

The Sleuth Kit (TSK)

http://www.sleuthkit.org/sleuthkit/index.php

ThumbsPlus

http://www.cerious.com/

VirtualBox

http://www.virtualbox.org/

VMWare, Inc.

http://www.vmware.com/

WinHex (now part of X-Ways)

http://www.winhex.com/

X-Ways

http://www.x-ways.net/forensics/index-m.html

Hardware

ACARD Write Block Kit, by ACARD Technology

www.acard.com

Cellebrite's Universal Forensic Extraction Device (UFED)

http://www.cellebrite.com/forensic-products.html

DriveLock and FastBloc, by Intelligent Computer Solutions

http://www.ics-iq.com

FastBloc, Guidance Software

http://www.guidancesoftware.com

ICS Solo-4

http://www.ics-iq.com

NoWrite, MyKey Technology, Inc.

www.mykeytech.com

UltraKit and UltraBlock, by Digital Intelligence, Inc.

www.digitalintelligence.com/products/ultrakit/

Training

AccessData Group, LLC

http://www.accessdata.com/training

Cyber Security Institute

http://www.cybersecurityinstitute.biz/

DIBS USA, Inc.

http://www.dibsusa.com/

EC-Council iClass online learning program

https://iclass.eccouncil.org/

Global Digital Forensics, Inc.

http://www.evestigate.com/Computer_Forensic_Training.htm

Guidance Software

http://www.guidancesoftware.com/computer-forensics-training.htm

High Tech Crime Institute

http://www.gohtci.com/index.php?q=category/division/training

Indiana Forensic Institute

http://www.ifi-indy.org/

International Association of Computer Investigative Specialists (IACIS)

http://www.iacis.com/training

Key Computer Service CCE Bootcamp

http://www.cce-bootcamp.com/

SANS (Sysadmin, Audit, Networking, and Security) Institute

http://www.sans.org

Security University

http://www.securityuniversity.com

Technical Resource Center

http://www.trcglobal.com

Appendix C

Forensic Certifications and More

Almost every day we read about some type of computer crime incident. Computer crime presents one of the fastest growth profiles for crime rates in the world, which means the need for computer forensics is exploding. Nowadays, not only law enforcement but also corporate IT and information security professionals perform proper, legally valid forensics on information systems.

Today, IT professionals need to know how digital crimes are committed, how to gather related evidence, and how to collaborate with law enforcement as a computer forensic case evolves. While performing proper computer forensics to prevent further damage to systems, evidence can be damaged, lost, or become inadmissible in a court of law. Given this, it is not surprising that numerous computer forensic certifications are available, ranging in coverage from computer crimes against children to file system recovery.

If you are interested in becoming a cybercrime investigator, earning a computer forensic certification can add to your credibility. This appendix covers some of the most popular and well-known computer forensic certifications. It also covers the related topics of licensing and accreditation as well.

Leading Computer Forensic Certifications

The following four credentials represent the most popular and well-respected computer forensic certifications, which we list along with their websites:

Certified Computer Examiner (CCE): http://www.certified-computer-examiner.com

Computer Forensic Computer Examiner (CFCE): http://www.iacis.com/certification/external_overview

Computer Hacking Forensic Investigator (CHFI) http://www.eccouncil.org/certification/computer_hacking_forensic_investigator.aspx

Professional Certified Investigator (PCI): http://www.asisonline.org/certification/pci/pciabout.xml

---

AccessData Certified Examiner (ACE)

One of three vendor-specific credentials in this compendium, the ACE certification, identifies individuals familiar with the FTK Forensic Toolkit, the Password Recovery Toolkit (PRTK), the FTK Imager, and the Registry Viewer. ACE-certified individuals are well-versed in proper forensic investigation and evidence handling, with particular emphasis on the AccessData toolset. The certification page includes links to preparation videos that cover the entire range of topics for the exam at

`http://www.accessdata.com/acepreparation.html`

A set of sample questions for the exam is available for download at

`http://www.accessdata.com/downloads/media/ACE_Study_Guide.pdf`

Candidates may challenge the exam to earn ACE certification, or take courses as described on the AccessData training page at

`http://www.accessdata.com/courses.html`

Advanced Information Security (AIS)

The Security University Advanced Information Security (AIS) certification is a hands-on computer security certification created for network IT and security professionals. This program covers key information security topics, tools, and technologies along with a very good hands-on, lab-oriented learning and testing program. The AIS is not an out-and-out computer forensic certification: it includes forensic topics among the many subject areas it covers.

To obtain AIS certification, security professionals must complete eight courses, including six tools-oriented classes on network penetration testing; firewalls and virtual private networks (VPNs); virus analysis, patch management, and incident response; PKI; intrusion detection and computer forensics, plus two management classes on network security policy and architecture security. Candidates must also take and pass a demanding exam to earn this credential. To learn more about this certification, visit

`http://www.securityuniversity.net/certification.php`

Certified Computer Examiner (CCE)

The Certified Computer Examiner (CCE) certification is one of the most complete and thorough evaluations available today for the computer forensic professional. This certification is offered in association with the International Society of Forensic Computer Examiners (ISFCE), and other institutions and forensic bodies.

The CCE certification is becoming the best recognized certification worldwide for both civilian and law enforcement examiners. Civilian examiners include information security officers and managers, IT administrators, consultants, systems and data security analysts, and even lawyers and HR managers.

The initial CCE process consists of a proctored online multiple-choice exam followed by the forensic examination of a floppy disk or CD-R disc. When the forensic examination has been been completed, the applicant begins forensic examination of the test media. These forensic examinations are designed to test the forensic knowledge and skills of the examiner.

The primary purpose of this certification is to measure an applicant's understanding and use of sound evidence handling and storage procedures and if they follow sound forensic examination procedures when conducting examinations. There are reasonable technical issues that must be resolved to recover the evidentiary data. However, most of the grade is based on following sound evidence handling and storage procedures and following sound examination procedures, not simply recovering the data. An 80 percent total average score is required to obtain CCE certification. The fee for the entire process is around $400. To obtain additional information about the CCE, visit http://www.isfce.com.

Certified Hacking Forensic Investigator (CHFI)

The CHFI comes from the EC-Council, an organization that specializes in anti-hacking, forensics, and penetration testing training and credentials. This certification covers forensic tools, techniques, and procedures necessary to obtain, collect, maintain, and present digital forensic evidence in a court of law.

This class includes an overview and introduction to computer forensics, the computer forensic investigation process, searching and seizing computers, digital evidence, first responder procedures, incident handling, the computer forensic laboratory, understanding hard disks and file systems, digital media devices, CD/DVD forensics, OS boot processes (with coverage of Windows, Linux, and Mac OS), data acquisition and duplication, recovering deleted files and deleted partitions, and much more. This is a thorough and comprehensive curriculum and exam.

EC-Council offers a 5-day training class (as do authorized parties) for the CHFI for around $2,900 (this includes the price of the exam). By itself, the exam costs $250 and is available through both Prometric and VUE testing centers.

For more information visit

http://www.eccouncil.org/certi"cation/computer_hacking_forensic_investigator.aspx

Certified Forensic Computer Examiner (CFCE)

The Certified Forensic Computer Examiner (CFCE) program is open to active law enforcement officers and others who qualify for membership in the International Association of Computer Investigative Specialists (IACIS). The external CFCE process can be particularly helpful to qualified examiners who cannot attend the annual IACIS training conference. You must submit an application, along with a fee, to be allowed to participate in the process. IACIS reviews each application carefully, and is the sole decision maker in its acceptance or rejection, as it deems appropriate.

Earning this credential requires completing a rigorous two-step testing process that includes both CFCE Peer Review and CFCE Certification phases. During the Peer Review phase, candidates are assigned four "problems" based on core competencies which must be solved. A mentor is assigned to each candidate to monitor their progress. Before proceeding to the CFCE Certification phase, candidates must successfully pass the Peer Review phase.

Candidates are required to enter the Certification phase within three months of completing the Peer Review phase. During the Certification phase, candidates work independently to assess a forensic image of a hard drive. Candidates are required to prepare a report documenting their activities (based on instructions provided) on that image. The report and evidence must be presented to IACIS in a way that demonstrates sound forensic procedures were used to conduct the examination and that the applicant understands the technical issues.

Candidates take a thorough written examination at the conclusion of this process. To earn the CFCE credential, candidates must score at least 80 percent on both practical and written exams. This process and these disk problems are the same problems that must be completed by IACIS-trained examiners. The cost of the certification process is about $750 and is nonrefundable after the application is accepted. Additional information about the CFCE is available online at http://www.iacis.com.

Certified Information Systems Auditor (CISA)

The Certified Information Systems Auditor (CISA) demonstrates knowledge of Information System (IS) auditing for control and security purposes. This certification is designed for IT security professionals responsible for auditing IT systems, practices, and procedures to make sure organizational security policies meet governmental and regulatory requirements, conform to best security practices and principles, and meet or exceed requirements stated in an organization's security policy. Thus, it is not a computer forensic certification either.

The CISA examination is offered twice a year in June and December. Certification requires a minimum of five years of professional information systems auditing, control, or security work experience. Go to http://www.isaca.org/ for further details.

Certified ProDiscover Examiner (CPE)

The CPE is one of three vendor-specific computer forensic certifications included in this collection (the others are the AccessData ACE and the EnCase Certified Examiner). This particular credential focuses on the popular and highly regarded ProDiscover Incident Response toolset. ProDiscover offers a Windows-oriented (but not exclusively Windows-focused) forensic application that covers collection, analysis, management, and reporting of computer disk evidence for Windows computers (FAT12, FAT16, FAT32 and all NTFS file systems including Dynamic Disk and Software RAID), as well as Sun Solaris UFS file system and Linux ext2/ext3 file systems.

The CPE exam stresses proper forensic techniques for collection, analysis, management, and reporting of computer evidence. The exam comes at the culmination of a 5-day, $2,500 classroom training exercise. For more information (including registration), visit the ProDiscover Training page at http://www.prodiscover.com/DesktopDefault.aspx?tabindex=4&tabid=9.

EnCase Certified Examiner Program

The EnCase Certified Examiner Program offers certifications for those who have mastered EnCase Guidance software. Candidates must submit an application demonstrating that they have a minimum of 64 hours of training in computer forensics (candidates who possess at least 12 months of documented experience in computer forensics may be exempted from this requirement).

Once approved, candidates may take the Phase I (written) examination. A minimum score of 80 percent is required before candidates can proceed to the Phase II (practical) examination. The Phase II examination must be completed within 60 days with a minimum score of 85 percent. Complete details about the EnCase certification program, including filing an application, and registering for and taking the two exams, are available online at http://www.guidancesoftware.com.

GIAC Certified Forensic Analyst (GCFA)

GIAC Certified Forensic Analysts (GCFAs) possess the knowledge, skills, and abilities necessary to handle advanced incident handling scenarios, conduct formal incident investigations, and carry out forensic investigation of networks and hosts. The GCFA is an intermediate-level certification, renewable every four years.

To earn the GCFA credential, a candidate must pass a 150-question written examination with a minimum score of 69.3 percent (correct answers to 104 of the 150 questions). The organization that sponsors the GIAC program is SANS, and it provides notification when exams are made available (normally this occurs 7–10 days after completing purchased SANS training, or within 24 hours after purchase of a stand-alone exam. Candidates must complete the exam within 120 days of its being made available. In addition, candidates must also complete a practical assignment that demonstrates their knowledge of the subject area.

The cost for the GCFA stand-alone exam is $250; the course (FOR-508, which includes the exam fee) runs for six days and costs from $3,950 to $4,300. Prices vary according to how far in advance of class dates one registers and pays: the longer you wait, the more you pay.

The GIAC website also includes information about other certifications that GIAC offers. Complete details about the GCFA are available at

http://www.giac.org/certifications/forensics/gcfa.php

GIAC Certified Forensics Examiner (GCFE)

The GIAC Certified Forensics Examiner (GCFE) focuses on the skills necessary to gather and analyze data collected from computers running Windows operating systems. Credential holders possess the skills and knowledge necessary to conduct all phases of forensic investigations. Candidates must pass a 150-question written examination with a minimum score of 71.3 percent. As with the GCFA, candidates must submit a practical assignment to demonstrate their knowledge of the subject area. Other stipulations described for the GCFA also apply to the GCFE (intermediate credential, four-year renewal period, exam as part of a paid-for course or stand-alone challenge exam, exam availability period, and so forth).

The cost for the stand-alone GCFE exam is $250, and the course (FOR-408, which runs for six days, and includes the exam fee) costs from $3,950 to $4,300 (prices go up as your registration date gets closer to the course start date). Complete details about the GCFE are available at

http://www.giac.org/certifications/forensics/gcfe.php

Professional Certified Investigator (PCI)

Professional Certified Investigator (PCI) candidates who want to take the PCI exam must first satisfy the following requirements (as stated on the PCI website):

◆ Five years of investigations experience including two years in case management

◆ High school diploma or GED equivalent

◆ Successful completion of an examination

◆ The applicant must not have been convicted of any criminal offense that would reflect negatively on the security profession, ASIS, or the certification program.

Eligibility for PCI certification and recertification is denied only when an applicant does not meet relevant security-related criteria, violates the PCI Code of Professional Responsibility, or commits an act that would reflect negatively on ASIS and the PCI program. The cost is around $300 for an ASIS member and $450 for a non-ASIS member. The PCI website is located at

http://www.asisonline.org/certification/pci/pciabout.xml

ASCLD/LAB Accreditation

The American Society of Crime Laboratory Directors/Laboratory Accreditation Board (ASCLD/LAB), is a non-profit professional society of crime laboratory directors and forensic science managers that seeks to promote excellence in forensic science through leadership and innovation. Among their various programs, the organization runs a crime laboratory accreditation program through an accreditation board (available online at http://www .ascld-lab.org). Obtaining accreditation is a time-consuming and expensive process, but accreditation results in crime labs operating on an equal footing with governmental crime laboratories like those operated by the FBI and the US Secret Service.

Individuals cannot seek such accreditation, but they should be aware of its existence and will be well-served if they seek out employers who hold ASCLD Lab Accreditation, or work with their employers to seek and obtain such accreditation.

Licensure

Professional licensure is required to work as a computer forensic professional in over one-third of the states in the United States and in other countries. For example, in the State of Georgia, the Board of Private Detectives and Security has ruled that computer forensic professionals fall under its jurisdiction and must earn a Private Investigator (PI) license to practice their trade in that state. (This credential is reciprocal with licenses in California and Louisiana, among other states). Be sure to check with your state or other local governing bodies to see if you must obtain a professional license to conduct computer forensic investigations before undertaking any such work. Failures to comply make you liable for both civil and criminal prosecution.

Appendix D

Forensic Tools

In Chapter 8, "Common Forensic Tools," you were introduced to some of the more popular and commonly used forensic tools. This appendix acquaints you with some additional forensic tools that are available on the market. Here, you'll find a high-level list of some of the many other tools you can use to assist in a forensic investigation. This summary list, along with the information in Chapter 8, gives you a great start in figuring out what you need to include in your forensic toolbox. You'll also learn about some of the vendors that provide forensic investigation training to help you become a better investigator.

Forensic Tool Suites

Forensic suites make processing and organizing large case files easier. These tools combine the functionality of many different, smaller applications and provide a common interface from which to conduct an electronic investigation.

Microsoft Computer Online Forensic Evidence Extractor (COFEE)

COFEE is a suite of software programs that assist law enforcement officers in collecting important forensic information from a running computer. The software makes it possible for personnel who are not trained forensic investigators to collect sound evidence. Owing to the powerful nature of such programs, COFEE is only available to law enforcement agencies. For more information on COFEE, visit their Web site:

http://www.microsoft.com/industry/government/solutions/cofee/

Vogon

Vogon Forensic Software is a collection of software tools for use when investigating personal computers. The Vogon software includes utilities to collect, manage, and analyze forensic evidence. For more information on Vogon Forensic Software, visit Vogon's Web site:

http://www.vogon-investigation.com/evidential_systems-03.htm

Password-Cracking Utilities

Forensic examiners often find encrypted or password-protected files during examinations of suspect computers. Password-cracking utilities allow you to view the contents of files.

Passware

Passware specializes in recovering passwords and decrypting media. The latest Passware forensic kit includes utilities to recover passwords and collect forensic evidence from over 180 types of files including decrypt media, files, and folders. Passware software ships as a complete forensic kit or various collections of utilities to meet the many needs of a forensic investigation. All Passware software is operated from an easy to use integrated user interface that makes it easy to collect evidence. For more information on Passware, visit their Web site: http://www.lostpassword.com.

ElcomSoft

ElcomSoft password-recovery software helps forensic investigators open files protected by popular computer applications. Elcomsoft is able to recover passwords from more than 80 different types of files, including the most popular archive and office applications. The product also helps recover files encrypted with the Microsoft Encrypting File System (EFS). For more information on ElcomSoft products, visit their Web site: http://www.elcomsoft.com.

Ophcrack

Ophcrack is a freely available password recovery utility for Microsoft Windows, Linux, and OS X. Ophcrack uses pre-built hash tables of common passwords, called rainbow tables, to quickly compare hash values to crack passwords. This tool is a handy addition to any forensic toolbox to help recover passwords. For more information on Ophcrack, visit their Web site: http://ophcrack.sourceforge.net/.

CD Analysis Utilities

At times, forensic examiners need to examine CDs or DVDs as part of their investigation. CD analysis utilities tools allow you to locate hidden sessions placed on optical media.

IsoBuster

IsoBuster is a utility used to perform data recovery from optical media (CD, DVD, and Blu-Ray) formats. IsoBuster shows the different tracks, sessions, and file systems stored on the suspect media, giving forensic investigators a complete view of all content. For more information on IsoBuster, visit their Web site: http://www.isobuster.com.

CD/DVD Inspector

CD/DVD Inspector is a utility for intensive analysis and extraction of data from CD and DVD media. The product targets professionals in data recovery, forensics, and law enforcement. CD/DVD Inspector reads all major CD, DVD, HD, and Blu-Ray file systems and provides forensic investigators with the information on all file systems on the suspect media. The product also provides complete reports on media contents. For more information on CD/DVD Inspector, visit its Web site: http://www.infinadyne.com/cddvd_inspector.html.

Metadata Viewer Utility

Microsoft Office files, among others, contain a vast array of information embedded inside documents. Metadata viewer utilities allow you to examine this type of data. Often, the discovery of metadata is crucial to a case.

Metadata Assistant

PayneGroup created Metadata Assistant in the late 1990s when they discovered that Word documents contain hidden information that could potentially expose their law firm clients to confidentiality breaches. Hundreds of thousands of law firms, government agencies, banking, oil, chemical, and pharmaceutical industries around the world now use Metadata Assistant products to remove metadata from Word documents and other file types. Metadata Assistant products remove metadata from Microsoft Word, Excel, PowerPoint, and RTF files. For more information on Metadata Assistant, visit the PayneGroup Web site: http://www.payneconsulting.com.

Miscellaneous Utilities

Forensic investigators must often bring creativity to investigations. Few cases are simple and scripted. The tools you've already been introduced to address many of investigators' needs. Some investigations have unique aspects that may require more specialized tools and utilities. This section covers a few example software utilities that address specialized investigative requirements.

WetStone Technologies, Inc.

WetStone Technologies, Inc. sells a range of forensic tools to help investigators collect and analyze evidence. Their products include utilities specially designed to identify known malware and collect evidence from running computers. Here are three of their most popular product lines:

- ◆ Gargoyle Investigator products: Software utilities used to rapidly uncover hidden evidence and malware instances on suspect computers.
- ◆ G-Flash: Mobile Malware Investigation software: Distributed on a convenient USB flash drive, G-Flash enables investigators to analyze suspect computers in the field and uncover hidden evidence.
- ◆ USB Live Acquisition and Triage Tool (US-LATT): This software utility, distributed on a USB flash drive, provides forensic investigators the ability to collect live information from a running computer.

For more information on WetStone Technologies, Inc. products, visit their Web site: http://www.wetstonetech.com.

XRY Complete

XRY Complete is a set of forensic hardware and software tools for mobile devices. XRY Complete includes the necessary hardware to connect to most mobile phones, PDAs, and GPS devices. The XRY software makes it easy to perform logical and physical data extraction processes. For more information on XRY Complete, visit the Micro Systemation Web site: http://www.msab.com.

Forensic Hardware Devices

Forensic investigators can process computer hard drives from standard PC hardware; however, the use of stand-alone, specialized hardware devices can make processing evidence both easier and faster. Several companies offer specialized hardware that collects, stores, and analyzes evidence. The companies listed in Table D.1 offer hardware products designed specifically for forensic investigators. Explore their Web sites for details on their product lines.

Table D.1   Companies offering forensic hardware products

Company	Web site
DIBS USA, Inc.	http://www.dibsusa.com
Digital Intelligence	http://www.digitalintelligence.com/forensichardware.php
Forensic Computer, Inc.	http://www.forensic-computers.com/
ForensicPC	http://www.forensicpc.com
H-11 Digital Forensics	http://www.h11-digital-forensics.com/computer-forensic-hardware.php
Intelligent Computer Solutions	http://www.ics-iq.com
LC Technology International	http://www.lc-tech.com/hardware/hardware.html

Computer Forensic Training

It is imperative for computer forensic examiners to obtain training to continuously improve and update their skills. Table D.2 lists some of the most popular organizations that offer specialized forensic training. Visit the Web sites of these organizations and explore their training offerings. You'll find many options that will help you learn how to become a more effective forensic investigator.

Table D.2   Companies offering computer forensic training

Organization	Web site
ComputerForensics	http://www.compuforensics.com/
Digital Intelligence	http://www.digitalintelligence.com
InfoSec Institute	http://www.infosecinstitute.com/courses/computer_forensics_training.html
SANS	http://computer-forensics.sans.org
Technical Resource Center	http://www.trcglobal.com
Key Computer Service CCE BootCamp	http://www.cce-bootcamp.com
AccessData	http://www.accessdata.com/courses.html
EC-Council	http://www.eccouncil.org/certification/computer_hacking_forensic_investigator.aspx
ProDiscover	http://www.prodiscover.com/DesktopDefault.aspx?tabindex=4&tabid=9

For more information about training and certification programs, please see Appendix C, "Forensic Certifications and More."

Glossary

A

Address Resolution Protocol (ARP) A protocol used on the Internet to map computer network addresses to hardware addresses.

admissible evidence Evidence that meets all regulatory and statutory requirements and has been properly obtained and handled.

allocation unit Another term for cluster.

ASCII (American Standard Code for Information Interchange) A single-byte character encoding scheme used for text-based data.

asymmetric key algorithm An encryption algorithm that uses one key to encrypt plaintext and another key to decrypt ciphertext. Also called public key algorithm.

auditing The process of tracking who's logging in and accessing what files.

B

Basic Input Output System (BIOS) Responsible for booting the computer by providing a basic set of instructions.

best evidence rule Whenever a document is presented as evidence, you must introduce the original document if at all possible. A copy may be introduced only if the original is not available.

best practices A set of recommended guidelines that outline a set of controls to improve internal and business processes, performance, quality, and efficiency.

bit stream backup Bit stream backups (also known as mirror image or evidence grade backups) are used to create an exact replica of a storage device.

Bluetooth A standard developed to allow various types of electronic equipment to make their own connections by using a short-range (10 meter) frequency-hopping radio link between devices.

body language Communication using body movements, gestures, and facial expressions.

brute force attack Attack that systematically tries every conceivable combination until a password is found or until all possible combinations have been exhausted.

C

cache Space on a hard disk used to improve performance speed by storing recently accessed data so that future requests for that data can be served faster locally.

CD/DVD-ROM/RW drive A drive, either internal or external, that is used to read and/or write CDs and DVDs. A compact disc (CD) can store large amounts of digital information (650 MB to 750 MB) on a very small surface. Single-sided, single-layer DVDs hold 4.70 GB, while double-sided double-layer DVDs hold more than 17 GB of digital information. CDs and DVDs are incredibly inexpensive to manufacture.

chain of custody Documentation of all steps that evidence has taken from the time it is located at a crime scene to the time it's introduced in a courtroom. All steps include collection, transportation, analysis, and storage processes. All accesses to the evidence must be documented as well.

checksum A value that can help detect data corruption. A checksum is derived by summing the number of bytes or other criterion in a string of data. At a later time, especially after the data has been transmitted or copied, the same calculation is performed. If the resulting value does not match the original value, the data is considered to be corrupt.

chosen plaintext attack   An attack to decrypt a file characterized by comparing ciphertext to a plaintext message you chose and encrypted.

cipher   An algorithm for encrypting and decrypting.

cloning   A process used to create an exact duplicate of one media on another like media.

cluster   Operating systems normally write in clusters. An entire cluster is reserved for each file even if the file's data requires less storage than the cluster size. The space that is not used by the file is called slack space.

Complementary Metal Oxide Semiconductor (CMOS) chip   On-board semiconductor chip used to store system information and configuration settings when the computer is either off or on.

computer evidence   Any computer hardware, software, or data that can be used to prove one or more of the five Ws and the H for a security incident — namely, who, what, when, where, why, and how.

computer forensics   Computer investigation and analysis techniques that involve the identification, preservation, extraction, documentation, and interpretation of computer data to determine potential legal evidence.

connector   The part of a cable that plugs into a port or interface to connect devices. Male connectors are identified by exposed pins. Female connectors are identified by holes into which the male connector can be inserted.

cookie   Small text file placed on a computer's hard drive as users browse Web sites. Each cookie file contains a unique number that identifies users to the Web site's computers upon the user's return to the site.

covert channel   Method by which an entity receives information in an unauthorized and obscure manner.

cross examination   Questions asked by opposing counsel to cast doubt on testimony provided during direct examination.

cryptography   The science of hiding the true contents of a message from unintended recipients.

cyclic redundancy check (CRC)   A common technique for detecting data transmission errors. Each transmitted message carries a numerical value based on the number of set bits in the message. The receiving device then applies the same formula to the message and checks to make sure the accompanying numerical value is the same, thereby verifying data integrity.

D

dd utility   Copy and convert utility. Originally included with most versions of UNIX and Linux, versions now exist for Windows as well.

decrypt   To translate an encrypted message back into the original unencrypted message.

demonstrative evidence   Evidence that illustrates or helps to explain other evidence. Usually demonstrative evidence consists of some kind of visual aid.

deposition   Testimony that is reduced to written form. (Video recorded depositions are also transcribed and reduced to written form, and both the written transcription as well as the video recording of the testimony may be admitted in court.)

desktop   A PC designed to be set up in a permanent location because its components are too large or heavy to transport easily.

dictionary attack   An attack that tries different passwords defined in a list or database of password candidates.

direct examination   Initial questions asked of a witness to extract testimony.

disaster recovery   The ability of an organization to recover from an occurrence inflicting widespread destruction and distress.

distributed denial of service (DDoS) attack   An attack that uses one or more systems to flood another system with so much traffic that the targeted system is unable to respond to legitimate requests for service or access.

documentary evidence   Written evidence, such as printed reports or data in log files. Such evidence cannot stand on its own and must be authenticated.

E

electromagnetic fields   Produced by the local buildup of electric charges in the atmosphere. They can damage computer components. They are present everywhere in our environment but are invisible to the human eye.

electronic discovery or e-discovery   The process whereby electronic documents are collected, prepared, reviewed, and distributed in association with legal and government proceedings.

electrostatic discharge (ESD)   Buildup of electrical charge on a surface that is suddenly transferred to another surface when it is touched.

e-mail header   Data at the beginning of an electronic message that contains information about the message.

encrypt   To obscure the meaning of a message to make it unreadable.

encryption key   A code that enables the user to encrypt or decrypt information when combined with a cipher or algorithm.

expert witness   A person called to testify in a court of law who possesses special knowledge or skill in some specific area that applies to a case.

Extended Binary Coded Decimal Interchange Code (EBCDIC)   A character encoding set used by IBM mainframes. Most computer systems use a variant of ASCII, but IBM mainframes and midrange systems, such as the AS/400, use this character set primarily designed for ease of use on punched cards.

extended FAT (exFAT)   Sometimes (and incorrectly) called FAT64, this extended version of the FAT file system was developed to keep FAT working with the kinds of large hard disks (1 TB and larger) now so widely installed in modern desktop and notebook PCs.

extension checker   A utility that compares a file's extension to its header. If the two do not match, the discrepancy is reported.

external hard drive   A hard disk in an external enclosure with its own power supply and data interface(s). Nearly all external hard disks support USB; many support higher-speed interfaces such as eSATA or FireWire (IEEE 1394).

external Serial Advanced Technology Attachment (eSATA)   Interface technology that permits external hard drives to use the same high-speed SATA interface that internal hard drives use.

F

Federal Rule of Civil Procedure 26   Federal Rule 26 states the General Provisions Governing Discovery and Duty of Disclosure. Section (a) states Required Disclosures and Methods to Discover Additional Matter.

File Allocation Table (FAT)   A simple file system used by DOS but supported by later Microsoft (and other) operating systems. The FAT resides at the beginning of a disk partition and acts as a table of contents for stored data.

file viewer   A utility that provides thumbnail images of files. Such tools are useful for scanning a group of files visually.

file system   An operating system's method for organizing, managing, and accessing files through logical structures on a hard drive.

FireWire   An IEEE-1394 technology that implements a high-performance, external bus standard for rapid data transfer and streaming multimedia (such as video).

forensic compression   The compacting of an image file by compressing redundant sectors to reduce the amount of space it takes up.

forensic duplicate   A process used to copy an entire hard drive that includes all bits of information from the source drive stored in a raw bit stream format.

forensic suite   Set of tools and/or software programs used to analyze a computer for collection of evidence.

forensically sound   Procedures whereby absolutely no alteration is caused to stored data. All evidence is preserved and protected from all contamination.

H

hard evidence   Real evidence conclusively associated with a suspect or activity.

hardware write blocker   A hardware device that is plugged in between the disk controller and the physical disk and blocks any write requests.

hash   A mathematical function that creates a fixed-length string from a message of any length. The result of a hash function is a hash value, sometimes called a message digest. Hash functions are one-way functions. That is, you can create a hash value from a message, but you cannot create a message from a hash value.

host protected area (HPA)   Area of a hard drive created specifically to allow manufacturers to hide diagnostic and recovery tools. (Sometimes referred to as hidden protected area or hardware protected area.)

hybrid attack   A modification of the dictionary attack that tries different permutations of each dictionary entry.

I

imaging   The process of creating a complete copy of a disk drive where the disk is copied sector-by-sector.

incident   A threatening computer security breach that can be recovered from in a relatively short period of time.

incident response   The action taken to respond to a situation that can be recovered from relatively quickly.

incident response plan   The actions an organization takes when it detects an attack, whether ongoing or after the fact.

incident response team (IRT)   A team of individuals trained and prepared to recognize and immediately respond appropriately to any security incident.

input/output (I/O)   Data transfer that occurs between the thinking part of the computer, or CPU, and an external device or peripheral. For example, when you type on a keyboard, that device sends input to the computer. Usually software directs the computer to output what you type on a screen.

International Association of Computer Investigative Specialists (IACIS)   International volunteer corporation comprised of federal, state, local, and international law enforcement professionals who are committed to education in the field of forensic computer science.

intrusion   Any unauthorized access to a computer, including the use, alteration, or disclosure of programs or data residing on the computer.

intrusion detection   Using software and hardware agents to monitor network traffic for patterns that may indicate an attempt at intrusion.

IP address   A unique identifier for a computer or device on a TCP/IP network.

J

Jaz disk   Older form of portable storage media consisting of a removable hard disk in a protective plastic shell introduced by Iomega in 1995. Production was discontinued in 2003.

K

key logger   Device that intercepts, records, and stores everything typed on a keyboard into a file. This includes all keystrokes, even passwords.

KISS method   KISS stands for "Keep It Simple, Stupid." This acronym reminds us to avoid making things more complicated than they need to be.

known plaintext attack   An attack to decrypt a file characterized by comparing known plaintext to the resulting ciphertext.

M

MAC time   Set of time stamps associated with a file. The time stamps describe the last time the file was modified (mtime), accessed (atime), and created (ctime).

malware   Another name for malicious code. This includes viruses, logic bombs, and worms.

Message Digest 5 (MD5)   MD5 is a one-way hash function, meaning that it takes a message and converts it into a fixed string of digits, which is then used to verify that the message hasn't been altered.

metadata   Data component that describes other data. In other words, it's data about data.

mobile device   A catch-all term that refers to handheld computing and communications devices, including cell phones, smartphones, handheld computers, and even so-called personal digital assistants (PDAs). All handheld devices have some of the following capabilities: general computing including web access and compact local applications (called apps), wireless Internet and networking components, wireless telecommunications, global positioning systems (GPS), e-mail access, and phone/address book capabilities. Mobile devices generally use flash memory instead of a hard drive for storage to keep them as light and small as possible.

modem   A shorthand version of the words modulator-demodulator. A modem is used to send digital data over a phone line. The sending modem converts digital data into a signal that is compatible with the phone line (modulation), and the receiving modem then converts that signal back into digital data (demodulation).

multiboot system   System that can boot, or start, and then run more than one operating system (though only one at a time).

N

Netstat   A utility that displays the active port connections on which the computer is listening.

Network File System (NFS)   Provides remote access to shared file systems across networks. The primary function of NFS is to mount directories to other computers. These directories can then be accessed as though they were local.

New Technology File System (NTFS)   A file system supported by Windows NT and higher-level Windows operating systems, including Windows Server 2000, 2003, and 2008, and Windows XP, Vista, and 7.

O

open source   Code that the code creator makes available under a license that permits end users to freely redistribute the source code, make modifications to the source code, and create derivative works.

operating system   Acts as a director and interpreter between the user and all the software and hardware on the computer.

P

packet   Unit of information routed between an origin and a destination. A file is divided into efficient-size packets for transmission.

passcode   A character string used to authenticate a user ID to perform some function, such as encryption key management.

password   A string of characters that security systems use to authenticate, or verify, a user's identity. Security systems compare passwords a user provides during login to stored values for the user account. If the value provided (password) matches the stored value, the security subsystem authenticates the user. Most operating systems store passwords when users create login accounts.

password cracking   Attempting to discover a password by trying multiple options and continuing until you find a successful match.

PC   A personal computer intended for generic use by an individual. PCs were originally known as microcomputers because they were built on a smaller scale than the systems most businesses used at the time.

personal digital assistant (PDA)   Tightly integrated handheld device that combines computing, Internet, and networking components. A PDA can use flash memory instead of a hard drive for storage.

port scanner   Program that attempts to connect to a list of computer ports or a range of IP addresses.

private key algorithm   An encryption algorithm that uses the same key to encrypt and decrypt. Also known as symmetric key algorithm.

protocol   A set of rules and conventions that govern how computers exchange information over a network medium.

public key algorithm   An encryption algorithm that uses one key to encrypt plaintext and another key to decrypt ciphertext. Also called asymmetric algorithm.

R

real evidence   Any physical objects you can bring into court. Real evidence can be touched, held, or otherwise observed directly.

relevant evidence   Evidence that serves to prove or disprove facts in a case.

Request for Comments (RFC)   Started in 1969, RFCs are a series of notes about the Internet. An Internet document can be submitted to the Internet Engineering Task Force (IETF) by anyone, but the IETF decides when and if a document becomes an RFC. Each RFC is designated by an RFC number. Once published, an RFC never changes. Modifications to an original RFC are assigned a new RFC number.

router   Device (or software) that determines the next network point to which a packet should be forwarded on the way to its destination.

S

search warrant   A court order that allows law enforcement to search and/or seize computer equipment without providing advance warning to its owner.

searching tool   A tool that searches for patterns (mostly string patterns) in large file collections.

Second/Third Extended Filesystems (ext2/ext3)   State-based file systems used by the Linux operating system.

security policies   Specifications for a secure environment, including such items as physical security requirements, network security planning details, a detailed list of approved software, and human resources policies on employee hiring and dismissal.

server   A computer with sufficient processing power and storage capacity to provide services to other computers over a network. Servers often include multiple processors, large amounts of memory, and many sizable hard drives. They also often incorporate two or more high-speed network interfaces (Gigabit Ethernet, also known as GbE, or better).

signature analysis   Technique that uses a filter to analyze both the header and the contents of the datagram, usually referred to as the packet payload.

site survey   Notes, photographs, drawings, and any other documentation that describes the state and condition of a scene.

slack space   Space on a hard disk between where the file ends and where the disk storage cluster ends.

social engineering   A method of obtaining sensitive information (for example, about a company) through exploitation of human nature.

software write blocker   Software that sits between the operating system and the disk driver that blocks all write requests.

spanning across multiple discs   Breaks the image file into chunks of a certain size so the image file can be backed up onto multiple CDs or other media.

steganography   Process of passing information in a manner that hides the existence of one message inside another file or message.

subpoena   A court order that compels an individual or organization to surrender evidence.

substitution cipher   A cipher that substitutes each character in the original message with an alternate character to create the encrypted message.

summons   A court order that compels a witness to appear in court and answer questions.

swap file   Space on the hard disk used as the virtual memory extension of a computer's actual memory.

symmetric key algorithm   An encryption algorithm that uses the same key to encrypt and decrypt. Also known as private key algorithm.

T

temporary Internet files   Copies of all HTML, GIF, JPG, and other files associated with the sites a user has visited on the Internet.

testimonial evidence   Evidence consisting of witness testimony, either in verbal or written form. Testimonial evidence may be presented in person by a witness in a court or in the form of a recorded deposition.

trace evidence   Traces of data either left behind or found with a criminal that can be used to prove that a crime was committed.

traceroute   A command used to see where a network packet is being sent and received in addition to all the places it goes along the way to its destination.

Transmission Control Protocol/Internet Protocol (TCP/IP) network   A network that uses the TCP/IP protocol.

Trojan horse program   In computers, a type of program or code that appears to be legitimate or harmless but contains malicious or harmful instructions that may allow unauthorized users access to the victim's computer system.

U

unerase tool   A utility that assists in recovering previously deleted files. In some cases, files can be completely recovered. At other times, only portions of a file can be recovered.

Universal Serial Bus (USB)   A connectivity standard that allows for the connection of multiple devices without the need for software or hardware.

UDP datagram   A message sent using the User Datagram Protocol (UDP), a network protocol used on the Internet. UDP allows applications to send datagrams to other hosts on an Internet Protocol (IP) network without requiring prior communications to set up special transmission channels or data paths.

USB flash drive (UFD)   A small, portable, high-capacity flash memory device that attaches to a computer or mobile device via a Universal Serial Bus (USB) port.

user ID   A string of characters that identifies a user in a computing environment.

V

Virtual FAT (VFAT)   Also called FAT32, an enhanced version of the FAT file system that allows for names longer than the 8.3 convention and uses smaller allocation units on the disk.

virus   A program or piece of code that is loaded onto a computer without the user's knowledge and is designed to attach itself to other code and replicate. The virus replicates when an infected file is executed or launched.

voluntary surrender   Permission granted by a computer equipment owner to search and/or seize equipment for investigative purposes.

W

war dialing   Automated software that attempts to dial numbers within a given range of phone numbers to determine if any of those numbers are actually used by modems accepting dial-in requests.

wireless access point (WAP)   Network device that contains a radio transmitter/receiver that is connected to another network. A WAP provides wireless devices access to a regular wired network.

workstation   A high-end desktop computer that delivers enhanced processing power, significant memory capacity, and performs special functions, such as software or game development, CAD/CAM design, finite element analysis, and so forth.

worm   Similar in function and behavior to a virus, except that worms do not need user intervention. A worm takes advantage of a security hole in an existing application or operating system and then finds other systems running the same software and automatically replicates itself to the new hosts.

Z

Zip disk   Older form of portable storage media, somewhat larger than a floppy disk. Stores hundreds of megabytes of data.

Index

Note to the reader: Throughout this index **boldfaced** page numbers indicate primary discussions of a topic. *Italicized* page numbers indicate illustrations.